Processing Varieties in English

This study of oral and written speech in English examines media as processing varieties and looks at their interaction with genre. To date the study of orality and literacy in English has been unsystematic; findings have been inconsistent and contradictory.

In this treatment, clear methodological parameters have been set up to ensure accurate and significant findings. All texts used are parallel texts arising out of the same or a similar context of situation. With this methodology, ideational meaning is clearly distinguished from textual meaning. Moreover, media and genre, two aspects of textual meaning, are distinguished so that representative features of each are isolated. Lastly, all texts are naturally occurring across representative genres. With such distinctions and criteria in place, the important interaction of media with genre is examined, while the character of oral and written speech as processing varieties is revealed.

Above all, this book demonstrates the non-neutrality of oral and written speech as language varieties. Especially important is the resultative/causative split between them in the representation of events. Written speech is not oral speech "written down," as Bloomfield and de Saussure originally claimed, but a very different system of syntactic and discourse organization which influences how we represent and see the world. Both varieties strongly influence the semantic content and generic function of any text they convey, indicating a very significant interplay of semantic variables in the processing of language.

Processing Varieties in English contributes to a wide range of linguistic areas and topics, including discourse analysis, socio-psycholinguistics, and cognitive science.

MARCIA I. MACAULAY received her PH.D. from the University of British Columbia and is currently a lecturer in the Department of English at the National University of Singapore.

Processing Varieties in English: An Examination of Oral and Written Speech across Genres

Marcia I. Macaulay

University of British Columbia Press
Vancouver

ISBN 0-7748-0334-7
Printed in Canada   ∞

Canadian Cataloguing in Publication Data
Macaulay, Marcia Irene
  Processing varieties in English

  Includes bibliographical referenes
  ISBN 0 7748 0334 7

  1. Oral communication. 2. Written communication.
  3. Literary form. 4. Mass media. 5. Speech acts
  (Linguistics). 6. Sociolinguistics.
  7. Psycholinguistics. I. Title.
  P95.M32 1990   302.2′24   C90-091198-0

UBC Press
6344 Memorial Rd
Vancouver, BC V6T 1W5

This book has been published with
the help of a grant from the Canadian
Federation for the Humanities, using
funds provided by the Social Sciences
and Humanities Research Council of
Canada.

To my parents

Contents

TABLES

Acknowledgments

Any work based on original research goes through numerous stages of development. At each stage I was fortunate enough to receive valuable advice and support from many colleagues and friends. Among these, I should especially like to thank Allen Specht, from the Sound and Moving Image Division of the British Columbia Provincial Archives, who went to great trouble helping me locate and select the Starret material used in this book. I should also like to thank my teachers Fred Bowers and Laurel Brinton, who helped me with the conceptual framework and analysis of my material. Further, I wish to thank the two readers from the Canadian Federation for the Humanities who gave me constructive criticism and commentary. Jane Fredeman from the University of British Columbia Press I thank for her continual support and for the care and attention she gave to the revision and editing of my manuscript. Lastly, I wish to thank Gail Fraser and Evanthia Tsiouria for their insightful feedback and generous support. Whatever strengths this book possesses owe much to the guidance of those named and others whom I have acknowledged here.

Processing Varieties in English

1

Introduction

Approximately two thousand years ago Aristotle noted in his *Rhetoric* that "The style of written prose is not the same as that of controversial speaking" (3.12). Modern linguists have given little attention to Aristotle's observation until very recently. During the nineteenth century, traditional grammarians and philologists concentrated on the study of written texts and derived phonological and syntactic analysis from the language in them, while in the twentieth century linguistic research concerning the differentiation of oral and written expression has been inhibited by a number of factors, but principally by what Jacques Derrida calls "phonocentrism," the view that orality is equivalent to language itself and that writing is merely a reflection of oral expression not requiring special attention. Although phonocentrism, in fact, goes back to Aristotle (*De Interpretatione* I),[1] in the twentieth century the phonocentric view has been most prominently taken up by de Saussure and Bloomfield. Both expressed themselves clearly and categoricaly on the subject of the relationship of written speech to oral speech:

Langue et écriture sont deux systèmes de signes distinct; l'unique raison d'être du second est de représenter le premier. (de Saussure 1916, 1967:45)

Writing is not language but merely a way of recording language by visible marks. In order to study writing we must know something about language, but the reverse is not true. (Bloomfield 1933:21)

Within the broad designation of linguistic structuralism, only Prague School linguists and isolated American Structuralists (Bolinger 1946) took it upon themselves to look at differences in media because they were interested in correlating linguistic function with

linguistic structure (Vachek 1948, 1976; Havránek 1955) and so perceived all structural differences as potentially meaningful.

Phonocentrism was not fostered as such by transformational-
generative theory; however, emphasis upon internal, genetic "competence" and, in turn, the construction of an "ideal speaker-hearer"
as the correct object of study discouraged the study of language in
actual situations and thus attention to variation in language. Yet
negative reaction to the idealization of speakers and hearers in trans-
formational-generative theory and concomitant interest in linguistic
variation in both the fields of sociolinguistics and discourse analysis
have caused renewed attention to be placed on the distinction made
by Aristotle.

The distinction between what I shall refer to as "oral speech" and
"written speech"[2] is important for the understanding of language
generally, but especially when analysis goes beyond the sentence in
isolation. Text cannot be considered apart from factors of production. The Saussurean *langue/parole* distinction and the Chomskyan
competence/performance distinction present a bifurcated view of
language, where *parole* is secondary to language as system in Saussure's analysis and performance is secondary to language as innate
capacity in Chomsky's. But it is not so evident that performance
factors are entirely distinct from the quintessence of language itself.
The media of language, oral speech and written speech, are not
simply vehicles or conduits of thought; they interact in profound
and complex ways with content to shape and modify, or, more accurately, to create meaning. They serve as processing varieties which
influence and contribute to a speaker's meaning and representation
of reality in language.

The very complexity and intricacy of such linguistic processing
has resulted in greatly differing descriptions of the media. Of the
many recent analyses, the two most significant are those of M.A.K.
Halliday and Wallace Chafe. They provide quite different treatments.
In Chafe's view (1982), based on a contrast of "idea units" (characterized by a coherent intonation contour bounded by pauses) in oral
and written speech, writing was found to be "integrated" and oral
speech "fragmented." Chafe derived his data from informal dinner-
table conversation, letters, lectures, and written academic papers
provided by the same group of subjects (faculty and graduate students). Examining word class distribution and phrase and clause
structure, Chafe found that formal written speech contrasts with
informal oral speech in having a greater number of nominalizations,
attributive adjectives, participles, genitive subjects and objects, con-

joined phrases, series, sequences of prepositional phrases, relative clauses, and complement clauses and phrases.

Chafe's characterization of oral speech as "fragmented" and written speech as "integrated" derives in large part from his observation of the nature of conjunction in oral and written speech and his observation of the strong nominal nature of written speech, an observation initially made by Havránek (1955) with regard to the written standard. In Chafe's view, oral speech is "fragmented" because "idea units" in oral speech are frequently strung together without connectives. When connectives are used, *and* is most common, followed by *but, so,* and *because*. For Chafe, oral speech exhibits little genuine integration of ideas and thought. Conversely, written speech is highly integrated because of its preference for embedded syntactic structures. Nominal constructions with adjacent structures such as attributive adjectives, participles, genitive subjects and objects, as well as complements and relative clauses create a high degree of compactness or integration of meaning in the written "idea unit."

Chafe further characterized oral speech as "involved" on the basis of the greater presence of markers of personal reference or experience in this variety. Written speech, in turn, is characterized by Chafe as being "detached" by virtue of its predominant use of passives and nominalizations. English passives permit detachment of agency from activity, while nominalizations permit the abstract reification of actions and processes and so also have the effect of detaching agency from activity.

As important as Chafe's overall analysis is, there are problems with the methods which he employs to arrive at his data. Chafe does not employ naturally occurring texts nor does he use parallel texts. Also, Chafe does not control his protocols for topic; therefore, many of the features he ascribes to written and oral speech could be causally related to topic and situational differences. Finally, Chafe's use of an "idea unit" is odd since he defines this as a coherent intonation contour bounded by pauses. This is a permissible unit of measurement in oral speech, but it is not applicable to written speech unless it is read aloud. Chafe's characterization of an idea unit in such strongly oral terms suggests again an unconscious translation of written speech into oral speech along Bloomfieldean or Saussurean lines.

Halliday's analysis (1978, 1987) compares in many respects with that of Chafe, but his view of oral speech is much different. Halliday characterizes written speech as "crystalline" and oral speech as "choreographic." From Jean Ure (1969) he takes the concept of "lexical density," which she defines as the proportion of content words per clause. According to Halliday, "What this [lexical density] means is that there are a large number of lexical items, content words, often including quite difficult words, of fairly low frequency, packed closely together; and typically, packed into what is a rather simple grammatical structure" (1978:47). Written speech is productive of high lexical density (more high content words per clause) in syntactically simple sentence structures, while oral speech produces clauses with low lexical density with much greater frequency of subordinate structures (noun, adverb clauses). In Halliday's view, oral and written speech are "complex" in two different ways:

The complexity of speech is choreographic—an intricacy of movement. That of writing is crystalline—a denseness of matter. In linguistic terms, spoken language is characterized by complex sentence structures with low lexical density (more clauses, but fewer high content words per clause); written language by simple sentence structures with high lexical density (more high content words per clause, but fewer clauses) . . . speech has complex sentences with simple words, while writing has complex words in simple sentences. (1978:49)

Much of Halliday's analysis accords with Chafe's view of written speech. While Halliday refers to written speech as "crystalline" and Chafe uses the term "integrated" to describe the medium, both point to the complexity of the nominal group in written English. For Halliday it is this complexity in the nominal group and the syntactic devices of modification and embedding which support this group that give rise to the lexically dense structure of the written English sentence.[3] However, for Halliday oral speech is not in any sense "fragmented" speech as it is for Chafe; rather it possesses its own distinct choreography.

Halliday (1987) also argues that there are certain semantic consequences in the use of each medium. Writing represents phenomena as product while oral speech renders them as process. Written speech, therefore, tends to display a high degree of "grammatical metaphor" by virtue of nominalization devices which render active processes as products and which in turn "background" such processes (e.g., *Smoking causes cancer* versus *If you continue to smoke, you will get cancer*). Also, such extensive use of nominalization in written speech can render meaning ambiguous, since it creates what Chafe terms "detachment" of agency from activity. The highly nominalized nature of written speech has for this reason ideological as well as semantic consequences.

Halliday's analysis is highly provocative since it challenges a number of dominant conceptions of both oral and written speech. Yet, although he recognizes the need to employ parallel texts, Halliday does not consistently do so, claiming that it is difficult "to find a pair of texts which match in all respects except that one is written and the other spoken" (1978:49). Halliday thus constructs his own "translations" of oral and written protocols (transcriptions from oral recordings of both children and adults as well as written texts). His hypothesis needs more empirical verification.

While the two principal theorists, Halliday and Chafe, differ in their analyses, some have argued that no major distinction between the media exists. Blankenship (1962) compared the oral and written speech of adults (the radio speeches and published articles of four public figures, including Margaret Mead) and found little variation between the two. Although Blankenship did find some differences in the referential use of adjectives in the written texts as well as a greater use of the present perfect tense and preferred use of the present progressive in her oral texts, she considered these preferences too minimal to be significant. She concluded that greater stylistic differentiation occurred between speakers than between oral and written speech.

Blankenship's inability to detect real differences results largely from her unconscious use of two written varieties. Modern speeches are seldom orally composed (though ideally they are written to be read aloud) and should show marked similarities with other forms of written composition. Texts written to be read aloud should demonstrate features which mark them as adaptations to a listening audience rather than to a reading audience; however, Blankenship does not employ this distinction and so does not categorize her texts according to true medium of use or audience type.[4]

Lakoff (1982b) has argued that the distinction amounts essentially to one between formality and informality, while Tannen (1982) has placed oral and written speech on a "continuum," which by definition obscures any clear distinction between the media. Ochs (1979) implicitly conflates oral and written speech with planned and unplanned discourse. Oral and written speech are also conflated with spontaneous and nonspontaneous discourse or emotive and intellectual discourse (Brown 1978; Vachek 1948, 1976; Havránek 1955).

As Mair has pointed out, "la définition du code parlé (ou de la langue parlée) pose des problèmes presque insolubles: même derrière la définition courante de la langue parlée comme 'discours libre et spontané effectué dans des situations de communication spontanées' peuvent se cacher tant de types de discours qu'on ne peut les assimiler à un système langagier commun" (1981:154). Equations of oral and written speech with spontaneous and emotive language and non-spontaneous and intellectual discourse respectively have overcast the issue of differentiation in oral and written speech and made analysis of these media susceptible to the criticism of Lakoff and Tannen that theoretically characteristic variables of oral and written speech are better understood as variables of language use and thus that oral and written speech co-exist on a continuum rather than being distinct sub-varieties of one variety in language.

Since different findings as well as the conflation of oral and written speech with other types of variety have resulted in a continued misunderstanding of the distinction, methodology is very important in the examination of these media. Three distinct methodological criteria must be met: one, data should be obtained from parallel texts; two, data should be collected across genres; and three, the data should be naturally occurring. Adhering to these criteria ensures that a researcher obtains data unobtrusively and in turn draws valid inferences from the data collected.

Of these criteria, the use of parallel texts is the most important. Sewell (1981) takes parallel texts to be stylistic variants of the same text type within a speech community. For Sewell, the various renderings of a particular news item would constitute parallel texts. Durmosoglu, on the other hand, defines parallel texts as "texts in two or more languages which have the same communicative purpose and render the same message (i.e., communicate the same meaning)" (1983:118). This more clearly defined conception of parallel texts also permits adaptation to the study of varieties within a given language. Parallel texts need not be produced by the same speaker, but they are likely to arise out of the same or a similar context of situation and to share features of genre (or register) as well as concern the same topic. By using texts with a comparable topic, content, and broad general purpose, a researcher can see how linguistic medium as a variable interacts with these other factors of production. Use of parallel texts also permits considerable control over variables since they can be isolated; most importantly genre can be distinguished from media.

The selection of parallel texts across genres permits even further control of variables. Unfortunately, at present there is no accepted typology of texts (Schmidt 1977). Although literary critics have extensively analysed narrative texts into major sub-genres (e.g., short story, novel, novella), major linguistic work has been done on narrative by Labov (1972b), and both Longacre (1983) and Werlich (1976) have both put forth theories of text-types, genre theory is still in its infancy.

Genre can usefully be compared to and distinguished from the concept of register in Hallidayean linguistics. Register corresponds to variety of language according to use and is situationally based. In such a view, medium itself is a variable of register because it represents one aspect of a speaker's linguistic response to situation. If we exclude considerations of media, however, register corresponds primarily to a speaker's choice of topic (what the speaker is talking about) as well as the role (function and, by extension, purpose) of the speaker in the situation. These basic factors govern the production of text.

Genre theory looks at texts not in production but as products. For example, in his text-typing of monologic discourse, Longacre (1968, 1976, 1983) examines two basic characteristics in the texts he analyses: agent orientation and contingent temporal succession. Texts are characterized according to the degree of orientation to the speaker as agent and the degree of chronological linkage present. Narrative is viewed as the base genre with procedural, behavioural, and expository text-types differing from it in one or more of the primary ways.

There is, however, a degree of overlap between these two approaches to text analysis. The general text-type categories which Longacre proposes—narrative, procedural, behavioural, expository—correspond grossly to speaker's role as well as speaker's general topic. Put simply, the situations speakers find themselves in can be constraining. Teachers are expected to teach; jocks in locker-rooms are expected to talk sports or sexual exploits, but not politics or current events. When linguists speak of registers, they are, in fact, speaking of specific speech genres or types which are associated with general or generic situations.[5]

We can think of genres as very broad categorical speech types which correlate with the general roles and functions performed by a given speaker. Within these categories individual registers more finely responsive to situation and actual speech production can be further identified. To analyse texts in this study, I take into consideration register variables, excluding media, but I also use the product orientations of Longacre and Werlich. Texts can also be analysed as speech acts and categorized into one "word to world" grouping (narrative, description, exposition) and a second "world to word" grouping (instruction and argument). Such an approach permits global analysis rather than the purely local analysis of text as register.

Analysing genres in terms of speech-act direction of fit affords insight into the principal properties shared by genres. Narratives, descriptions, and expository texts all fundamentally concern representation of the world by the word. Narrative differs from description and exposition primarily in its orientation to the past. Description and exposition differ in that the former is oriented to physical objects or processes in space while the latter is oriented to concepts or conceptual information. In the second grouping of "world to word," instruction and argument differ in the requirement of instruction for mimesis. Instruction has not occurred unless the "world" has replicated the "word." Conversely, in argument there is an equivalent future orientation but no requirement for mimesis.[6] On the basis of a speech-act analysis, central features (and particularly those in the predicate of clauses) of each genre can be isolated and so differentiated from those of media.

Of further importance is the need to collect data which is naturally occurring. Such texts arise out of situations determined by speakers or writers rather than those governed or controlled by researchers. Labov (1972a) has drawn attention to the phenomenon of what he terms the "observer's paradox." Language observed is language altered, and therefore it is important for the researcher not to intrude on any variety studied. Otherwise, misrepresentation of data may occur.

All the texts which I have collected and shall analyse in subsequent chapters adhere to the criteria delineated above. By using such controls, I have tried to respond to the fact of variety in language by clearly identifying, distinguishing, and describing it. Since, methodologically, description must precede explanation, the more finely one can describe any variety of language, the more plausibly one can explain it.

Each chapter examines the specific interaction and interplay of media with one genre. In this way, the influence of media on genre can be examined. By clearly distinguishing language according to use (register/genre) from media, we are better able to see how these varieties interact and influence one another. The primary focus here, however, is upon the influence of media on genre, since this is also the dominant direction of influence. Individual genres are differentiated by a processing medium, either oral or written.

Chapter 2 examines three sets of parallel narrative texts taken from one speaker, Martin Starret. Starret was a mountain man who died in 1962. He recorded an extensive series of interviews with Imbert Orchard for the Canadian Broadcasting Corporation recounting his life and adventures in late nineteenth- and early twentieth-century British Columbia. His reminiscences are invaluable for the historian, but also for the discourse analyst, since Starret kept journals, now in the British Columbia Provincial Archives, which serve as parallel written texts to his recorded oral narratives and descriptions.

Starret is also important because he is a gifted natural narrator with a broad range of experience. I examine three types of narrative in this chapter: personal, historical and mythic (or anthropological). We can see from Starret's narratives how complex a genre narrative is since the past is not so much recreated as created in personal, cultural, or mythic terms. Specifically, oral and written narratives differ in their treatments of plot, character and structure. Perspective also differs in oral and written tellings of the same story because different syntactic choices, such as that between the active and the passive voice, can alter the organization and analysis of a recounted series of events. Especially important is the distinction between resultative and causative analysis of events in oral and written narrative texts. Oral and written speech promote very different analyses of events in chronological sequence and thus different expressions of past experience.

Chapter 3 examines two parallel descriptive texts also taken from Starret's reminiscences and journals. In this discussion, I examine the treatment of space in oral and written speech. Starret uses different strategies of discourse organization in his oral and written texts. The oral description relies heavily on narrative or pseudo-narrative structures, while the written description employs thematic focus and a very specific syntax of attribution as well as an analytic problem-solution text structure.

Chapter 4 examines oral and written exposition. Since speakers in academic exposition tend to read from written scripts rather than orally compose lectures from prepared notes, I examine a set of parallel expository texts taken from a popular writer/speaker, Leo Buscaglia, who does not read from notes. His lectures, therefore, are genuinely oral in their structure and organization. Moreover, they are also examples of planned oral expository texts and so permit comparison of planned oral and written discourse.

Exposition differs from other genres in foregrounding the transmission of new information. Buscaglia's treatment of new information differs greatly in his oral and written texts. The problem of discourse generation and organization is more clearly in evidence in the oral text, where very specific strategies of lexical, syntactic, and ideational repetition serve the oral expositor. The written exposition, while equally exploiting repetition, does so unobtrusively, to avoid perceived awareness of repetition by the reader. There are also very different interactions between speaker and audience in contrast to writer and reader. The rhetorical problem of transmitting new information is differently achieved by Buscaglia in each medium.

Chapter 5 treats instruction, for which I have selected a very common variety of popular instruction, the cooking lesson. Cooking programmes are now commonplace on television and so provide a resource for analysis of oral instruction. There is also common interaction between the medium of television and that of print since many television cooks, such as the one I have chosen, Jeff Smith ("The Frugal Gourmet"), use their series of programmes to sell their books. As an instructor, Smith needs to transmit both conceptual and practical knowledge to his students; they must understand and then re-enact his directions. In oral instruction, he achieves his aim through extensive elaboration and complex cognitive association, while in written instruction he employs a problem/solution frame to give salience to the written recipe which serves as his principle means of instruction. In this genre the aural/visual dichotomy between oral and written speech is most obvious. The oral text appeals exclusively to the student's ability to process through the ear, while the written text exploits visual gesture and cues from the spatial domain of the page.

Chapter 6 examines an argument between Noam Chomsky and Fred Halliday in conversation and in print regarding the New Cold War between the USA and the USSR. I have used a taped broadcast of Chomsky and Halliday originally made for the British television programme *Voices*. I compare their oral argumentation with written argumentation found in Chomsky's essay "Towards a New Cold War" (in *Towards a New Cold War*, 1982) and in Halliday's *The Making of the Second Cold War* (1983). As in oral and written narrative, the resultative/causative split between oral and written speech is prominent since it permits very different approaches to the logical representation of ideas. Also important is the degree to which interpersonal information in discourse is given prominence in argument. Although technically argument is about"content," the degree to which it foregrounds interpersonal meaning is significant. Indeed, ideational content often takes a back seat to the relationship between co-speakers or co-writers. Oral argument is particularly governed by interpersonal meaning and requires very specific strategies for its continuance. Written argument, having the advantage of being monologic, permits greater expression of disagreement and harsher evaluation of the opposition. The syntax of written speech becomes itself a feature of written argumentation.

I have personally transcribed all the oral data collected from tape recordings. However, I have not attempted transcription of all information. I am primarily concerned to transcribe wording, including hesitation phenomena (e.g., *uh*, *ah*) and to stress (in gross terms), syntax and discourse organization. I mark stress by bolding in the case of a full word and by letter capitalization in the case of a phoneme or morpheme. Heavily stressed words I both italicize and bold. A circumflex ˆ is used when a particular sound carries its own intonation contour and for short pauses between words, phases, or clauses. The playfulness of speakers with a given sound cannot be fully rendered in written speech, but it is this playfulness that I am graphically alluding to by such a mark over a word. Sentence boundaries are marked in oral texts largely on the basis of pauses. It is not always the case that a speaker concludes a sentence by means of pausing (pauses can occur sentence internally), but in general this principle applies. An oral sentence, then, can consist of three or more main clauses in additive sequence.

A discourse-based approach to the study of oral and written speech extends previous analysis and effects a change in analysis from the quantitative to the functional. Features of a given variety can be determined and counted, but it is necessary besides to understand the functional properties of those features. Oral and written speech must be examined for their generative capacities in discourse and for their ability to influence and differentiate texts within genres. We best understand these media as processing varieties which interact with ideational content as well as with genre and other factors in discourse to produce meaning. Meaning itself cannot be distinguished from its production.

2

Oral and Written Narrative

Narrative is the most universal genre. All human beings across cultures relate stories of the past. It is this ability that allows people to understand one another and transmit knowledge of themselves to others in or beyond their group. Narrative conventions may differ from culture to culture, but the fact that human beings conceptualize and experience the past in narrative form permits them to know themselves in a way not possible for other living creatures. Conventionally thought of as simple, narrative is, in fact, a complex discourse type concerned with experiental knowledge:

"Narrate" is from the Latin *narrare* ("to tell") which is akin to the Latin *gnarus* ("knowing," "acquainted with," "expert in") both derivative from the Indo-European root *gnâ* ("to know") whence the vast family of words deriving from the Latin *cognoscere*, including "cognition" itself, and "noun" and "pronoun," the Greek *gignoskein* whence *gnosis*, and the Old English past participle *gecnawan* whence the Modern English "know." Narrative is, it would seem, rather an appropriate term for a reflexive activity which seeks to "know" (even in its ritual aspect, to have *gnosis* about) antecedent events and the meaning of those events. *Drama* itself is, of course, derived from the Greek *drân* ("to do or act"); hence narrative is knowledge (and/or *gnosis*) emerging from action, that is experiential knowledge. (Turner 1979:163)

Formally, narrative has been defined by Labov as "one method of recapitulating past experience by matching a verbal sequence of clauses to the sequence of events which (it is inferred) actually occurred" (1972b:359–60). Labov's definition of narrative overlaps with a speech-act definition of narrative as a discourse whose direction of fit is word to world rather than world to word. Thus, Labov focuses on why human beings tell stories, what he calls the "so what factor."

If an audience responds to a given narrative with an evaluation of "so what," the narrative is unsuccessful and, in effect, does not count. To be successful, a narrative must be "tellable" for both audience and speaker. Evaluation occurs, then, throughout the telling of a story and is conveyed linguistically through use of comparators (adjectives, modals, negatives, futures, imperatives) and intensifiers (expressive phonology, repetition, qualifiers). Evaluation can be both internal and external. In external evaluation, the narrator comments directly upon events, while in internal evaluation, comments are embedded as the thoughts of the narrator at the time of an event or in the remarks of one character to another. Of the linguistic devices for evaluation, the most celebrated are metaphor and simile, which are comparators.

Labov divides narrative structurally into initial abstract, which summarizes the story or point of the story; orientation, which provides background, usually in the form of a time and space frame of reference; complicating action; result or resolution; coda, which marks the end of a story and "bring[s] the narrator and the listener back to the point at which they entered the narrative" (365); and evaluation. Labov further distinguishes narrative clauses which are not freely permutable and thus must be temporally ordered from those which are "free" and thus can serve either the function of orientation or evaluation. Labov defines a minimal narrative "as a sequence of two clauses which are *temporally ordered*: that is, a change in their order will result in a change in the temporal sequence of the original semantic interpretation" (360).

Labov's definition of narrative provides a very detailed account of the major linguistic features of narrative as well as a partial analysis of why we tell stories, but Labov's focus on narrative as a means of conveying past experience does not fully explicate this most basic genre. When narrative is compared with other principal genres, what stands out is the strong dual orientation narration has to action and agency or what is referred to in literary criticism as plot and character. In narrative, the past actions of a given agent or agents lead to a resolved state. Oral and written narratives treat these two principal dimensions of narrative very differently.

Research on the distinction between oral and written narrative has been done recently by Wallace Chafe (1982), Deborah Tannen (1982), and Walter Ong (1981, 1982). Examining oral and written narratives, Chafe argues that the distinction between "colloquial" and "ritual" oral language parallels that between oral and written speech. He therefore correlates features which he identifies with written speech with those he observes in oral ritual speech (as narration): "We might then expect to find in ritual language something like the integration of written language, as opposed to the fragmentation of spoken" (50). Further, Chafe argues that oral ritual performers are as detached as writers are from their audience. In Senecan oral ritual performance Chafe found an extensive use (36 per 1000) of an impersonal reference marker comparable to *one* in English and *on* in French. Chafe states that "As with the passive, this prefix allows the omission of specific reference to the agent of an action, and thus appears also to be evidence of detachment" (51). Deagentive passives where the *by* phrase is deleted permit such omission, but such structures are not comparable to those where agency is marked, even by such impersonal deictics as *one* or *on*. Moreover, where English frequently permits the deletion of agency by means of the passive, French almost always requires the use of *on* to mark the presence of an agent. It is possible that the impersonal reference marker Chafe isolates in ritual Senecan narratives is a device for speaker detachment, but his comparison of English *one* and French *on* to the deagentive passive in English—a structure found primarily in scientific discourse—is questionable.

Tannen's analysis is in large part a development of Chafe's analysis concerning integration and involvement in oral ritual narratives. She maintains that there is a continuum between oral and written speech because oral and written narratives share features in common, features which she ascribes primarily to oral speech. Tannen collected parallel narrative texts from one graduate class in discourse analysis. In her sample she found that written narratives, when they approximate short stories rather than exposition, exhibit many of the features theoretically assigned to oral speech (informal register, direct quotation and greater degree of detail). Tannen, therefore, arrives at a similar thesis to that of Blankenship (1962), that is, that oral and written speech do not contribute significantly to differentiation in discourse.

Although Tannen attempts to control her data for genre, she defines written narrative implicitly as "integrated" because written speech is integrated. She equates written narration with what is more traditionally thought of as written expository report and isolates as "aberrant" a narrative which is comparable to a short story. The features which Tannen accepts as those of oral speech—informal register, direct quotation, and a high degree of detail—are postulated of oral speech by Chafe, but as yet they do not have any empirical status. Formality of speech does not necessarily correlate with written speech, while quotation is certainly found in written texts. The detail of which Tannen speaks correlates with what is termed "evaluation" by Labov (1972b), a feature of narrative as a genre and not of oral speech as a medium.

Examining one "aberrant pair of spoken and written narratives," Tannen makes the following observation which pertains to her working, if unstated, definition of narrative:

> One pair of narratives collected was not typical. First, the written version was not shorter, but rather much longer than the spoken one. The spoken version contained 383 words distributed over 64 idea units; the written 693 words contained 51 sentences and 85 clauses or phrases. Furthermore, the written version did not seem less personal or imageable; if anything, it seemed more so. The reason is that it was not expository prose, but a short story. (11)

In this analysis Tannen is assuming that written narratives, because written, should be short and concise just as written expositions (summaries, reports) are. In her view, the presence of features of involvement (self-reference, monitoring, "fuzziness," use of quotation) postulated as features of oral speech by Chafe has theoretically elongated one narrative and in effect transformed it from "exposition" into "creative writing." There is a continuum between oral and written speech, therefore, because features of orality show up in certain written texts.

Genre has not been closely examined in this analysis. Summaries or reports have been categorized as narratives, but they do not report events in the past. For example, Tannen cites one sentence from a written text which represents in her view the highly integrated nature of written speech: "Dale, in the ninth grade, will go to junior high school, which for this academic year consists of only the 8th and 9th graders, for a total of 2,000 students" (9). This sentence is not a narrative clause. Tannen herself notes that, "The spoken version uses the present continuous tense, whereas the written uses the more formal *will*" (10). She is correct with regard to the formal and informal distinction provided by the two tense forms, but futurity conveyed by the periphrastic form *is going* or by the modal *will* is consonant with an oral or written report, not with narrative, which is characterized linguistically by the simple past or the past imperfect.

Ironically, the aberrant set of parallel narratives Tannen cites are the only genuine narratives present in her data. The written narrative is longer than the oral narrative in this set because the narrator has built on the original oral version by expanding upon the complication in events and in so doing has made the story more interesting.[1] Such expansion could also have been effected by the narrator in a second oral telling. It is common for narrators to embellish upon, change, and improve stories in the course of subsequent retellings. Embellishment and the presence of greater evaluation in a narrative text do not derive from oral "involvement" but rather are features of narrative itself. Imprecise definition of narrative and presuppositions about the length of oral and written texts have led Tannen to ignore the features of narrative as defined by Labov (1972b). Her view that there is a continuum between oral and written speech does not really hold because she is remarking upon features of genre which are shared between these two texts.

Ong has found significant differentiation between oral and written narrative discourse in his examination of the epic. Building on the work of Lord (1960) and Havelock (1963), he has pointed out that oral epics are a principal means by which oral cultures convey and maintain cultural knowledge over time. He argues that not words but oral formulaic expressions are the basic linguistic units of oral cultures. Oral epic poetry is replete with oral formulaic utterances conveyed in heavily rhythmic, balanced patterns with extensive repetition or antithesis, alliteration, and assonance. Oral speech is additive rather than subordinate, epithetic in its use of terminology and names, and, in particular, it is redundant or copious in expression.

With regard to thematic organization, Ong maintains that the oral epic differs from the written epic in the way the bard manipulates standard thematic subject matter. He points out that Milton may start *Paradise Lost in medias res* because he has a preconception of the epic's beginning, middle, and end. But the oral bard, in contrast, can have no such preconception.[2] Singing in response to an audience which influences the ongoing structure of a song, the oral bard strings together a huge repertoire of episodes juggling their selection as he sings. The Greek term for this bardic behaviour was *rhapsodien*, "to stitch together song." The *Beowulf* poet makes explicit reference to this bardic practice when he states that in singing "word oder fand," "one word finds another." What is most likely meant by this phrase is the evocation of one episode or theme by another in the sequential chain-like construction of story in song.[3]

Ong's analysis seems to indicate that in oral and written narration, at least, there are media constraints in the way information can be processed. Significantly, Pawley and Syder argue for a "one-clause-at-a-time constraint" in oral speech which "underlies the characteristic 'clause-chaining' style of spontaneous connected discourse" (1983:565).[4] However, the "one-clause-at-a-time constraint" they hypothesize does not entirely account for the strong ordering differences in oral and written speech these researchers themselves observe. Although oral speech may largely be made up of linear sequences of clauses, the features which Pawley and Syder isolate (e.g., delayed relative clauses) show that often clausal structures are interrupted or suspended to be completed later as speech progresses. The "one-clause-at-a-time constraint" they put forth is, therefore, a tendency or general processing behaviour in oral speech. Nonetheless, such processing interacts significantly with other factors of text production in narrative.

In the three sets of naturally occurring parallel texts to be examined in this chapter, processing is a significant factor in the generation of narratives. Of course, it is not possible for two stories, no matter how much they share the same topic or content, to be the same. Fundamental changes take place in the telling. As Chafe (1979) has pointed out, "subchunking" is performed differently on different tellings. However, as suggested by the work of Ong and Pawley and Syder as well as by subsequent analysis here, the media of oral and written speech perform a role in the transformation of content.

PERSONAL NARRATIVE: THE BOY IN THE MIRROR

"The Boy in the Mirror" is a personal narrative told by Martin Starret, the famous British Columbia mountain man, about an event in his childhood. In both oral and written accounts Starret recalls his first strange experience in seeing himself in a mirror and his brother's mischievous instructions to hit the apparition which he sees there. The fundamental facts are provided in both narratives: Martin returns home to find that the bed he shares with his older brother has been moved; the bed is now adjacent to a mirror; he is able to see himself in the mirror but does not understand that the reflection which he sees is his own; he asks his brother who the boy in the mirror is; his brother tells him to punch the boy; he does this; the mirror cracks and in so doing makes a noise; his mother hears this noise; she enters the boys' room to determine what has happened.

The two stories share a basic narrative core, but in a number of important ways they diverge from each other. In terms of factual presentation, Martin's brother, Willie, does not volunteer to tell his part in the "accident" in the oral version. It is Martin who is blamed and must vindicate himself. He informs his mother that Willie told him to punch the mirror. The point of the oral version is that Martin himself is not punished but is "let out" and that his mother is a forgiving and gentle person.

In the written version, Martin is to a greater extent portrayed as a victim of both his brother and the adult world in general. The passive serves to facilitate the child's perspective: he is consistently in the patient role, consistently being done for or done to. The point of this telling is that Martin learns to be less trusting and more sceptical about those who tell him to do things. He learns to make decisions for himself. The story, then, is about the transition from a state of childhood to an incipient state of adulthood. Also, the function of the mother in this telling is more directly that of a judge. His brother immediately admits his part in instigating the event and is physically punished by his mother. Martin is not required to vindicate himself. His mother is the source of justice and in this telling she physically exits the room once her work as judge is done. Since in this version his brother is punished by his mother, Martin learns that trust is not something to be granted freely, even to kin.

Clearly, these two tellings provide very different versions of the same event. But why are they so different? Why does one concentrate on escape and the other on trust? Why is the mother in one version an angel of mercy and in the other a stern judge who would have been a great deal tougher on the two boys had she not had "important company"? What part are media playing in the selection of perspective and events in the telling of the basic story?

How media influence the structure of narrative discourse can be determined to a certain extent by a breakdown of syntactic constructions in discourse. The syntactic profile in Table 1 reveals the syntactic makeup of the oral and written versions of Martin Starret's narrative "The Boy in the Mirror" about one of his childhood experiences.

Examining this profile, we can see that in the oral text simple sentences predominate, since they occur in 50 per cent of all syntactic structures. Also, there are overall fewer subordinate structures (relative, adverbial, and noun clauses) in the oral version, although there is a slight increase in "embedded" or intervening clauses. Interestingly, however, there are more complex sentences in the oral narrative than in the written version. This difference is explained by the fact that compound/complex sentences, rather than complete sentences predominate in the written text. Fifty-three per cent of all sentences in the written version are compound/complex, while only 15 per cent are compound/complex in the oral version.

Adjectival constructions (relatives, participles, attributive adjec-

TABLE 1
Syntactic Profile/The Boy in the Mirror

Sentences	Oral 20 (286wds)	Written 13 (339wds)
Simple	**10 (50%)**	**03 (23%)**
Compound	02 (10%)	02 (15%)
Complex	04 (20%)	01 (07%)
Compound/complex	**03 (15%)**	**07 (53%)**
Embedded	01 (05%)	00 (00%)
Relative clauses	**00**	**05**
Adverbial clauses	02	04
Noun clauses	05	05
Co-ordinate clauses	**16**	**09**
Conjoining phrases	01	04
Participle phrases	03	04
Gerund phrases	02	03
Infinitive phrases	05	04
Passives	**01**	**08**
Exist. *There*/clefts	02	00
Attributive adjs.	**12**	**24**
(participles)	02	06
Nouns in apposition	00	01

tives) and passives are also more fully present in the written narrative. Only in the frequency of infinitive phrases does the oral narrative differ in dominance with the written narrative.

The syntactic profile of "The Boy in the Mirror" does not support Halliday' s view that oral speech is more "choreographic" than written speech. Excluding relative clauses, which Halliday identifies as embedding devices, there are, in fact, more adverbial clauses in the written version and an equivalent number of noun clauses. Chafe's general view, then, that co-ordination is favoured in oral speech and subordination in written speech is supported in the grammar of these two texts. However, a syntactic profile does not allow more than a superficial and quantitative analysis of any text. To determine if the additive syntax of oral speech produces what Chafe refers to as "fragmentation," while the presence of a high percentage of adjectival structures produces "integration" requires examination of the use of those structures in any given set of parallel texts. A syntactic profile can provide only a general grammatical outline. Ultimately, all structures must be examined in terms of the role they play in discourse itself.

The broad contexts of situation in which each story is told are roughly the same, although certain specifics differ. In the oral telling, Martin Starret is responding to Imbert Orchard's request to explain childhood memories of growing up in Hope, BC, at the turn of the century. Starret is asked to explain his sensual response to his environment at the time, that is, his response to the natural environment in which he lived as well as to his home environment. The story of the mirror arises when Starret remembers what his room looked like to him as a boy. In the written telling, the story is part of a chronological telling of events in his childhood. Orchard had encouraged Starret to keep a written record of his boyhood and other memories. The tellings of the story arise, then, in somewhat different ways, although the purpose in each telling is fundamentally the same.

But this does not really explain why the stories differ. Different choices are made in the actual tellings of the main events during the course of active narration. The question is whether these choices are constrained by media and whether certain choices predetermine other choices in the construction of each story.

One important difference between the stories is that the oral version provides an abstract, while the written version does not. In the oral version, Starret tells Orchard that he remembers the mirror because it is cracked and because he cracked it. He then proceeds to tell Orchard how this came about. In contrast, there is no abstract in the written version to focus attention upon the essential "how" of events. The story is told as part of a larger story in which Starret visits his grandfather in Vancouver. The story of the mirror is part of his account of his return home from this major event in his child's life. The state of his childhood is the more dominant focus. We can say, then, that the written version is about an aspect of what it is to be a child, while the oral version is more directly about the breaking of a mirror.

The oral version is embedded in a vivid description of Starret's actual home environment:

And I remember the **sun** hitting it [window] there and you'd wake up some mornings you wouldn't be dreaming till you'd just wake wide up and there's the sun. And I'd look around move the neck this side and the other and I'm **home**. **This** this is my **room** I would think. And I'd look on on the **wall**. And the mirror'd be over there. There was an old fashioned **wash**stand with a **bowl** and a **picture** and so on. But there was a there was a **loôking** glass and I remember that that looking glass because it had a a crooked **break** in it. It just **cracked** in the **glass** and then sometimes I'd **smile** a little because I'd remember **breaking** that glass as a very small boy.

The primary concern here is with the sense the child has of having a home and of being home. What Labov refers to as the "so-what" factor in this story has to do with the potential threat to that feeling of belonging, of being home and safe. Understandably, then, Starret's coda in this version has to do with an ongoing sense of protection and belonging. He is not evicted from his home despite his aggressive act: "I got let out and he [brother] was **told** not to **tell** me to do things like that any more."

In oral speech, information which is thematically important, often where theme and new information co-occur in the theme slot in the sentence, or information which is new and therefore focused, is typically marked by emphatic stressing during pronunciation. Thus Starret stresses "**sun**," "**home**," "**this**," "**room**," "**wall**," "**wash**" in "**wash**stand," "**bowl**," "**picture**," "**looking**" in "**looking** glass," "**break**," "**cracked**," "**glass**," "**smile**," and "**breaking**." All these stressed lexemes convey crucial new information to the text. In particular he stresses the "**break**" in the glass and the "**breaking**" of the looking glass in the room. Where we have clear lexical cohesion in this text, we also have literal co-association. The break in the glass is an ongoing reminder (the conditional is employed: "I'd remember") of the actual event of breaking the glass, important to Starret because of the more symbolic potential break or disruption it may have caused in his own home environment. Interestingly, in his teens the family did separate into two groups, Starret living with his father and his brother Willie going with his mother. Only much later was he reunited with his mother.

Orally, Martin introduces the new topic of the mirror or looking glass by means of an existential *there are* construction, which can be compared functionally to a cleft construction. Existential *there* is used as an explicit new topic marker. Moreover, Starret employs both "there was" and stressed intonation, "**loôking** glass," to signal the importance of this new topic and the story that it calls to mind. Notably, he refers to the mirror in his room as a "**loôking** glass" rather than as a "mirror." Starret more extensively uses the composite or phrasal construction *looking glass* in oral speech, whereas he employs the synthetic lexeme *mirror* in written speech.[5] However, "glass" also better serves the topic of breakage since one of its semantic features is certainly +break.[6] The gerund "looking" is topically useful as well. Starret stresses "**looking**" in his description of the glass because, of course, it is the act of looking that precipitates the act of breaking in this narrative about breakage.

Of great importance in this oral narrative is that Starret presents himself as an active agent in the story. It is in this respect that the oral version principally contrasts with the written version where Starret portrays himself more extensively as a victim. In the oral abstract Starret remembers actively "**breaking** that glass." The gerund in this phrase is transitive in construction with glass as the literal and grammatical object of "**breaking**." Starret appropriately nominalizes the action as one event, but he suppresses information about how the event took place, how he did what he did. Nonetheless, agency is clearly marked through his use of the transitive verb *break*.

This difference in perspective is equally evident in the narrative cores of the two versions of "The Boy in the Mirror." In both the initial orientation is provided by gerund constructions providing temporal and circumstantial context.

After being away visiting my grandparents I returned one time and the **bed** had been **moved** in the room to right alongside of the **glass**, my mother not thinking anything a the **glass**'ed be broken. (Oral narrative)

Upon arriving at Silvervale we were greeted by Father and Mother who were busy at milking time. Being evening we were at once taken into the house where we enjoyed a belated meal, and I was undressed and put into my accustomed bed with my Brother Willie. We were left alone with the bedroom door shut; we could hear our elders conversing in the next room. Our bedroom appeared familiar to me except that our bed had been moved around to a different side of the room so the large old fashioned mirror which hung on the wall and within easy reach was reflecting our likenesses, and the long summer evening gave ample light to show our every movement and detail. (Written narrative)

In the oral version, Starret specifies the sequence of his actions through use of the orienting phrase "after being away visiting my grandparents." We know what he has been doing before his return. He then focuses solely on his own return in the first narrative clause of this version: "I returned one time." The verb which he uses is intransitive, but it is active and there is an implicit locative goal, home. This action is abruptly juxtaposed to a description of a state of affairs: "and the **bed** had been **moved** in the room to right alongside of the **glass**, my mother not thinking anything a the **glass**'ed be broken." As protagonist he is confronted immediately with the complicating action of the story: his mother has moved his bed.

The conjunction "and" here does not merely link the action and the state; it serves to juxtapose them dramatically. There is an iconic use of the syntax whereby the syntax mirrors the real events (or rather mirrors the teller's perception of the events at the time of telling). Rather than explain to his listener, Orchard, that he discovered a new state of affairs immediately upon return, Starret simply juxtaposes the new state with the information of his return. The new state is conveyed to the listener as it was perceived by the returning boy in the real situation he is telling about. *And* functions as an evaluator by drawing the listener's attention to the remarkable or special, thus serving what Labov calls the "so-what" factor in narrative discourse.

In contrast to the oral version of "The Boy in the Mirror," the orientation in the written version is both more fully descriptive and radically different in terms of perspective. The dramatic juxtaposition of events afforded by an additive syntax is absent. We are immediately oriented to a receptive world defined by the strong presence of a "Father and Mother." *Father* and *mother* are both capitalized, and by assigning these lexemes status as proper nouns, Starret textually emphasizes his parents' importance to him as a child. The deictic centre of the discourse is further specified as that of the parents since the phrase "Upon *arriving* [my italics] at Silvervale" orients the reader to the time and place of the parents and not to that of the child. Starret expands upon this orientation by indicating the parents' activity at the time of his arrival: "we were greeted by Father and Mother *who were busy at milking time* [my italics]." In keeping with this receptive orientation, he employs the passive. The child is greeted by his parents, taken, fed, undressed, put to bed, and finally left alone. The boy is the recipient of an entire sequence of events before the events of the narrative take place. His status as a child is made explicit and concrete by virtue of this extensive use of the passive and by virtue of the strong temporal and physical deictic centring of his parents and their home environment.

In the written version of Martin Starret's story of the boy in the mirror, use of the passive in large part creates the perspective of a child in a world of adults. Once selected by means of the passive voice and use of other-orienting verbs such as *arrive*, the view Starret has of himself as a recipient maintains itself throughout the discourse. Thus, he states in his written coda: "However the *unexpected* act on my part, and the warning I *received* at the time, had a tendency to not do always as others *advised* me to" [my italics]. The sentence is not entirely grammatical as Starret phrases it, but we do have use of a past participle, "unexpected," a conceptual passive, "received," and grammatical conceptualization of Starret as a recipient by means of the dative "advised me to." In the use of a nominal construction such as "the unexpected act," he grammatically divorces the behaviour from himself in keeping with the explicit warning from his mother to behave differently. But the act is also "unexpected," presumably by his parents and specifically his mother. Again the deictic centre in this narration is that of the parents and not of the boy himself, as it most definitely is in his oral version of the story. The passive, then, has significant implications for the structure of written discourse and, in particular, for the construction of perspective and viewpoint.

Temporal events are also handled differently from those in oral speech. In the first sentence of the written narration three distinct events are collapsed into one: "Upon arriving at Silvervale we were greeted by Father and Mother who were busy at milking time." In the oral text events are treated discretely, each event being related to a subsequent event by use of *and* or another conjunction. The "one-clause-at-a-time constraint" proposed by Pawley and Synder, though seldom a constraint, is a strong tendency. Oral speech employs a primarily linear syntax, whereas written speech does not. In the written narrative, therefore, events, as above, can be collapsed into one. A "constellational" rather than an additive syntax occurs. Events that would be separate and distinct in oral speech have lost their separate and distinct status and, like planets, revolve around a central event which becomes the focus of all other actions or events in the sentence as a whole. Moreover, we do not get more for less in such a syntax as Chafe, Beaman, and others have argued;[7] meaning is altered in a written "constellational" syntax.

In the sentence cited above, three distinct events are described: arriving, greeting, and milking. Any of these actions could have been designated as central, but greeting is chosen. The other events do not so much support greeting, though one is adverbial and the other is adjectival, as convey an illusory sense of simultaneity. "Arriving" and "milking," by virtue of being gerunds, have lost information about tense provided by finite verbs. Present participles and gerunds, however, are aspectually imperfective and so convey a conception of ongoing process, which in turn conveys the implication that the actions they describe co-occur with the activity in the main verb in a given sentence. More specifically, the conventional implicature provided is not just that the activities in the finite and non-finite verbs overlap, but also that they occur simultaneously. Perception of time in written speech is thus frequently non-real. Events are organized synoptically so that events which are quite distinct are temporally rearranged and seen as interrelated and connected. Conceptual cohesion results from loss of temporal information in the use of non-finite verbs and in turn supports the illusion of a world where once-distinct events interact simultaneously and coherently. In the written narrative, we lose time but gain order.

Order is also gained by virtue of syntactic orientation to a causative rather than resultative analysis of events. Cohesion is created in the written narrative through devices such as left-branching participles, which can convey causative meaning. For example, in narrating his mother's involvement in the story of the boy in the mirror, Martin Starret represents her actions and behaviour in very different ways in the written and oral versions:

Hearing the unusual noise, Mother came in to investigate. When she noticed the cracked mirror, she asked Willie how it had happened and he said,"I told Martin to punch the boy in the glass." (Written narrative)

My mother came in to see what the noise's about an' she said uh "Wh Why, what happened to the **mirror**?" "Oh Martin **punched** it." (Oral narrative)

In both versions Starret has just punched the mirror as his brother told him to do. Both versions then deal with the mother's response to this previous event. However, the written version collapses two events into one: the mother's hearing of the noise and her entrance into her sons' room. Yet the participle here does not convey the idea that hearing, coming in, and investigating go on simultaneously; rather, it serves to interrelate all these actions causally. The participle "hearing," in left-hand position to the noun it modifies, conveys a meaning of cause for the events which follow both literally and grammatically: Starret's mother comes in because she has heard an unusual noise, which serves as the prime mover to her later action. Moreover, the participle in left-hand position, by virtue of its placement between two clauses, serves to link graphically the event of the boy's punching the mirror with his mother's aural awareness of this action and her subsequent response and reaction to it. Left branching participles, then, function very much like conjunctions and promote an analysis of cause rather than result.

Gunther Kress and Michael Rowan (1982) have argued that causation is differently expressed by children and by adults. Children express causation via an additive syntax: "Yesterday when we played Red Rover Jody and Stephen smashed into each other and Jody had a blood ear and she couldn't hear very well and then she had to go and clean her ear" (157). Causation in children's language is expressed by means of a regularity view which "sees causal processes as merely the regular succession of states of affairs; a cause and an effect are things which happen together in sequence, and there is no more to causality than this togetherness" (161). The powers view, in contrast, "embodies the idea that one thing causes another by making it happen: that a causal connection is a real, active process, by which one thing produces another" (161). The explicit marking of cause, according to Kress and Rowan, distinguishes the speech of adults from that of children. They further suggest that written and oral speech are implicated in this distinction between a regularity and a powers view of causation, but only to the extent that each medium may facilitate the development of one view or the other. Writing, they argue, "speeds up the development, use, and frequency of occurrence of the powers view" (176).

The distinction Kress and Rowan make between a regularity view and a powers view underlies a fundamental difference between oral and written speech, although I believe it is more accurately expressed as a distinction between resultative analysis and true causative analysis. The regularity view is evident in Starret's oral version when he states: "So I **punched** the **glass** and that's how it got **cracked**." This is a more explicit representation than that of the child above and focuses more explicitly on result. "Got" is an inchoative marker which expresses change of state, while the participle "**cracked**" marks the new state or result. Cause rather than result would be expressed if Martin were to have said *So I punched the glass and cracked it*. However, his actual phrasing parallels that of the child cited by Kress and Rowan and conveys resultative rather than causative analysis.

Pragmatically, the additive linear syntax of oral speech can convey numerous readings. Quirk et al. identify eight uses of *and* as a coordinator. *And* can have resultative, sequential, contrastive, conditional, comparative, additive, and explanatory force (1985:13.22–7). *And* can also be used stylistically when it is stressed to mark the introduction into discourse of important new information. In addition, *and* can have purposeful (*I went to the store and I brought some groceries*) and simultaneous force (*I went out and Margaret stayed home*). With resultative force, a concept of result links any two events but puts emphasis on the second. Where cause is conceptualized, the first event is emphasized. Cause involves a "prime mover" and so a predisposition to examine the initiation of an event rather than a given effect or result.

Oral and written speech, then, do not merely affect perspective in terms of the preference of one for the active voice and of the other for the passive; they affect perspective in that events are viewed, sequenced and related in fundamentally different ways. The oral predisposition to result, what Kress and Rowan refer to as the "regularity view," requires that attention be given to the specifics of what happened, whereas the focus of written speech on cause, or the "powers view," promotes attention to why events happen. Thus, in his written version of "The Boy in the Mirror," Martin Starret explains his fascination with the mirror newly placed on the wall: "This was the first mirror I have any recollection of looking at." The mirror itself is seen as a prime mover because it ignites his curiosity which in turn causes him to ask his brother about the boy he finds residing within it.

In the oral version, Starret also narrates the events in sequence, but each event is discrete: "And and I looked over to **glass** here 'twas evening then and my I see a little **boy** in there and I said to my brother, 'Who who's that what little boy is that there beside you?'" The *and* which links the first and second clause in this long sentence is an *and* of result. This *and* can be stressed if the result is of particular significance or narratively unusual. However, in this sentence "my" conveys Starret's response to what he unexpectedly sees in the mirror. The events here are not seen as causally linked. Starret does not explain that this was the first mirror he had ever seen. The listener deduces this information from the events as narrated. Focus is not on how events began but on precisely how each event happened in terms of its immediate temporal context or the immediate context of preceding events. Causal linkage or analysis is not imposed on events which exist in temporal or resultative relation.

HISTORICAL NARRATIVE:
THE LEGEND OF GUNNINUTE THE OUTLAW

"The Legend of Gunninute" told by Martin Starret is an example of narrative as historical account. In his two parallel histories, Starret tells the story of a famous Canadian outlaw who eluded capture by the police for many years before finally giving himself up to the authorities. Such narratives are second-order narratives; that is, Starret does not recount his own past experience but rather past experience that is shared by those in his culture and generation. As a second-order narrator, Starret functions as an historian, often the traditional function of the bard or singer in oral cultures.

Starret's two accounts of "The Legend of Gunninute" differ fundamentally in their structuring of and perspective on the basic events of this story of a famous BC outlaw at the turn of the century. Syntactic differences are highly evident, although not identical to those in the two versions of "The Boy in the Mirror," as shown in Table 2.

TABLE 2
Syntactic Profile/The Legend of Gunninute

Sentences	Oral 87 (1260wds)	Written 20 (707wds)
Simple	**38 (44%)**	**05 (25%)**
Compound	11 (13%)	02 (10%)
Complex	**26 (30%)**	**08 (40%)**
Compound/complex	08 (09%)	03 (15%)
Embedded	04 (04%)	01 (10%)
Relative clauses	09	09
Adverbial clauses	09	05
Noun clauses	31	06
Co-ordinate clauses	43	05
Conjoining phrases	09	04
Participle phrases	04	07
Gerund phrases	07	04
Infinitive phrases	12	02
Passives	01	07
Exist. *There*/clefts	03	00
Attributive adjs.	**52**	**65**
(participles)	01	05
Nouns in apposition	02	04

Simple sentences and co-ordinate clauses predominate syntactically in the oral version of this history, as they do in the syntactic profile of "The Boy in the Mirror." There is, nonetheless, a high percentage of complex structures in the oral version (30%), although not as high as that in the written version (40%). Noun clauses are also slightly more dominant (31/87 sents. or 33%) in the oral version than in the written version (6/20 sents. or 30%). This difference is explained by the fact that the nature of narration in the oral version is often indirect; Starret reports events as he has heard them from other sources and so employs a high percentage of noun clauses. Chafe's contention that quotation is a major feature of oral speech would seem to be supported by this fact. Moreover, the written version is not highly influenced by additive structures, with the majority of its complex structures being in complex sentences alone.

Yet clause and phrase percentiles in "The Legend of Gunninute" are essentially comparable to those in "The Boy in the Mirror." Adjectival structures (attributive adjectives, relative clauses, and participle phrases) are dominant in the written version as is the passive voice. There is also a similar dominant use of infinitive phrases in the oral version. Generally, the nominal/verbal split that is apparent in the earlier narrative set is equally apparent in the two versions of "The Legend of Gunninute," as is the split between an additive and a synthetic syntax.

The versions of this history are also structurally very different. In the oral version of "The Legend of Gunninute," Martin takes great care to incorporate the story of his acquisition of the facts into his telling of the story itself. The story, then, is structured episodically with each episode supplying a new piece of information to the listener in the same order as Martin received it himself. In only one episode is Martin a first-order narrator.

In assigning status to the primary narrators whose stories he is retelling, Starret stresses their last names or Father Coccola's epithet: Bob **Hume**, Bill **Hamilton**, Father Coccola, the **missionary**. This is important new information in the text and clarifies the exact sources of Starret's information. In oral narration such sources are important since one need not be believed unless one can, in effect, produce one's sources. Starret, therefore, embeds himself in an oral tradition whereby the story has legitimacy as part of the historical record.

The written version, unlike the oral, is organized thematically rather than episodically. As a result, only one aspect of the story of Gunninute, his eluding capture at that time, is given narrative prominence. Also, the written version of "The Legend of Gunninute" is told directly by Starret with no concern for the sources of his information. The story functions as part of his overall journal account of events during the year 1907, but it is presented as one complete story about Gunninute and the BC police's attempt to capture him with the conflict between Indian and white culture as the sub-text.

What can be termed "plot" is understood and treated very differently in these two parallel texts. In his work on oral epics, Ong has shown that they are constructed episodically and cannot genuinely commence *in medias res* because the overall structure of the text is not or cannot be known beforehand by the narrator. In contrast to the oral epic poet, Ong argues, "Milton had in mind a plot, with a beginning, middle, and end (Aristotle, *Poetics* 1450b) in a sequence corresponding temporally to that of the events he was reporting. This plot he deliberately dismembered in order to reassemble its parts in a consciously contrived anachronistic pattern" (1981:14). Equally, as a natural oral narrator Starret has no means by which he can "deliberately dismember" the events of his legend of Gunninute for evaluative effect. There is no thematic focus, as, for example, Milton provides in *Paradise Lost*: "I thence/Invoke thy aid to my adventurous song. . . . That, to the height of this great argument/I may assert Eternal Providence/And *justify the ways of God* [my italics] to men."

What Ong argues about the discourse properties of oral and written epics is true of oral and written narratives longer than the simpler personal narrative such as "The Boy in the Mirror." However, we need to consider whether or not plot is, in fact, only a written convention, as Ong maintains. Oral narratives are far more concerned with plot in the sense of action than are written narratives. It is not for nothing that in his *Aspects of the Novel* E.M. Forster takes up his debate on narrative with Aristotle over the importance of plot. Where Aristotle sees plot as primary, Forster relegates it to second place giving character and characterization greater emphasis. Forster understands literary narrative as a written art; Aritotle's conventions are based on oral Greek theatre. Plot is not absent from Starret's oral version of the history of Gunninute because it is episodically structured; rather, plot as chronological action is expressed through this episodic structure. Each episode is conveyed in clear sequence; there is a beginning and an ending. "Middle," however, is not at some specified conceptual centre but instead exists as an infinitely expandable possibility having one or more episodes in its ultimate makeup. Middle is plastic rather than focal or crucial.

The rhapsodic technique employed by the oral narrator focuses upon discrete actions related conceptually to one another, while the thematic technique employed by the writerly narrator focuses upon cause and characterization. Indeed, the discourse properties of oral and written narrative are very much like those of the syntax of oral and written speech. In oral syntax events are most commonly linked together by the conjunction *and*; episodes in oral narrative are linked or "stitched together" one episode at a time, each bringing to mind another in coherent sequence. In written speech events are constellationally organized; written narrative focuses attention upon one event of a possible number in an effort to organize experience centrally around it. These differences in structural organization would indicate that quite distinct processing behaviour is employed in oral and written composition which traverses the boundary of syntax into that of discourse.

Topic or coherence is further differentiated in Starret's two versions of the Gunninute legend. This is especially evident in the openings where the use of active and passive voice as well as topic-marking are contrastive:

In the fall of nine ss hundred and **seven** I was working in the Whitworth ranch in the Skagit close to the international **border** and a man came to work

on that ranch name of Bob **Hume**. He told me about Cataline the packer and
he told me about this **Gunninute** the outlaw who who had **killed** these two
men at **Hazeltown** and who was out in hiding in the **mountains**. (Oral
narrative)

During this season 1907 at Two Mile, the first camp out of Hazelton, a horse
wrangler named Alex McIntosh, a half breed, native of Hazelton who was
working with one of the most prominant [sic] trains, was shot and killed
dead early one morning while out herding in the pack animals from night
grazing to Two Mile Campground, where the cargo had been placed the
previous evening. Another horse haser of another outfit was shot and killed
dead that forenoon also by apparently the same Murderer, who by these
terrible acts proved or appeared to prove that both deeds had been committed by the same crackshot ability. (Written narrative)

The oral version immediately introduces Gunninute as the main
topic of discourse and does so in two distinct ways, while the written version first focuses upon Gunninute's murdered victims and
only later, in dramatic revelation, introduces Gunninute as topic and
explicit agent. In the oral version Starret first employs the demonstrative *this* before "**Gunninute**." Such a non-deictic or non-referen-
tial usage in oral speech serves to indicate that the noun modified is
a new topic in discourse. Benji Wald has pointed out that Modern
Oral English has developed what he terms new-*this* to introduce
"new referents which were not previously shared by the conver-
sants" (1983:96). Moreover, in keeping with Perlman's observation
(1969), he notes that new-*this* fundamentally functions as a new
topic marker and so supplies the strong implication that "*more information* about the referent is imminent as the discourse progresses"
(97).One can say that new-*this* is not anaphoric but cataphoric in
terms of focus in discourse. Starret also specifies Gunninute as a
new topic by stressing his name in speech and so reinforces the
function of new-*this*. Since Starret was in his eighties when he told
this oral version of Gunninute's story in the 1960s, new-*this* must
have been a feature in Modern Oral English for at least one hundred
years and not for only the last thirty as Wald suggests.[8]
Once Gunninute is established as a topic and in turn further
identified by epithet as "**Gunninute** the outlaw," the listener of the
oral version of the story is prepared to listen to the storyteller's
account of events as they pertain to him. Thus, Gunninute as a topic
unifies all the episodes making the overall oral version coherent.
However, the oral version is not centrally organized only around
Gunninute's doings as it would be in a written version told from

Gunninute's perspective. After Starret has recounted the main events in Gunninute's killing of Alex McIntosh, and his escape and subsequent killing of another packer, and his further flight to elude the police, he then recounts other related events often from a different perspective, which expand upon the listener's understanding of the murder of McIntosh, and Gunninute's hiding out and the eventual reasons for his surrender. Each subsequent episode is an elaboration of some aspect of the previous episode.

The written version is coherent in a very different way. In it, Gunninute is introduced as a topic dramatically or climactically by means of the passive voice and not by new-*this* or heavy word stress. Unlike the oral version, the written version commences from the perspective of the murdered man, Alex McIntosh, or rather from that of the white community, since McIntosh as grammatical subject of a syntactic construction in the passive voice is grammatically a subject in the role of patient, someone therefore done to or for, in this case done to as a victim: "a horse wrangler named Alex McIntosh . . . was shot and killed dead early one morning." The deagentive passive focuses upon the fact of McIntosh's killing and thus suppresses mention of the agent of the main action. However, given that narrative must always be about agency, this deletion of the agent has the stylistic effect of producing curiosity about the source of this action: who committed the crime? This information is deliberately withheld from the reader until the second paragraph. In the intervening sentence, a statement of agency is provided, but as a characterization of that agency, not as an identification of agency. The reader still does not know who the killer is but is informed that the action performed was murder and that it was accomplished with great dexterity. The agent is both characterized as antisocial and defined in abstract terms: "Another horse haser of another outfit was shot and killed dead that forenoon also *by apparently the same Murderer*, who by these terrible acts proved or appeared to prove that both deeds had been committed *by the same crackshot ability* [my italics]." These two designations of agency dehumanize the agent who is seen first as a deliberate killer and then entirely in abstract terms as a "crackshot ability."

In its use of a factual passive the written version is not told from Gunninute's perspective. Before we learn his name, we see the main agent in this version as a negative and abstract "crackshot ability." The combined use of the agentive passive and the abstract latinate "ability," which in itself denotes agency of a skilful kind, as well as further use of the agentive noun "Murderer," in large part govern the reader's perspective on the events and conception of Gunninute, supporting a generally hostile view of Indians and Indian culture. This version provides no information about Gunninute's motives nor any other counter-perspective as the oral version does: "And my uncle C.V. Smith of Hazeltown was a fur trader at that time then. **He** said that this fellow that was killed deserved killing. He says, 'I sympathize with **the Indian**. I don't believe in any these people imposing on **the Indians** at all.'" Through sophisticated use of embedded internal evaluation in the oral version, the same speaker, Martin Starret, provides his listener with the second point of view. However, a dual perspective is not encouraged by the selection of the passive voice and the noun types used to fill the agent *by* slot in the written version. One perspective for the reader is syntactically chosen by the assignment of roles and others are excluded.

As explicit new topic Gunninute is finally introduced in the second paragraph (third sentence) of the written version. The effect of this late identification is stylistically dramatic. The killer is finally identified in response to the unstated question: Who committed "these terrible acts"? The response is structured as an hypothesis: "A BC Police Constable named James E. Kirby formally from Port Essington Detachment, had reason to believe these two murders had been committed by a Kispiox native named Simon Gunninute, a young capable Indian not only being very capable but also of good repute." The register Martin duplicates in this statement is, of course, that of an official police report. The effect of the very cautious phrasing "had reason to believe" is to suggest methodical, professional examination of the facts before the hypothesis that a given native of Kispiox is the agent in question was arrived at. Officialness is equally highlighted in the construction of the subject of the sentence. Rather than *James Kirby of the BC police believed*, officialness is stressed in the placement of the title before the name: "A *BC Police Constable* [my italics] named James E. Kirby had reason to believe." Even Gunninute as the suspect is identified cautiously and indirectly in this third passive construction since a more general designation, "a Kispiox native," precedes the actual naming of the agent, "named Simon Gunninute."

Although he is finally designated as a new topic by means of the third passive structure in the discourse, Gunninute is nonetheless a hypothetical topic since he is a hypothetical agent. The grammatical delaying of identification of agent in this written version is not only dramatic stylistically, causing the reader to wonder "who done it," but it is also in keeping with the characterization of the police as methodical, cautious solvers of crime. They are not rushing to judgment and so Gunninute is not immediately identified. The facts and problem are first presented before a solution is suggested. The written version, then, views events thematically as a "police matter," while in the oral version Starret seeks simply to tell the listener exactly what Gunninute did and what happened to him. Gunninute does not become an antagonist, nor is he subsumed as a topic by that of his desired capture by the police.

It should be clear that the passive is an extremely flexible and multi-purpose construction as employed primarily in written speech. It permits both the suppression and the explicit statement of agency and can stylistically counterbalance these two possibilities to create dramatic tension as Martin Starret does in his sequencing of three passives in the opening of his written version of the story of Gunninute. It also allows an agent or agency itself to be introduced into a discourse as a new topic. Moreover, the two uses can be combined. Starret introduces the topic of Gunninute into his discourse in a dramatic way by finally responding to a question he himself has created in the mind of his reader: "Who did this?" The written version of "The Legend of Gunninute" is not a murder mystery, but like murder mysteries it focuses upon characterization of agency and orientation to the solving of a problem since Gunninute is seen as a negative cause which needs to be "caught."

Further differentiation in the "characterization" of Gunninute can be seen in the way the next events are treated. In the oral version Gunninute's actions are simply actions or reactions stemming from events or circumstances occurring at one point in time; in the written version, thematic consistency of action is created by elimination of any competitive perspective. Thus in the oral version Martin clearly spells out the steps in Gunninute's escape from the scene of his first crime:

And morning after a **drunk** of some kind he'd shot this **packer** and then he'd gone home and shot some of his horses. He only took one or two with him and the dogs I think he left with his wife. His wife **stayed** there. And then he came **back** toward Hazeltown to **get** out to Babine on the Babine trail ˆ to get over to Takla Lake and then **up** Takla Lake and **up** the Driftwood River to a tributary of the **Skeena** up in there ˆ the **Sustut** near Bear Lake. That's where he was heading for Bear Lake or old Fort Connolly north of 56° somewhere. And **it seems** that on his way back into **Hazelton** there was a a **drover** or a **pack train man** running in a bunch of horses just coming out of a **side** road to the one that **Gunninute** was travelling on on his escape toward Babine and he saw this cloud of dust and he saw the man behind it and he **shot** him by mistake. He didn't mean to shoot that man at all he just on alert and he thought that man was after him and he shot him. That was accident pure accident.

In this passage both existential *there* and stressed intonation introduce the new topic of the "**drover**"/"**pack train man**." Grammar and intonation work together to indicate topicality. The sentence in which the drover is introduced is dominated by additive constructions: "*And* **it seems** that on his way back into **Hazelton** there was a a **drover** or a **pack train man** running in a bunch of horses just coming out of a **side** road to the one that **Gunninute** was travelling on on his escape toward Babine *and* he saw this cloud of dust *and* he saw the man behind it *and and* he shot him [my italics]." Martin does not pause in speaking this long, co-ordinated sentence, and although pausing in oral speech is not always a key to sentence completion or structure, in a long series of co-ordinate constructions it generally is. While the first *and* functions with "**it seems**" to foreshadow a significant event, the following two *and*'s indicate sequence in time. By conventional implicature we know that first Gunninute saw "this cloud of dust" with new-*this* introducing"cloud of dust" and then afterwards "saw the man behind it." The listener is then told "and he **shot** him by mistake," with stress on "**shot**." This last *and* relates the proposition it contains [shot (Gunninute, man)] to events which preceded it in time, indicating that this last event comes as an unintended result of the two preceding. Moreover, focus is not upon the first event in this sequence but upon the last which Martin signals by actually stressing "**shot**" and so calling attention to the unhappy result. The additive constructions in this long sentence work together to build heightened interest in the ultimate result, which has been foreshadowed by the first of these constructions. This sequence of four *and*'s in ongoing combination also suggests iconically the rapidity of events and thus the confusion which such speed entailed for Gunninute.

In marked contrast, the written version does not supply such a detailed account of Gunninute's movements. Rather, it chooses to evaluate those movements in keeping with its theme of capture:

Native Telegraph travels fast and far in one day only most of the countryside knew Simon Gunninute had in the forenoon of the eventful day ridden to his home and shot almost all his pack horses and all his train dogs and alone by a round about way had succeeded in dodging the Police road block and hit the trail to Fort Babine mounted on his best saddle horse and the then capable Police had as much chance of catching him as a mountain Goat which may have been seen on the mountainside the week before last, as so it proved as Gunninute was never found or captured in his vast wilderness domain, from Kispiox North to Telegraph Creek or nearly so thence West to the upper Skeena Waters and East to the Driftwood Valley whose waters head near Fort Connelly or Bear Lake.

This very long sentence has as its central concern the predicate "succeeded in dodging." All information in the sentence supports the concept of Gunninute's elusiveness, which is the central concern of the narrative. Again Gunninute is portrayed by such evaluation as a skilful agent who succeeds in "dodging" the police. The second crime, which he committed during his flight from the first, is entirely left out of the written narration, since it does not support the characterization of an agent successfully dodging his pursuers.

Where the oral version shows us Gunninute making a very serious mistake in his haste to flee from the law, the written version has assigned him status as topical agent via the passive voice and further characterized him through negatively denoted agentive nouns in the agent *by* phrase, and so it simply ignores happenstance and unhappy result. Further, while the oral version tells its listener that Gunninute is simply "out in hiding in the **mountains**," the written version speaks of "his vast wilderness domain." The Latinate "domain," of course, again connotes mastery and command since a domain is a place governed by a lord.

The only mention of the second crime in the written version comes at the very beginning of the narration and functions as part of the abstract. As already noted, in this initial abstract Starret explains that *"Another horse haser* of another outfit was *shot and killed dead* that forenoon also *by apparently the same Murderer,* who by these terrible acts proved or appeared to prove that *both deeds had been committed by the same crackshot ability* [my italics]." This, of course, is a radically different interpretation of events from that in the oral version. Extended use of the passive again explicitly marks Gunninute as an agent, while the formal "deeds" elevates his action of killing the second packer to a conscious and deliberate as well as connotatively negative act. The "deed" done by Gunninute in the written version is very different from the inadvertent reaction resulting from confusion presented in the oral version. Gunninute is marked as a causative agent rather than simply an actor or, more accurately, a reactor.

To a much greater extent the written version has to be seen as a particular interpretation of a particular set of events. From the beginning analysis is involved since the acts "proved or appeared to prove" a link between themselves. The unstated analysts are, of course, the police who have methodically and logically built a case against Gunninute.[9] The plot has been sculpted to suit the theme and the theme itself is influenced by the grammar of the passive voice. Moreover, the written version achieves integration by selecting an initial focus available in the grammar and in turn eliminating all competing foci. The oral version, in contrast, is not cycloptic; multiple perspectives are possible and can be provided by the episodic structure of its discourse. With regard, then, to the uses oral and written speech are put to in recording history, although oral histories are homeostatic and so can be easily modified from telling to telling, they also permit a greater range of experience to be recorded since episodic construction allows flexibility and plot as action is foregrounded over characterization and theme.[10]

MYTHIC NARRATIVE: THE LEGEND OF ASTACE

The legend of Astace is a Carrier Creation myth, and, in keeping with Victor Turner's definition of narration as a way of knowing, it exemplifies one culture's understanding or explanation of its origins. In both oral and written versions of the legend, the Indian Astace creates a new world, the Northwest and the Pacific Ocean. Significantly, Martin Starret is not a member of the culture whose narrative he transmits, and so in his telling we encounter the phenomenon of one culture interpreting another.[11]

There are parallels in the Carrier Creation myth with the Christian myth of creation and with the story of Christ since Astace's own origins are supernatural. Parallel also are the different versions of the legend told by different Carrier clans. However, there are marked differences between the oral and written versions of the legend as told by Martin Starret. Yet superficial syntactic analysis would indicate almost no difference between these two parallel texts, as shown in Table 3. From an analysis of sentence types alone, these two texts are indistinguishable. However, they do differ in their percentages for clauses and phrases. Although there is only a slight increase in complexity in the written version by virtue of its 19 per cent compound/complex structures to the 13 per cent compound/complex structures in the oral version, a characteristically marked difference in the exploitation of adjectival constructions exists in the written narrative with its far more extensive use of attributive adjectives, participles, and relative clauses. Noun clauses and infinitives are also dominant in the written narrative rather than the oral narrative as is the case in the two previous profiles, a fact which suggests that these features may be topically dependent rather than media depen-

TABLE 3
Syntactic Profile/The Legend of Astace

Sentences	Oral 104 (1740wds)	Written 123 (2637wds)
Simple	43 (42%)	49 (40%)
Compound	18 (17%)	21 (17%)
Complex	24 (23%)	30 (24%)
Compound/complex	13 (13%)	23 (19%)
Embedded	05 (05%)	00 (00%)
Relative clauses	**11 (7 rest)**	**27 (9 rest)**
Adverbial clauses	26	31
Noun clauses	**10**	**22**
Co-ordinate clauses	**68**	**37**
Conjoining phrases	31	38
Participle phrases	**06**	**39**
Gerund phrases	13	10
Infinitive phrases	**11**	**29**
Passives	06	06
Exist. *There*/clefts	05	03
Attributive adjs.	**108**	**218**
(participles)	02	08
Nouns in apposition	15	04

dent. In contrast, there is a greater number of co-ordinate clauses in the oral than in the written version. Thus, the written version exhibits a typically nominal, synthetic syntax, while the oral version exhibits an equally typical additive syntax.

We also see characteristic differences in plot and treatment of agency in these two parallel texts. Perspective is much differently achieved, although not as a result of distinctive use of active and passive voice as in "The Boy in the Mirror" and "The Legend of Gunninute." There are, in fact, an equal number of passive constructions in the oral and written versions of the legend. In the oral version Starret focuses little on the agent and extensively on the "how" of the creation of the world, whereas in the written version focus upon the creator or agent of creation is his dominant concern. Responding to his listener, Imbert Orchard, in his oral telling, he asks if Orchard wants to hear "the InDīan story the Indian legend *how* [my italics] that was ˆ how it happened to be there or how she was created." Starret, however, entitles his written version "Astace The Indian," thus indicating that the story is primarily about Astace himself. Even more than in the Gunninute parallel texts plot as action is foregrounded in the oral myth, while agency as "character" is foregrounded in the written.

In the oral version Starret first orients his listener to the culture out of which the creation myth comes and in turn sets the scene in terms of place and time. There is no mention of Astace. Starret immediately contextualizes his story for his audience, indicating very clearly his sources of information as well as relevant differences between cultures that might cause difficulty for his audience: "They **always** knew about a supreme being the Indians in that country and they differ a whole lot from the Indians in the in the southern states like the Navaho or tho the Apaches those gentlemen down there. They only believed in **one** supreme being one god." Such anthropological digression is non-existent in the written version since it is not thematically important or useful.

Starret's projection of himself as a cultural interpreter in this oral telling stems in part from his very conscious awareness that he is not the source of the story. As in "Gunninute," he is concerned that the listener know his sources, since it is largely through acceptable sources that he asserts tellability, the "so what" factor in his narrative:

Well, now I'm **telling** you what the Indians told me and that was **not one** Indian but **several** and from two **sections** like from the Babine ˆ tribe and from the Stuart **lakers**. They're both **Carriers** but they're kinda cousins you know, different **clans** like. One of them told me I remember the the other one was just ˆ **partly** the same thing that ah **years** ago before there wasn't they didn't know anything about any white man.

In this passage Starret uses stress as his primary means to assert tellability. First he stresses "**telling**," indicating his belief that what he has to tell is important, and also, through this explicit performative, that he is about to embark on an extended turn in the conversation. Martin is urging his co-conversationalist Imbert Orchard to give up his equal status as a speaker and accept the role of audience as complement to his own role of narrator. When Orchard fails in this regard and does interrupt Starret on one occasion to correct him (Starret unintentionally includes the Fraser as part of the Peace River system), Starret simply notes the correction, reiterates the correct answer, and returns to his story. But, from the tone in his voice and speed of his reply, there is an indication that he is annoyed by the interruption and thus the challenge to his authority as a knowledgeable backwoods man. One of his digressions on Indian culture follows shortly afterward as a means of re-establishing his former narrative authority and of maintaining the floor against any further possible incursions from Orchard.

Stress in the passage cited above is placed also on the words "**not one**" and "**several**," "**two sections**," and "**Stuart lakers**." Through stress on numerical information about the number of sources he has for his story, the legitimacy of what Starret is about to tell is enhanced. The more sources he has, the greater the weight his own telling carries. Starret, himself, then, can be considered an authoritative source and his telling of the myth an important event in itself, in further support of his decision to stress the explicit performative verb "**telling**."

In the written version of the legend, tellability is conveyed largely through formal and Latinate vocabulary and through evaluation of the topic. Specifically, Starret's description of Astace in the orientation is highly formalized, in keeping with his epithetic designation of Astace as "The Great":

He was also ambitious, more so than others of his tribe. This territory in which he was reared seemed too small for him, and he longed for a new world or country . . . something entirely his own . . . where he could hold despotic sway. Being very proud like most aborigines, he reasoned that he was much superior in every way, shape, and form to every other man in the tribe or even in the world.

In this passage formal Latinate and Anglo-Saxon vocabulary such as "territory," "reared," "longed," "despotic sway," "aborigines," and "reasoned" suggests elevation of topic and seriousness of purpose on the part of the narrator. Moreover, there is an extensive description of Astace while in the oral version little description is provided. There are approximately four lines in the oral version devoted to such description and approximately a page and a half in the written version. Through primarily adjectival description of the main character or agent in the written version, an indirect argument is conveyed that the story of this agent's doings will be interesting and thus worthy of the reader's undivided attention.

In Starret's long description of Astace, which functions as the orientation in the written version, there are thirty-six attributive adjectives as well as many other descriptors which are not as equally integrative. The reader is given a very full description of the main agent of the story. Starret introduces Astace as the topic of the discourse in the first sentence of the written version using existential *there* as topic marker: "Many hundreds of years ago there lived an Indian beyond the place now called Winnipeg." This initial orientation sentence in the narrative provides both a time and space frame for the reader while simultaneously introducing the topic, "an

Indian." Thematic focus, then, is upon the agent, just as it is in Starret's written version of "Gunninute." The topic of the written version is not the creation but the creator:

At the time this story commences Astace was a young man of about twenty-five years of age. He was mean, a liar and a thief and an all round rogue generally; but, as has been mentioned, the vicinity in which he lived seemed too small for him. He longed for expansion, and to be great in the eyes of the other young people of his tribe.

In the written version Astace is motivated by his hubris to create a new world and even dies in the final grand act of creating the Pacific Ocean. The abundance of adjectives used to describe Astace and his situation serve to mark him as an unusual and thus especially tellable topic. They also serve to explain his behaviour rather than simply to describe it. In the oral version of the legend Starret's digressions also explain Astace's behaviour, but not in the same way. Astace's behaviour is seen as exemplifying that of his culture as a whole. Thus, in describing Astace's swimming skills, Starret states that "*They* [my italics] were **trained** that way those days." But at no time is Astace ever portrayed as an individual entity possessed of individual ambitions and motivations. Only his supernatural origins distinguish him and supply his fitness for his great task. In the written version, however, Astace is centre stage as the defined topic and is extensively evaluated by adjectival modification:

He was slightly over *six feet tall, erect of carriage,* with *long black* hair, *coarse like a horse's mane* which he wore parted almost in the centre of his head. He had a *hard, cunning hatchet* face with *typical high* cheekbones and *sharp, cruel, small black* eyes; a *somewhat prominent* nose, *straight* mouth *with jaws resembling a steel trap* and a *very determined, strong* chin. (my italics)

In this passage a syntactic pattern of description is evident. The nominal thematic information in each sentence is minimal; the pronoun "he" fills the subject and theme slot of each sentence. The verb slot is filled either by the copula *be* or the transitive *have*. As Fillmore (1968) has pointed out, *have* functions in such constructions as a filler verb allowing the possessor of an inalienable attribute to fill the subject slot in the sentence. In Latin a copula construction is used: *Mihi* **sunt** *capilli nigri* (*To me are black hairs* [*I have black hair*]). *Have,* then, is not a true transitive but equivalent functionally to a copula. *With* used in conjunction with copula structures functions as does *have*; that is, it equally marks inalienable attribution. In describing

Astace, Starret employs a combination of the copula and the preposition *with* to cite Astace's features: "He was slightly over six feet tall, erect of carriage, *with long black hair* [my italics]." "With long black hair" is semantically equivalent to *had long black hair*. *Be*, *have*, and *with* all function simply to correlate thematic information with new nominal or adjectival information.

Throughout his long description of Astace, Starret uses these structures over and over varying their combination only slightly. However, he uses a NP Cop Adj sequence as his main syntactic structure. It is, of course, precisely what we would expect in any description. Yet as simple as this structure is, it is dominant only in the written narrative. In fact, the structure is a vehicle for the introduction of new nominal and adjectival information. Combined, the thematic and rhematic information in such a structure supply information concerning direction. This is explicit in Latin or Anglo-Saxon attribution: *Liber **mihi** est* (a book is *to* me), while in Modern English this clear sense of direction is lost: *I have a book*. New information is supplied in the rheme of the clause by nouns and adjectives acting as complements: "His body was [strongly constructed] [with broad shoulders, a small waist and legs and hips] [built like those of a long distance runner] [whose every move showed capability of great speed and endurance]." Processing such nominal and adjectival information is very easy because once subject (theme) and verb are in place syntactically at the front of the clause, information can simply be added on at will, thus producing deceptively complex structures from what in reality is a fundamentally simple one. Moreover, since the structure is simple it can be repeated with minor variation at great length. In this way a great deal of new information about an object or character can be supplied.

In the oral narrative, new information of this kind is supplied not through nominal and adjectival attribution but through separate episodes or episodic digression. What correlates with the long description of Astace in the written version is the second episode of the oral version concerning Astace's origins. This episode is a narrative of the events culminating in Astace's birth. Astace's mother is thirsty; she goes to a spring to get water. After she has drawn water, a mosslike substance remains in her cup despite her efforts to eliminate it. She eventually drinks the water with the substance in it and shortly after becomes pregnant with Astace. This story within a story serves the same orientation function as the extensive description of Astace in the written version and is likewise told or placed at the beginning of the narrative as a whole. But, of course, the two techniques of providing background to the main character are very different. In the oral version the story of Astace's origins is embedded within a larger story of the origin or creation of the world. We learn through a narrative concerning the impregnation of Astace's mother that Astace is not a child of man but of some supernatural force. We learn about Astace by learning how he came into being, not by learning what sort of being he is.

In oral epics genealogy is also common as a method of orientation and characterization.[12] *Beowulf* commences with a genealogy providing its audience with the particular historical knowledge necessary to understand the principal relationships within the narrative. The Bible, of course, is equally replete with genealogies. However, not only are agents supplied with histories, but also objects such as scars and swords. In an essay in *Mimesis*, Erich Auerbach cites the example of Odysseus' scar in the *Odyssey*. On Odysseus' return home he is recognized by a distinctive scar. The narrative at this point departs from the central concern of Odysseus' return to narrate the adventure whereby Odysseus received his distinctive scar, thus explaining its origins.[13] In *Beowulf* a history of the sword used by Wiglaf to defend Beowulf is provided over twenty lines before Wiglaf actually addresses the king he has saved. These long narrative digressions seem odd to any reader used to written narration, yet they are "seamlessly" introduced into long oral narration, often presented very much like flashbacks in film: "Then [Wiglaf] *remembered* [my italics] what Beowulf had given him, the wealthy dwelling place of the Waegundings and the rights to land his father had had. He could not restrain himself and his hand grasped the yellow limewood sheath and drew the ancient sword" (2606-9). In the written narrative, exploiting as it does nominal and adjectival information, a sword or character or scar would be described more directly, if at all, via the syntax of attribution.

Characterization rather than agency alone is also facilitated by participles in the written myth. A left-branching participial construction is used to explain Astace's behaviour and ultimate act of creation: "*Being very proud* [my italics] like most aborigines, he reasoned that he was much superior in every way, shape, and form to every other man in the tribe or even in the world." The participial construction *being* used in left-hand position promotes a causal connection between character and behaviour; "being" in left-hand position links Astace's desire ("and he longed for a new world or country . . . something entirely his own . . . where he could hold despotic sway") with his realization of his own ability to fulfill his desires ("he reasoned he was much superior in every way, shape, and form to every other man in the tribe or even in the world"). Iconically, desire is linked with the fulfillment of desire. Such linkage between character and behaviour is not in evidence in the oral version, since cohesion is created through an additive syntax rather than through left-branching participles.

The written myth puts emphasis on Astace as an agent and makes his actions a reflection of his character. This emphasis also occurs in the written version of Gunninute. Action becomes "behaviour." In contrast, action is primary in the oral myth, and it is through action that agency is revealed. The primacy of action is equally evident in the oral versions of "The Boy in the Mirror" and "Gunninute," where the transitivity (choice between intransitive and transitive verbs) of verb structures largely governs the expression of agency.

In the three main episodes which Starret narrates in his oral version of the legend of Astace after he has asserted tellability and provided an abstract ("And **it seems** ˆ **they** credit the country like of being created by **that** person."), action rather than agentive character is foregrounded. The first episode provides time and space frames for the narration as a whole. Starret explains that there was a particular Indian family which lived in the Peace River district. He then describes this family in terms of what it did to survive: "It was way up on top there a family lived and they set snares and caught animals and had fish nets." Starret could easily have described this family in nominal terms as trappers and fishers, but instead he describes the people from whom Astace is descended by means of verb constructions and thus in terms of what they do.

Starret next narrates a second episode wherein "an Indian maiden" goes to a spring to get a drink of water. Her actions are concentrated upon:

And she went to get a drink of water. She dipped in the spring and had this vessel almost full of water but she noticed that there was a a piece of **moss** had come from the bottom or some foreign substance and a small piece of dirt and she put her fingers in and tried to throw it out and it eluded always.

Again, primary information in the passage is supplied by verbs and verb constructions. All reference to the Indian maiden is pronominal; her actions are depicted through a series of narrative clauses. The pronoun "she" conveniently fills the subject or theme slot in each clause, while new and rhematic information is supplied by verbs: "went to get a drink of water," "dipped," "had this vessel almost full of water," "noticed," "put her fingers in," "tried to throw it out."

Only one other competing nominal concept is introduced in this passage. A new theme is introduced by existential *there* within a noun clause complement to the experiential verb *notice*: "she noticed that there was a a piece of **moss** had come from the bottom or some foreign substance and a small piece of dirt." In the course of processing this new theme, "piece of **moss**," Starret reinterprets the theme syntactically as a subject and commences a new sentence: "a piece of **moss** had come from the bottom."

Apart from elaboration which Martin supplies with regard to the second theme, "a piece of **moss**," verbal information strongly outweighs nominal information in the above passage. The second theme is quite extensively modified, but Martin's orientation to the piece of moss is conveyed through verbal rather than adjectival information: "a piece of **moss** had come from the bottom." The moss is further portrayed actively by means of a transitive verb construction (with ellipsis of the assumed object *her*) in the last narrative clause of the passage: "and it eluded always." Through such verb constructions, the moss is subtly personified as it would not be if it were simply described as a slippery substance on the top of the water. Agency is conveyed through transitive and intransitive verb constructions in the oral narrative and not through an attributive syntax or participles.

This means of conveying agency is most evident in the third episode of the oral version which concerns Astace's creation of the world. An additive syntax and concentration of information in verbs preclude the kind of analytic characterization of Astace that we see in the written version. In the oral version of the legend, Astace does not consciously choose to create a new world; rather, his actions result in this creation. Moreover, his character is revealed by his actions and reactions rather than functioning as a motivating force which precipitates or causes action.

Astace's main adventure begins when he attempts to capture some swans by swimming under water and tying their feet together. In this activity Astace has the tables turned on him:

Well he he must of got three or four of these tying and tied together and somehow or another when he tried to drag them ashore he wasn't **heavy** enough. ˆ The swans were **heavier** than **he** was. And so they started to **fly** and he hung on and they lifted him right above the lake and carried him above the tree tops and **landed** him right on the edge of the cloud so the story goes.

Events here are resultatively related to one another. Astace' s attempt to haul away the tied swans produces a counterattempt by the swans to fly away. In turn, Martin employs an additive conjunction of result in describing their reaction to Astace's action: "*And so* [my italics] they started to **fly** and he hung on and they lifted him right above the lake and carried him above the tree tops and **landed** him right on the edge of the cloud so the story goes." The swans' action produces further resultative reaction from Astace: "and he hung on." Action is linked to action and reaction in resultative sequence, and narrative plot is achieved. Once above the land on this cloud, Astace produces a basket when it starts to rain:

So he sat on this cloud and pretty soon it started to **rain**. And by some reason or other he hada **cup** or a **basket**. The Indian told me a **birch bark***basket*. He was carrying it around like like you'd carry a **powder** horn or something. He's carrying this. And he happened to have it when he sat on this cloud and he waited till it **rained** and he held this to get the water. And that got **brim** full of water and when it was full, the rain just about stopped and this Astace straightened up and he walked the cloud and he saw he was on top. And he was inspired by some way or some unknown power and he walked in a kind of **half** circle around put it carried this in the crook of his left **hand** this this vessel of water and he **sprinkled** the water right out the same as a a **sower** many centuries ago woulda like in the Bible time would have sowed seed on the land or **corn** barley or anything like that.

The events which follow are further related in terms of time and result. Thus, in temporal sequence the rain next stops: "and when it was full, the rain just about stopped." Two further events follow in temporal sequence: "and this Astace straightened up and he walked the cloud." Finally, as a result of these two actions, a realization comes to Astace: "and he saw he was on top."

Throughout these two passages concerning Astace's adventure with the swans and his collecting of rain and walking the cloud, reference to him is almost exclusively pronominal. The pronoun "he" serves the function of theme but adds little or no information to the narrative. At no point in the oral narrative is action ever momentarily halted to facilitate an evaluative pronouncement of the kind evident in the written version: "I, Astace the Great, will shew that I can create a world of my own, which no one shall enter but those that I wish. I have spoken." Such elements of oral speech are not evident in the oral version because dialogue used in written narrative is present to serve characterization, whereas oral narrative concentrates almost exclusively on the agent's activities or the advancement of plot. In one instance in the oral version where Starret does characterize Astace, he does so by evaluating Astace's action of throwing water: "and he **sprinkled** the water right out the same as a **sower** many centuries ago woulda like in the Bible time would have sowed seed on the land or **corn** barley or anything like that." Here sprinkling water is compared to sowing seed with explicit reference to corn and barley. Astace is characterized in terms of his actions; his actions are not a reflection of his character.

As Halliday (1971) has shown with regard to transitivity structures in English, the agency of a particular character in narrative is accentuated by transitive rather than intransitive constructions. In his novel *The Inheritors* Golding deliberately uses intransitive rather than transitive constructions to characterize the theoretically inferior Neanderthals: "[Lok] smelled along the shaft of the twig." In such constructions there is one participant only, the experiencer. By virtue of the intransitive structure there is no interaction of the experiencer and the object of his experience. Direction of action alone, "along the shaft of the twig," is supplied. Agency, then, is heightened in transitive structures: *He smelled the rose.* Two participants are engaged by one activity.[14]

In Starret's oral version of the legend of Astace transitivity structures also delimit agency. The narrative actively depicts Astace tying swans or dispersing water until the narrative's conclusion when an ironic twist in the plot occurs:

And he walked this circle round like and then he followed **down** hill away. He didn't want to be up anymore and he followed down till he got **tired** and he was throwing water all the time, for **hours** according to the way the story goes. And when he got down near Spokeshoot which is Port Essington he **tripped** and fell down and the water all spilled. That formed the salt water. That was the Indian story how this world was created according to the **Carrier** legend.

At the commencement of this passage, Astace is portrayed as an active agent: "And he walked this circle round like," "and he was throwing water all the time." In the first verb structure, a normally intransitive verb *walk* is used transitively denoting the purposeful agency of Astace. However, intransitive structures replace transitive structures: "and then he followed **down** hill away." Starret stresses the locative goal of Astace's movement. Movement replaces action and so characterizes the agent of the oral narrative in a new way. The narrative ends ironically because Astace's greatest achievement, the creation of the Pacific Ocean, is effected indirectly by his movements rendered in intransitive verb constructions rather than by his directly agentive actions: "And when he got down near Spokeshoot which is Port Essington he **tripped** and fell down and the water all spilled." Astace's agency is diminished by the intransitive structures, but irony is achieved because his accomplishments are not.

In marked contrast to the conclusion of the oral version, Starret's written version of the legend of Astace ends with the destruction of both Astace and his basket, focusing attention on the agent and his means:

In the half light he glanced down into his precious basket and saw that it was still about half full of water. Just then he stubbed his right foot, and poor Astace, tired after such a long run without rest or food, was unable to recover his balance and fell down hard on his right side crushing his faithful basket beneath him and striking his head. Everything turned black and Astace knew no more. The water thus spilled by Astace in his fall formed that part of the Pacific Ocean west of British Columbia.

Astace does not lose his status as agent since he is assigned the role of agent via the *by* phrase of the passive voice used in the last sentence. Moreover, while in the oral version Astace's tripping results in water spilling, in the written version a causal analysis is supplied. A past participle phrase "tired after such a long run without rest or food" is inserted after the subject Astace and before the predicate "was unable to recover his balance." Embedded between subject and predicate in this way, the phrase has explanatory force and so functions as a *primum mobile* for the predicate, which is read as an effect of this cause. In the oral version Astace's tiredness is also noted, but it is analysed resultatively in conjunction with inchoative *got*: "He didn't want to be up anymore and he followed down till he got **tired** and he was throwing water all the time, for **hours** according to the way the story goes." There is no causal connection between the character's state and his actions, while in the written version participles again serve to link action to character.

The oral and written versions of the legend of Astace exhibit marked differences, particularly in their treatment of agency. We see the same plot differences as those exhibited by the two versions of "Gunninute," with the exception that one narrative episode is used as orientation in the oral version of "Astace." Agency, however, is differentiated in a quite significant way, not through a contrast of active and passive voice, but through a contrast between transitive and intransitive verbs and an attributive syntax which can exploit both copula verbs and the passive voice. Use of an attributive syntax and access to adjectival constructions permit what might be referred to as "characterization" in the written version. Moreover, this characterization is very closely connected to plot, since action on the part of Astace is consistently tied to features of his personality. Conversely, in the oral version Astace is a vehicle of the plot, and his agency is an expression of his activity.

CONCLUSION

In the three types of narrative examined in this chapter, personal, historical, and mythic, there are marked differences in the lexical, syntactic and discourse properties of these narrative texts. The sets of parallel narrative texts do not reveal identical differences, but nonetheless a high degree of consistency exists respectively among the oral and written versions of these parallel texts. The oral and written narratives are consistently differentiated in their preferences for specific syntactic structures. A gross syntactic profile reveals the broad outlines of these differences, as shown in Table 4.

The real story here is not revealed in the preference for different sentence types. Simple sentences are only marginally preferred in the oral texts, and there is an equivalent number of complex sentences. Complexity is only more favoured by the written narratives in their greater use of compound-complex sentences. From even a cursory look at this profile, it is easy to see why competing analyses of oral and written speech have been put forth, since simple, compound and complex sentences are almost equivalent in number. However, this data does not favour any one model.

Major differentiation is evident only in clauses and phrases. Adjectival structures and passives are clearly favoured in the written narratives. These structures promote both what I have termed an attributive syntax and a constellational syntax. Access to such syntactic structures promotes or influences in turn a specific structure in written narratives. Equally, the additive, linear syntax of written speech is revealed in the preference for co-ordinate clauses and cleft-like constructions in the oral texts, although nouns in apposition and embedded clauses are also more prevalent, suggesting that the one-clause-at-a-time constraint is a tendency rather than a true constraint in oral processing. Sequences can be interrupted and returned to in this syntax.

Although I have not examined word morphology to any great extent in this discussion, it is interesting that in one oral narrative Martin Starret prefers the compound word *looking glass* to the more synthetic *mirror*, as he equally prefers the oral phrasing "to see what the noise's about" to the latinate "investigate" in writing. There is a parallel between synthetic Latinate words and other synthetic struc-

TABLE 4
Syntactic Profile/All Narratives

Sentences	Oral 211 (3286w)	Written 156 (3683w)
Simple	**91 (43%)**	**57 (36%)**
Compound	31 (14%)	25 (16%)
Complex	54 (25%)	39 (25%)
Compound/complex	24 (11%)	33 (21%)
Embedded	11 (05%)	01 (00%)
Relative clauses	**20**	**53**
Adverbial clauses	37	40
Noun clauses	46	33
Co-ordinate clauses	**127**	**51**
Conjoining phrases	41	46
Participle phrases	13	51
Gerund phrases	22	19
Infinitive phrases	28	35
Passives	**08**	**21**
Exist. *There*/clefts	18	03
Attributive adjs.	**172**	**307**
(participles)	05	19
Nouns in apposition	17	09

tures, such as participles, which predominate in the written texts. A further parallel is evident when we see how much more thematically focused and synoptic the written narratives are. In contrast, a compound, predominantly Anglo-Saxon vocabulary also parallels an additive syntax as well as an episodic or rhapsodic strategy of discourse composition in the oral narratives. There seems to be a very similar processing strategy which underlies word, clause, and discourse composition.

Syntactic preferences also influence how action and agency are treated in individual texts. Agency in oral narratives is conveyed largely through verb structures; action determines agency. Agents are depicted through actions rather than features. Agency is particularly heightened through transitive structures which involve actor and an affected or patient in the clause. Thus *John* in the clause *John hit the ball* is exclusively agentive while *John* in *John ran home* combines agent and patient in one category (i.e., *John ran himself home*). Moreover, there is only one participant in the second clause which depicts movement, while in the first clause two participants are involved and the agent has impact on his environment.[15]

Agency in written narratives is also marked syntactically. However, this is largely achieved through the *by* phrase of the passive voice. The passive voice is a principal means by which agency can be marked as new information. Stylistic effect is produced if agency is either marked through the *by* phrase or deleted. Furthermore, an other-oriented perspective can be created through the passive if the main participant in a narrative is placed in the subject slot of a passive construction. Through this use of the passive voice, the narrative becomes one about what was done to this participant, rather than what the participant did. However, when the main participant is the marked agent in a passive construction, this participant can be viewed as either a doer or as a negative doer. Marked agency in the passive also promotes the view of the main participant in a narrative as a cause, one who initiates a sequence of events deliberately or consciously. The passive, then, is a principal means of role assignment and characterizing relations between a patient and an agent in written narrative. Further, selection of the passive can preclude other roles or behaviours not consistent with initial characterization as patient or agent, thus promoting both thematic coherence and monolithic perspective.

To the extent that written speech much more fully exploits nominal and adjectival constructions via an attributive syntax than does oral speech, one major effect in narrative is increased interest in agency itself and, indeed, the thematization of agency as in the case of the written version of Astace. To provide background or orientation information about a character, oral narrative must rely on episodic digressions or stories within stories, while written narrative can rely on a syntax which allows new information to be back-directed or attributed to a defined topic in the subject slot of a given syntactic structure. An analysis of the features of an agent is thus provided by an attributive syntax, while the history of an agent is episodically provided in oral narrative orientations. In turn, what may be termed the behaviour of the agent is related to his or her character and so action becomes a reflection of the character of the agent in written narrative.

Action or plot is also extensively affected by differences in oral and written speech. Oral and written narratives are structured along very different lines. Plot is expressed through rhapsodic composition in oral narratives longer than the simple personal account of "The Boy in the Mirror." Thematic composition is more common in written narratives. The episodic structure of long oral narratives permits a multiplicity of perspectives, whereas the topically focused structure of long written narrative eliminates all but one central perspective, in effect choosing a point of view in the selection of topic. Coherence in oral narratives should not be seen as absent simply because episodic digression is employed. In fact, "digressions" are not organizationally disruptive in oral discourse, since it is only from the perspective of thematically organized written narrative that evaluative commentary or the incorporation of orienting stories within stories could in any way be thought of as "off topic." The structure of written narratives is largely closed, while that of oral narratives is open-ended, and therefore coherence or topicality is differently achieved in these two sub-varieties of narrative.

Different means of achieving cohesion in oral and written speech further differentiate oral and written narratives. An oral additive syntax promotes resultative analysis of events, while the constellational syntax of written speech promotes causative analysis. Causation can be expressed explicitly in oral speech through conjunctions, but the fuller pragmatic exploitation of *and* creates the dominant view of events as temporally ordered or in resultative relation. In contrast, written speech promotes a causative analysis of events in narrative. Participial constructions not only synthesize events in time creating the illusion of interrelation and simultaneity, but also link events causally. What is distinct and pristine in oral speech becomes integrated and ordered in written.

Narrative as a way of knowing, to use Victor Turner's definition, is not one process but two. We know the past differently in oral and written narrative. Action and agency are understood in fundamentally different ways. Written narrative, to a much greater extent, analyses the past it conveys, conceptualizing it first as a whole and then subdividing it into parts. It conveys character rather than agency alone and relates action to character. Events, too, can lose their distinctness and become elements of a broader phenomenon. Oral narrative concentrates on action and characterizes the agent through his or her actions. Moreover, actions seldom lose their temporality and integrity by participating semantically or syntactically in other actions. Participles and gerunds are little used as constructions. The constellational and attributive syntax of written speech and the verb-oriented, additive syntax of oral speech structurally and semantically differentiate narrative as a genre.

3

Oral and Written Description

Description, like narration, adheres to a speech-act direction of fit which is word to world. Our strongest intuitive sense of description is that it provides or should provide in language a direct representation of the world itself. Description tells us how something or someone is or was by factually representing attributes and features. However, to be more precise, description is also a way of representing beings, things, states or processes as they exist in space. Werlich (1976), for example, defines descriptive discourse as focusing on factual phenomena in their spatial context. Description, then, explicates how something is or was in space rather than in time. We expect to see descriptive discourse replete with locative rather than temporal constructions.

To what extent description achieves in language a correlation between word and world is difficult to say. In his analysis of room descriptions, Benny Shanon points out that "descriptions are not based on any direct mappings of things onto words, and . . . the patterns they reveal are not immediate reflections of patterns which are external. Rather descriptions are the products of the regular functioning of mediating rules and they are subject to internal constraints" (1984:227). As a psychologist, Shanon seeks to demonstrate that descriptions are moderated by cognitive constraints on the processing of information. Thus not all possible information about a room is coded in a room description. In the act of describing a room, Shanon' s subjects employed a very selective strategy to encode information. They first characterized the shape of the room they were describing and then isolated and described its main parts including walls, floor, and ceiling. They then gave attention to windows and doors. Major pieces of furniture were next described and afterwards objects with a definite place of their own followed by objects without a definite place of their own. Shanon found that given linguistic structures would predominate at a given stage in description. For example, he found that a certain type of relative clause (NP{rel VP loc}) was employed largely to introduce new information at the later stages of room description, that is, with regard to furniture and objects in the room. For Shanon, language encodes strategically selected information about a given entity in space. Language itself plays no part in the strategic representation of reality.

Labov and Linde (1975) have also studied description with a view to better understanding the relationship between language and thought. Unlike Shanon, they found that two strategies were employed by their subjects rather than only one. Labov and Linde's study differed from Shanon's not only in its larger goal of apartment description, but also with regard to the medium employed by their subjects. Shanon's subjects produced room descriptions in written Hebrew, while Labov and Linde's subjects responded orally to their investigative question: "Could you tell me the lay-out of your apartment?" To this question Labov and Linde found that "The great majority of such lay-outs are imaginary tours which transform spatial lay-outs into temporally organized narratives" (924). In a few instances subjects also responded with what Labov and Linde refer to as a MAP layout. In the map layout subjects responded very much as did Shanon's subjects; that is, they started first with a general overview ("I'd say it's laid out in a huge square pattern, broken down into four units."), after which they proceeded to break down the apartment into its main components or structural parts ("If you were looking down at this apartment from a height, it would be like—like I said before, a huge square with two lines drawn through the center to make like four smaller squares."). These subjects provided their audience with a perspective from which to view an apartment as a whole before providing more specific and detailed information, much as Shanon's subjects had done in their room descriptions. The question, of course, is why this strategy, which seems more efficient, was not more employed by Labov and Linde's subjects. Do the two strategies cited by Labov and Linde correlate with linguistic medium, the pseudo-narrative or tour being a product of oral speech and the map layout conversely a product of written speech? Labov and Linde found the map layout in only 3 per cent of their subjects, while Shanon reported only this strategy in his analysis of written room descriptions.

In the process descriptions to be examined in this chapter there are differences in strategy comparable to those found by Labov and Linde in their study of apartment descriptions. The oral description is very much closer to narrative, while the written description often more closely approximates analysis and exposition. The medium in which these descriptions is encoded significantly affects their treatment and presentation of content, their rendering of the direction of fit between word and world. Description is less a "useful site for the study of the translation of thought into language," as Labov and Linde put it, and more a useful means to study the relationship between cognitive and linguistic constraints in the representation of beings, entities, states, and processes.

PROCESS DESCRIPTION: CATTLE DRIVING

In interviews with Imbert Orchard and in his journals, Martin Starret describes the process of cattle driving as it was done circa 1890 at Hope in the Fraser Valley of British Columbia. Cattle were herded through the streets of Hope and onto waiting barges at the town's docks and then shipped downriver to New Westminster. However, his accounts exhibit maximal difference in their treatment of perspective on the event and the event itself. The oral description of the cattle drive heavily exploits narrative structures, whereas the written description comes closer to being a process analysis.

A syntactic contrast between the two parallel process descriptions concerning cattle driving reveals a typical breakdown between oral and written speech. Co-ordinate clause formation is a much more dominant feature of the oral syntax than the written, which is characterized by its use of adjectival structures (relative clauses, participles, and attributive adjectives). Gerunds are also dominant in the written syntax as is the passive voice.

Also consistent is the fact that there is no marked differentiation between adverb clauses. This finding supports Halliday's view that oral speech exhibits hypotaxis, but not that written speech prefers simple, "crystalline" sentences. Equally, it supports Chafe's view that written speech exhibits hypotaxis, but not that oral speech prefers simple sentences. However, we can say generally that we find a typically additive syntax in the oral version and a typically nominal or attributive syntax in the written version. The preference written speech has for coding information in nominal/adjectival structures as well as in the passive is revealed in the profile below, while the preference oral speech has for active declarative and additive cohesive structures is equally revealed in Table 5.

The cattle drives Starret describes were special events in his childhood. In both accounts he introduces his topic with accompanying evaluation:

TABLE 5
Syntactic Profile/Cattle Driving

Sentences	Oral 28 (615wds)	Written 21 (828wds)
Simple	08 (29%)	07 (33%)
Compound	**06 (21%)**	**03 (14%)**
Complex	**07 (25%)**	**09 (43%)**
Compound/complex	04 (14%)	02 (10%)
Embedded	03 (11%)	00 (00%)
Relative clauses	**04**	**11**
Adverbial clauses	06	07
Noun clauses	03	00
Co-ordinate clauses	**31**	**06**
Conjoining phrases	14	12
Participle phrases	**06**	**19**
Gerund phrases	**01**	**09**
Infinitive phrases	11	11
Absolute constrs.	00	02
Passives	**03**	**12**
Exist. *There*/clefts	03	01
Attributive adjs.	**29**	**89**
(participles)	**05**	**16**
Nouns in apposition	02	00

When the cattle started coming I don't know what **date that** was but it was kind of a an interesting **sight** to to see those **cattle** being loaded. (Oral description)

From the Hudson's Bay pasturefield or from Joe Bowes's feed lot probably the most activity of the season would occur, when the cattle would be moved or driven from these holding enclosures through the edge of town to the waterfront thoroughfare (known now as Water Street) where the Boat Landing corral was located (opposite where Marshall' s gift Shop, and Pope's Garage now stand). (Written description)

The topic arises in both descriptions in the course of Starret's explication of life in Hope during the 1890s when he was a child. In the written journal, events are oriented around the year 1892, while in the oral context of situation, Starret's description of cattle driving results from his ongoing explanation and description of the physical environment of Hope at the turn of the century and life at that time.

In the oral interview with Orchard, cattle driving has been brought up in other related discussions. In the course of Starret's general account of his life and times the topic, then, has become a potential topic, which he may or may not develop at a later date. He only takes this topic up fully after a short description of the town of Hope itself in which he notes the presence of holding stalls or corrals for beef cattle being readied for shipment to New Westminster. However, between this description of the stalls and the actual process description of cattle driving, more physical description of the town and area intervenes. Starret does not go directly from a description or functional explanation of the stalls to a process description of cattle driving itself as he does in the written version. In other words, the actual cognitive mechanism by which topics are taken up and treated is not entirely clear in conversation. All that is clear is that topics, once introduced, do become potential topics for full treatment at the time of introduction or at a later date.

In the written process description of cattle driving, the topic comes into play by association with steamboat sailings, which in turn are introduced through association with a telegraph service in the area enabling residents to "be informed on the time of Steamboat sailings on River and any changes in stage schudles [sic] on the Cariboo Rd." A series of associative links is made, then, before the topic of cattle driving is selected over any of the other topics introduced beforehand. The associative links are quite easy to follow in Starret's journal entry, but topic saliency is less easy to understand, that is, why he chooses one topic over another and treats it more fully.

However, Starret's evaluation of this topic in both versions explains saliency to some extent. Clearly, in both cases he feels he has hit on an interesting topic for his respective readers and listener. The co-occurrence of the introduction and evaluation of topic indicates that this topic has been selected for its narrative value, its tellability. Topics, then, are not just randomly introduced into conversation or journals but are selected for their value or acceptability to an audience.

Exclusive of evaluation, the descriptions also provide very different perspectives on the event to be described. Using a topic-introducing cleft construction, in the oral version Starret states that "it was kind of a an interesting **sight** to to see those **cattle** being loaded." In the written version, his discourse topic is not visually descriptive, but rather descriptive of an overall process or generalized action: "From the Hudson's Bay pasturefield or from Joe Bowes's feed lot probably the most *activity* [my italics] of the season would occur."

The lexeme *activity* is both Latinate and abstract; such a word or term is highly appropriate in a process description since *activity* denotes purposeful movement. It is in keeping with the idea of process which concerns action in the abstract, rather than that personified or performed by a given actor. In Longacre's (1976) feature analysis of procedural discourse (process description), orientation to agency is replaced by orientation to the patient. Whether the process is making cookies or driving cattle, the actor is given little weight in the discourse while the actions performed coalesce into a given depersonalized overall activity or process. However, "sight" meets none of these criteria. Although *sight* is technically an abstract noun, it is not abstract in the way *activity* is. *Sight* denotes an evaluated event worthy of being seen by an observer. The adjective "interesting" which modifies "sight" is in fact redundant, used only for added emphasis of its denotative content. "Sight" in the oral version also specifies interpersonal engagement in the event, that is, the presence of a human observer.

Orally, Starret both characterizes his topic as a "sight" and proceeds appropriately to create a visual stance or perspective for his listener. He does this by first locating his listener before actually describing the cattle being driven through town:

But they you'd see them everybody was ah these storekeepers if there's policemen I never knew any policemen here but there might have been at one time told the people to keep back off because the cattle 'ud be along. So they'd peek through **windows** kids and they'd keep **quiet**. And then the **dogs** would be either **tied** up or or ah put in an **outhouse** or somewhere **warehouse** so they wouldn't bother the **cattle**.

Starret begins this passage with some difficulty in processing. It is important, though, to note that he makes a major strategic decision in the course of reprocessing. He begins by continuing to talk about the cattle which he has just described ("A lot of them were rather **four** sore footed coming across the rocky **trail** and the **wire** edge of the **wild**ness had been **taken** off them en route."), but he changes his mind about topic and so changes pronoun reference from "they," referring back to cattle, to "you," referring not to any second person in particular, but to a generalized audience of which Starret's specific audience, Orchard, is potentially a part. Strategically, Starret decides to assign Orchard both a role to play and a stage on which to play it.

Starret's decision to adhere to his original designation of topic as a "sight" causes him to employ a form of lexical repetition and cohesion: "you'd see them." His use of the generalized "you," comparable in formal English to *one*, affords Orchard entry to the scene Starret is about to describe, while the modal "would" indicates that the event to be seen is equally generalized or customary. Like the participants in e.e. cummings' poem "anyone lived in a pretty how town," the viewer is anyone and everyone, both anonymous and all-inclusive. Orchard, then, is made to identify with the anonymous "you" watching a customary event in Hope during the 1890s.

What Chafe (1982) refers to as "involvement" seems to be a factor in this oral discourse. However, Chafe's definition of involvement does not accord with the form of involvement present in this description. Chafe defines "involvement" largely in terms of features in speech which indicate the presence of the speaker and the speaker's processing of information: first person references, references to the speaker's own mental processing and monitoring of information flow as well as emphasis, "fuzziness," and use of direct quotes. But these features do not as a whole manifest one phenomenon which can be termed "involvement." Use of direct quotes in oral speech occurs when the speaker feels the need to gain authority for his or her position by quotation from another source, but quoting is common in written discourse generally as it is in written narration, where writers illustrate character through quotation. It does not appear to be a feature exclusively of oral speech.

It is hard to see how "fuzziness" is a feature of "involvement," since phrases such as *and so on* or *sort of* are phenomena of processing which remain in recorded oral speech but are eliminated in sequential drafts in written speech. "Fuzziness" is not so much a feature of any medium of expression as it is a general processing feature, which can be edited out in the case of written speech. References to mental processing are also processing phenomena, but they have little to do with a speaker's involvement with audience. When they occur, they do so because a speaker is in the process of making strategic decisions about topic or topics, in effect making meaning in the course of speaking.

It is difficult as well to understand how first person reference is a feature of involvement. Natural narratives, whether oral or written, are commonly told in the first person, as will be any discourse which pertains to the direct experience of the speaker. However, first person reference is little employed by Starret in either his oral or his written process description of cattle driving. First person reference is therefore appropriate in some genres but, as in process description, inappropriate in others.

If involvement is not processing behaviour on the part of a speaker, what is it? The presence of such constructions as "you'd see," "you'd hear," or "you know" indicates that the speaker is strategically involving the listener in the situation of the discourse.

However, such phrases are not, as Chafe suggests, a way of monitoring speech flow to see if the listener is following. They actually place the listener at the scene of an event so that he or she can "observe" first-hand what takes place. The tour strategy used by 97 per cent of Labov and Linde's subjects in describing their apartments fulfils the same function; that is, the listener becomes a participant in the description: "*You* [my italics] walk into a long, narrow foyer, leading into a smaller, squarer foyer, eating place, dinette-area." "*You* [my italics] walked in the front door. There was a narrow hallway." The inclusive second person is employed to position the interviewer at the scene and so assign him or her a role to play in the discourse, that of tourist to the speaker's tour guide. In Starret's oral process description the interviewer becomes, through Starret's strategy of involvement, any citizen of Hope circa 1890. Involvement, then, is an actual strategy employed by speakers and is here effected through phrases such as "you'd see," "you'd hear," and "you know."

Once Starret has engaged or involved Orchard in the actual scene he wishes to describe, he then more fully contextualizes the scene of which Orchard is now a part. He explains that "these storekeepers ... told the people to keep back off because the cattle 'ud be along." A behavioural sequence which begins with the admonitions of storekeepers to the adult population produces a chain reaction ending only with the tying up of dogs. The storekeepers move the adults who then move the children and the dogs. Starret thus explains the perspective of children, of whom he would be one, and the further placement of dogs: "So they'd peek through **windows** kids and they'd keep **quiet**. And then the **dogs** would be either **tied** up or or ah put in an **outhouse** or somewhere **warehouse** so they wouldn't bother the **cattle**." All the townspeople of Hope are characterized as an expectant audience in position for the main event to begin. Only the dogs are excluded, for practical purposes, from the stage. The scene, then, is set, and the orientation for the interviewer, now an observer at the scene, is effected.

Use of verbs such as "peek" in relation to the children's actions evaluates the scene as one of importance necessitating care. So, equally, does the stated fact that the children would "keep **quiet**." Starret's stressing of "**quiet**," of course, draws attention to the unusualness of such behaviour on the part of children, indicating further the specialness of this particular event for the community, which has been transformed from a collection of citizens going about its everyday affairs into a positioned audience waiting for the big event to occur.

In contrast to the drama of the oral process description with its scenic orientation and role involvement for the listener, the written process description orients and creates perspective for the reader quite differently:

From the Hudson's Bay pasturefield or from Joe Bowes's feed lot probably the most activity of the season would occur, when the cattle would be moved or driven from these holding enclosures through the edge of town to the waterfront thoroughfare . . . where the Boat Landing corral was located.

There is a very different set of relations pertaining to writers and readers as opposed to speakers and listeners. Writers and readers are removed from one another physically in a way speakers and listeners are not. Functioning, then, at a remove from one another, writers and readers come to rely on less direct and more oblique methods of meaning transmission. Since the writer does not have the game option of saying to the reader, "You be the tourist and I'll be the tour-guide" or "You and I'll be citizens on the street watching and I'll provide commentary," he or she must use other devices or conventions.

To a much greater extent the writer exploits stylistic uses of word order in the language, using words, phrases or clauses in a marked sense to alert the reader to specialized meaning. For example, Starret might have constructed his orientation sentence without fronting prepositions as he does above:

Probably the most activity of the season would occur from the Hudson's Bay pasturefield or from Joe Bowes's feed lot . . . (unmarked)

In such an unmarked construction there is no signal or cue to the reader. The prepositional phrase simply modifies the verb "occur," indicating place or location. However, in marked position the thematized prepositional phrase becomes a conventionalized indirect speech act on the part of the writer to effect direction of gaze and thus perspective for a distanced reader:

From the Hudson's Bay pasturefield or from Joe Bowes's feed lot probably the most activity of the season would occur . . . (marked)

Through such a marked locative construction, Starret provides his reader with what Labov and Linde refer to as a map or general outline of the specific region in which the cattle drive takes place. In written description such an overview permits the selection of more salient or special aspects of the process being described. To employ

a cinematic metaphor, the writer can go in for a close-up at a strategically selected "point" in the description. Moreover, by virtue of
such strategic selection, written description takes on the character
of an analysis. This use of the principle of word order contrasts
fundamentally with the strategy of involvement in the oral description. Even so, the writer must rely on the reader' s general competence to take the word order cue. If the reader's skills are deficient,
the intended perspective exists only as a potential guide. Readers,
then, must collaborate much more than listeners in the creation of
meaning in texts, for they must respond to a very different set of
conventions or a different semiotic order than that employed in oral
speech.

  As direction is thematized through the fronting of the first prepositional phrase in the sentence, so the entire sentence primarily
concerns itself with the matter of location and direction which is
foregrounded not only by prepositional phrases in sequence, "*from*
these holding enclosures *through* the edge of town *to* the waterfront
thoroughfare [my italics]," but also by choice of lexemes with a high
degree of locative information: "enclosures," "edge," "waterfront,"
"thoroughfare," "Boat Landing corral," "located." Linguistically
rather than graphically, Starret gives his reader an overview of the
scene and the operation to be described. From such a perspective
the reader/viewer gains comprehensiveness, but loses direct contact
with the scene and event itself.

  Once perspective has been achieved for the reader and the listener
respectively in the descriptions, Starret turns his attention to the actual process of cattle driving. Major differences are evident in the two
treatments. The written description concentrates attention on the last
and most problematic phase in the process; the oral description, in
stark contrast, delineates all phases, giving equal weight to each.

  In the written description, the initial orientation sentence serves
to supply the reader with all the information he or she will receive
about two-thirds of the event, while the remaining description concentrates on two functionally salient or problematic aspects of the
cattle drive. Martin continues his description of the cattle drive by
transferring topically from a general overview of the scene and activity to a specific and functional description of the Boat Landing
corral where the beef cattle are funnelled into a holding area and
then driven onto the ships waiting to transfer them to New Westminster:

A substantial gate in the exit of the log fence when being opened allowed
the cattle to be driven into a log schute which would allow perhaps three

animals to walk abreast down the steep incline to an additional gangplank, built with extra strong braced sides, as the cattle always balked at this point as this was a new experience they were being compelled to pass through.

This very long sentence is analytic and causative in orientation. Thematic focus is given to the means by which the cattle are transferred from land to water. The forced transition from land to water is the stage in the process most particularly disliked by the cattle and so one which attracts particular topic salience in Starret's written account. However, despite efficient use of lexical and syntactic cohesion, the readability of the above sentence introducing this problematic last stage in the process is affected. The description of the Boat Landing corral commences not with the entry of the cattle into the corral, but with their transference from the corral onto a gangplank leading to a steamboat. The kind of sentential cohesion effected by Starret, termed tail-head linkage by Longacre (1968), where a topic introduced at the end of one sentence becomes the subject of the next, promotes readability. There is only the problem of relating "corral" with "gate," but since gate is a meronym of corral, that is, lexically a part of its larger whole, lexical cohesion is also strong from sentence to sentence. But the sentence is nonetheless difficult to read, because strategically Starret has decided to focus only on the last stage of the process he is describing. The reader has no explicit information that the cattle have been driven into the corral, only that they are at the corral stage of the process.

Processing is difficult for the reader because readers and listeners alike share a script or frame to the effect that entrances precede exits in descriptions of movement. While the oral description adheres to such psychologically prior frames, the written description requires the reader to supply missing semantic gaps or stages in the process, participating in the creation of a subtext where aspects of cohesion are weak. Cohesion is not only a property of lexico-grammatical linkage, but also of exploited "frames" of reference or stereotypical frameworks of experience to which we relate any new experiences in the course of life and in the course of reading and listening.[1]

Still, the strategic placement of locative information in the sentence does aid the reader in achieving perspective. Once the reader connects the gate with the corral and "reads" the sentence as being about exiting rather than entering, he or she is able to locate a point of reference or deictic centre ("A substantial gate *in* the exit *of* the log fence [my italics],") and follow visually the sequence of events leading up to the cattle' s actual transference from land to water by means of a gangplank.

Starret describes the event of cattle driving phenomenonologi-
cally, that is, as an event occurring without human agency in keeping with Longacre's definition of procedural discourse or process
description. Yet agency is marked in the text through what Halliday
(1985) refers to as "grammatical metaphor." Noticeably, the verb
allow is used twice. Given that human agency is backgrounded by
means of deagentive passive constructions, the metaphorical use of
a transitive verb such as *allow* is highly striking:

A substantial gate in the exit of the log fence when being opened *allowed* the
cattle to be driven into a log schute which would *allow* perhaps three animals to walk abreast down the steep incline to an additional gangplank. [my
italics]

The world described in this sentence is nonreal in the sense that
human agency is replaced by the agency of inanimate objects. The
past participle passive construction "when being opened" supplies
no human agent as the physical means of causing the gate to
transfer from one state, being closed, to another, being opened.
Starret could easily have supplied such human agency: *A substantial
gate . . . when being opened by one of the cattle drivers allowed*. However, he
does not do so. Inclusion of human agency would conflict with what
is metaphorically being transferred to the gate itself.

This conflict is more evident if human agency is supplied to another past participle construction in the sentence: *A gate . . . allowed
the cattle to be driven by the cattle drivers*. Agency already denoted by the
verb *allow* does not permit any further marking of agency in the
sentence. By grammatically deleting human agency and metaphorically supplying the gate and the chute with agency, Starret can
focus on the process itself rather than on the participants while also
analysing the structural properties of the crucial holding pens.

The analysis Starret supplies is both causative and implicit. His
use of a metaphorical construction frees him from stating explicitly
that the gate being described was so structured and constructed by
human agents that when they opened it, only small numbers of
cattle could walk through into a chute. The verb "allowed" indicates
that a causative correlation is being made between the gate (that is,
its implicit structural properties) and the effect produced, the relo-
cation of cattle into a log chute. Thus, this sentence is fundamentally
about control and power, specifically that of human beings over
animals, but nowhere is this point explicitly stated. Like the causative analysis supplied, power relations are implicit. Yet they are also

meant to be, for any explicit structural analysis of the gate and the chute would undermine the reader's ability to follow the process sequentially. Two kinds of meaning, then, interact in this sentence: one directional and the other analytic. Though it is consistently supplied, analysis is also consistently subordinated to locative and directional information necessary for the reader to follow the process. The sub-theme of control functions as a secondary message at this point.

A number of marked differences are evident between the two versions. I have already alluded to some. First, strict sequence of events is maintained in the oral version. The listener observes the entire process from its initial to its later stages:

And then one fellow'd be on **point** down the street and the cattle'd be following and there' d be a lot of fellows **wooing** at them and calling and **chasing** them along you know 'n 'casionally you'd hear a **whip** crack from a drover **whip** crack you know but I never see 'im abusin' the cattle any. And they'd get along this street till and and they had a kind of a a receiver **fence** I guess you'd call it along the bank so they wouldn't get over **there** and the gate would open on the other side to make a funnel shape and they'd get them into that corral. And then they'd get the gate shut. And then they'd try uh try to get them **down**. There were **two gates** that closed this now what a **lane** like. A lane was also funnel-shaped down to the water's edge from this corral. Ah it was independent of the corral altogether. It was you had to open a gate to get **inta** this lane and then the lane narrowed up till only one at a time could get through the end of it.

The additive syntax of oral speech ensures the adherence to sequence in this passage. Even were an overview or abstract supplied, strict sequence of events would be maintained.

A second fundamental difference between the oral and written versions is that the oral process description is very close to narrative, being what Wald (1973) originally defined as a "pseudo-narrative." The first stage of the process is described as a citizen of Hope would see it on the street during the 1890s. "Street" is designated as given information in the first clause through use of the definite article as a descriptor: "And then one fellow'd be on **point** down the street." The viewer/listener is given a fixed perspective on the street and so is able to "see" the drover. Here, as in the written description, locative information combined with given information cues the listener to where he or she is imaginatively in relation to the cattle drive and in turn where imaginatively to look. The listener can see the event in linear sequence not only in terms of what happens first but also in terms of who comes first. There is a strong element of parade or spectacle in the oral process description Starret provides for his interviewer.

In his description of the initial stage of this cattle driving process, Starret combines five clauses in one sentence. On the one hand such a combination of clauses allows the listener to follow the events of the first stage in sequence, while, on the other, it creates stylistically an experience of simultaneous or rapid action and thus heightened experience by virtue of the energy portrayed:

And then one fellow'd be on **point** down the street and the cattle'd be following and there'd be a lot of fellows **wooing** at them and calling and chasing them along you know 'n 'casionally you'd hear a **whip** crack from a drover **whip** crack you know but I never see 'im abusin' the cattle any.

This is not an analytic but a highly visual depiction of the process being described. Indeed, it would be more appropriate to term such a description an "event description" rather than a "process description." In sequence, the listener first "sees" the lead drover directing the entire drive and then the cattle accompanied by other drovers verbally and physically driving them through the town. All participants are fully accounted for in the sequence in which a fixed observer would see them.

Quite unlike the written description of the cattle drive, human agents as well as cattle patients are clearly in evidence in Starret's oral process description. The agency of the drovers is also clearly heightened by the use of transitive verbs. Understandable, then, is a perception of this process description as being story-like, for the description both takes place in the past and has a strong orientation to agency inherent in narrative. What distinguishes this description from a narrative is the use of the modal *would* with habitual force or meaning. Four of the five clauses in the sentence employ a modal *would*+ verb construction marking the action designated by the verb as habitual or customary in the past. The tense designation is correct for narrative since the actions Starret is describing take place in the past, but the simple past marks action as perfective, while the modal *would* marks action as habitual in conjunction with imperfective uses of the verb. The first verb structure of the first clause, " 'd be on **point**," is imperfective combined with habitual meaning as is the following verb structure: "cattle'd be following." The presence of four present participles, which are aspectually imperfective, in two of the clauses and one present progressive verb construction designates the description appropriately as one of process, while the modal *would* marks the process as habitual in the past.

The features of genre interact significantly with the features of oral speech to produce the story-like quality of this oral process description, thus differentiating it maximally from its written counterpart. With features of involvement, "you know," "you'd hear," and the presence of evaluation, "but I never see 'im abusin' the cattle any," the features of oral speech also combine to heighten the tellability of this story-like process description adding to it an aesthetic quality not possessed by Starret's written version with its greater causative and analytic orientation. In oral description preference for active declarative structures as well as additive cohesion between sentences causes an "objective" discourse such as description to take on selected features of oral story-telling, in particular expression of human agency and action. However, to the extent that such description enhances agency, the properties of such discourse are assumed to be enhanced, since connotatively rather than in terms of strict denotation, we evaluate such texts as being even more highly "descriptive."

In the next stage, where Starret must explain the corralling of the cattle, the oral process description declines in quality. Whereas the written description combines analysis and sequence well, the attempt to treat sequence and analysis together in the oral version causes Starret a number of processing difficulties not at all evident in his description of the previous stage:

And they'd get along this street till and and they had a kind of a a receiver **fence** I guess you'd call it along the bank so they wouldn't get over **there** and the gate would open on the other side to make a funnel shape and they'd get them into that corral. And then they'd get the gate shut. And they'd try uh try to get them **down**. There were **two gates** that closed this now what a **lane** like. A **lane** was also funnel-shaped down to the water's edge from this corral. Ah it was independent of the corral altogether. It was you had to open a gate to get **inta** this lane and then the lane narrowed up till only one at a time could get through the end of it.

While the first stage in the oral description is descriptively exciting, the second stage is descriptively confusing. As indicated, Starret is attempting to perform two descriptive acts simultaneously. With the drovers in the role of agent/subject in each main clause, he wishes to continue "narrating" their actions in strict sequence. As well, he wishes to describe and explain the structure of the new topic "corral" so that he can continue to describe the transference of the cattle through it. For purposes of comparison, we can again briefly examine the written description to see how this problem of organization is dealt with:

A substantial gate in the exit of the log fence when being opened allowed the cattle to be driven into a log schute which would allow perhaps three animals to walk abreast down the steep incline to an additional gangplank . . .

By backgrounding human agency, which creates aesthetic value in the oral version, the written process description is able to correlate analysis and sequence. Conversely, in the oral version, the presence of human agents in the subject slot of most of the main clauses creates a form of breakdown in the second stage of the description. Starret's first processing difficulty comes when he must introduce the topic of the corral itself. He does this awkwardly by employing a descriptive clause with the verb *have*, thus adhering to the preference in oral speech for animate grammatical subjects in declarative sentences:

And they'd get along this street till and and *they* [my italics] had a kind of a a receiver **fence** I guess you'd call it along the bank so they wouldn't get over **there** and the gate would open on the other side to make a funnel shape and they'd get them into that corral.

Although Starret does meet the psychological needs of the descriptive frame requiring that entrances precede exits, his oral description of the cattle entering the corral is difficult for a listener to follow. In effect there are two competing topic/subjects in this long co-ordinated oral sentence: the cattle drovers and the receiver fence. This competition is further complicated by the presence of a third topic/subject, "they," referring to cattle. Also, deictic "**there**" and "on the other side" with unspecified reference make perceptual difficulties for the listener, who has been very well cued with regard to perspective and scenic features up until this point in the description. Physical reference continues to be vague while the two topics compete. However, Starret adheres to his selection of the human agents in subject slot for two further sentences until he finally employs existential *there* to introduce the new subject of "**two gates**," clearly related to the topic of the "receiver fence":

There were **two gates** that closed this now what a **lane** like. A **lane** was also funnel-shaped down to the water's edge from this corral. Ah it was independent of the corral altogether.

To achieve coherence, Martin finally eliminates the drovers as competing topic/subject with the corral or "receiver fence" and so concentrates on those features of the corral which pertain to the transmission of the cattle out of this holding pen. Intersentential cohesion also becomes strong within this grouping of three sentences. Between the first and the second there is tail-head linkage where the object of a preceding sentence becomes the subject of the next, and between the second and the third there is head-head linkage where the subjects share the same referent, "lane." Briefly, Starret abandons the pseudo-narrative strategy and adopts a strategy of describing physical data in the environment only. While he could have easily repeated the descriptive clause structure used to introduce the receiver fence (i.e. *And then they'd try uh try to get them down. They had* [my emphasis] *two gates*), Starret chooses to introduce the gates as an entirely new subject via existential *there*, so altering processing strategy and more successfully producing coherent and cohesive text: "There were **two gates** that closed this now what a **lane** like."

With the necessary elimination of human agents as competing topic/subject in the oral description, the phenomenon of metaphorical transference of agency to an inanimate object takes place in the oral version as it does in the written description. Thus changes of state must be expressed metaphorically or not at all once human agents are eliminated from a scene. However, although the verb "closed" is causative, meaning "caused to become closed," the oral process description at no time employs conjunctive verbs which causally analyse structural phenomena, as the written version does, where Martin states that a gate or a chute "allows" the transmission of the cattle in particular sequence or groupings. Moreover, Martin's shift in strategy from the pseudo-narrative to the analytic is brief. Almost immediately he reverts to pseudo-narrative sentence structures to complete his description of the corral and its adjunct lane leading down to the gangplank of the waiting steamboat:

It [lane] *was you had to open a gate to get **inta** this lane and then the lane narrowed up till only one at a time could get through the end of it.* [my italics]

Although the gate has been metaphorically analysed as agentive in an earlier sentence, Martin reanalyses the gate and its physical relation to the lane a second time significantly reintroducing a human agent, the generalized "you," into the subject slot of the sentence so that a change of state, opening, is effected nonmetaphorically by a human agent. Commencing the above sentence coherently and

cohesively with the subject "it" referential to lane, Starret repro-
cesses the sentence in keeping with the oral preference for active
declarative sentences with animate agents in subject slot.

The second clause of this sentence reverts to "lane" as a grammatical subject only because human agency is not competitively available in its further description. Noticeably, however, Starret does not
describe this lane as a "schute" as he does in his written description.
Where the written description presents the lane as a functional vessel, or "schute," which metaphorically "allows" only a tight formation on the part of the cattle, the oral description presents the lane in
exclusively visual terms, highly depictive of the scene or setting, as
"narrow[ing] up till only one at a time could get through the end of
it." The analysis is not causative, but resultative. The particle "up"
marks effective aspect, which focuses attention on the final stage of
an activity and, in particular, on the final result of that activity. The
adverbial clause "till only one at a time could get through the end of
it" is also resultative, although, technically, it is an adverb clause of
time. While the funnel-like structure of the lane determines that the
cattle must realign themselves, this structure is not described as
causing such realignment, having no necessary agentive force assigned to it. Predisposition to human agency, as well as a strong
orientation to strict sequencing of events in time where results are
marked at the end point of a temporal sequence, favours the non-
analytic over the analytic in oral process description.

This dichotomy between an analytic and non-analytic or narrative
strategy continues to hold in the respective treatments of the last
general stage of the cattle driving process, transference of the cattle
to the steamboat where, in both versions, this stage in the process is
depicted as being fraught with difficulty and thus necessitating
problem solving. In the oral version, "trouble" is introduced as the
new topic of the last paragraph of the description ("And they used to
have trouble to get that first **cow** on"), whereas the problem of the
cattle balking while on the gangplank is introduced at the end of the
second sentence of the written description which takes this problem
as its principal theme.

Although it marks human agency very little, the written description focuses to a much greater extent on the control and contain-
ment of the cattle in their passage from land to ship. In the oral
version, "the problem" as theme is seen simply as one of manoeuv-
ring the cattle once they get to the gangplank where they balk:

And they used to have trouble to get that first **cow** on. The cow would go
there and it'd see the gangplank. Well the the uh the effect of the **motion** of

the **river** would cause this steamboat just to vary a little to wave a little see to go up and down to plop just a little bit. And the gangplank would move just that little bit and the cow would balk there and wouldn't go. So the fellow'd say the fellow that **owned** the cattle would generally be **right** there and the man that owned the cattle, **head** of the cowboys and he'd say, "**Hey Tom**, bring that **buckskin** horse here and a **lariat**. Get that **leader** in **there**."

In this analysis, despite the presence in one clause of the conjunctive verb *cause*, action produces a reaction, which, reanalysed as action, produces another reaction. Thus the cows get to the gangplank, see the motion of the water, implicitly become frightened and so refuse to go further. Starret provides evaluation in terms of cause ("Well the the uh the effect of the **motion** of the **river** would cause this steamboat just to vary a little . . ."), but he analyses the behaviour of the cattle in terms of result: "And the gangplank would move just that little bit and the cow would balk there and wouldn't **go**." The behaviour of the drovers results in turn from this reaction on the part of the cattle: "*So* [my italics] the fellow'd say." Although the drovers are technically in command, they are analysed here as responding to the cattle when necessary, rather than as governing them every inch of the way.

In contrast, control is manifest at every point in the written version. The physical environment as constructed by human agency is designed to control and contain the cattle as if the cattle were not simply animals but a kind of force requiring constant constraint. The environment itself becomes agentive, functioning as a counterforce to the cattle. In addition to the gate and the chute "allow[ing]" the cattle to exit or walk in a certain way, the gangplank, "built with extra strong braced sides," constrains the force of the cattle. Further, the written description continues to articulate features of the environment which promote mastery of the process for the human agents involved. Having described the gate, the chute, and the gangplank as agents in his written description, Starret next analyses the steamboat waiting to receive the cattle:

The Steamboat facing down stream was securely tied to the shore by immense hawsers on from the stern whose shore end was fastened to an iron ring attached to a Deadman buried to a secure depth on top of the band, which held the stern of the Boat against the beach. The Bow of the craft was held in place against the shore by another hawser which was secured by tying to a convenient tree or stump up on shore.

To thematize the NP in the role of patient, Starret employs the passive voice. However, he does not delete agency as he has done in other preceding passive structures. Agency is clearly marked, although the agent, "immense hawsers," is non-animate. Again, metaphorical transference takes place, for it is the "hawsers," instruments in case grammar terms, which become agents in the passive structures above. This transformation of instrumentation into agency itself characterizes the treatment of agency in the description as a whole, foregrounding the concern with control lexically explicit in the verb "secured" in the second clause of the second sentence. Control is seen to be enhanced when instruments themselves govern situations.

Yet despite such instrumental control over the environment of the cattle in their journey through the town and subsequent passage onto the waiting boat, the cattle do not cross the gangplank smoothly; as a force they are contained but not entirely governed. Analysing the cattle as he had earlier analysed the physical environment to contain them, Starret focuses on their wildness and their terror in this intermediate situation. His analysis is almost entirely causative, concentrating on efficient cause which produces on the cattle the negative effect of balking:

Whenever the Cattle started to walk over the gangplank, their weight would cause the far end to move down a little, and mostly the Boat would rock a little by the action of the river current coming in contact with the moored craft.

This gang-plank motion seemed always to terrify the already half wild cattle and they would start to mill around in their confined space; the animals, crowding in from behind, sensing matters at hand being out of the ordinary, refused to advance any further, so a dead lock ensued.

In the first sentence above, the weight of the cattle as well as the river current are analysed as prime movers in the creation of "gang-plank motion," which is further analysed ("seemed" is explicitly interpretive on the part of the writer, being what Halliday [1985] refers to as a marker of modality, the writer/speaker's comment on a situation) causatively as producing terror in the animals. Their terror, then, results in chaotic behaviour: "and they would start to mill around in their confined space." Simultaneously, those animals following refuse to move further because of the crowded conditions which they interpret as unusual and thus dangerous. All structures in the passage above excluding one *and* of result are causative and so produce a strongly analytic description of the cattle balking on the gangplank. The psychology of the cattle is as important to this highly analytic treatment as is the attention to instrumentation.

Both process descriptions end by detailing the actions of a "Puncher," whose function it is to rope the lead cow and forcibly drag it onto a waiting steamboat, thus unstemming the logjam of cattle on and in front of the gangplank. In each version, description of the problem is logically followed by description of its solution. The solution, however, is explicitly presented as such in the written description, while the solution in the oral description functions more as a resolution in plot arising out of a complicating action, that of the cattle refusing to move.

We can see this distinction in the respective commencements of this solution stage in each description:

At this unusual change of events, the drovers on the rear of the cavalcade would draw together and decide on a more effective manner than having the Cowboys shouting, and whipping the stock in the rear. (Written description)

So the fellow'd say the fellow that **owned** the cattle would generally be **right** there the man that owned the cattle, **head** of the cowboys and he'd say, "**Hey Tom**, bring that **buckskin** horse here and a **lariat**. Get that **leader** in **there**." (Oral description)

The written description differs from the oral not only in its democratic rendering of decision making, but also in its articulation of decision making as a separate and discrete act in the overall process. A collective decision-making act on the part of "the drovers in the rear" both separates the problem from the solution structurally in the discourse and imposes an explicit contrapuntal organization upon it, while it also explicitly and simultaneously supports the theme of problem solving in the discourse.

In the oral description it is presupposed by the listener that the "**head** of the cowboys" has made a decision before explicitly directing one of the cowboys, Tom, to act. His direction, "Get that **leader** in **there**," presents solution as direct narrative action rather than the outcome of analysis.

The two endings, in fact, serve separate ideals of what is "descriptive." The oral description fosters its connections to narrative by detailing the actions of a single actor, the puncher Tom. The listener "watches" Tom rope and drag the leader cow onto the steamboat waiting to take the cattle down to New Westminster. The actions described seem to be taking place in real time and are performed by a real person:

So he'd come down with a horse an' hit these cattle over the nose and **get** them to other side and **get** them back and then get ah throw a a **rope** over this cattle's **horns** . . . (Oral description)

The written description promotes another kind of ideal—that of generality. The actions of the puncher, therefore, are the actions of any and every puncher at any and every cattle drive:

A Puncher mounted on one of the strongest horses would edge down one side of the shute toward the boat and eventually with much slapping with his stock whip or doubled up rata clear a passage so his horse could get through onto the gangplank at the spear head of the stubbern milling critters. In this position with his mount faced to board the craft, the rider . . . (Written description)

The use of formal vocabulary, "mount," "craft," as well as agentive nominalizations, "puncher," "rider," and a gerund construction, "slapping with his stock whip or doubled up rata," distance the reader from the activity and generalize its actions and its sequences.

The oral description concentrates on a very specific action and so supplies specific locative detail such as the goal of the blow, "over the nose," in conjunction with an *and* of purpose to explicate final cause in the structure, "an' hit these cattle over the nose and **get** them to other side." In the written description a gerund phrase, "with much slapping with his stock whip or doubled up rata," is used. Thus, a specific action in the oral description is combined syntactically with a specific purpose, whereas a generalized action in the written description is syntactically subordinated to a generalized goal: "clear a passage." The gerund phrase in the written description syntactically, as well as semantically, removes the action from the immediate and specific context of cattle and drovers and quite literally objectifies it as the object of the instrumental preposition *with*. Through such mechanisms of abstraction, generalization is created. Although less detailed and so less "descriptive" on one level, on another the written description achieves descriptive power because it can concentrate in its predicates those goals which literally predicate solution.

CONCLUSION

Oral and written speech influence process description in fundamentally different ways. The oral process description examined in this chapter corresponds to a pseudo-narrative. Processing in oral speech does not permit extensive exploitation of the passive, which features prominently in the phenomenalization of description in written speech. Written speech, conversely, with its access to the passive and use of nominalizations, can produce an abstract conception of process itself. Action as activity can be focused on by either backgrounding human agency grammatically or transferring it metaphorically to features of the environment or by producing marked agency where instruments take on agentive force or meaning.

In the oral and written process descriptions very different strategies are also used by the same speaker to create perspective and effect thematic coherence. Perspective is achieved in the oral text by a strategy of involvement, which engages the listener in a form of role playing as a means of comprehending actions and events. However, whereas perspective is created through involvement in oral process description, it is created in written process description by cues to the reader effected through marked word order. As Prague School theorists have pointed out, sentence structures in English can be examined from the point of view of grammar, semantics, and communication (Danes 1964). They employ the term "functional sentence perspective" to explicate how any sentence exists as an utterance from a speaker/writer to a listener/reader. They have pointed out that word order as well as intonation can be used in English, once it becomes an analytic language, as a means of expressing given and new distinctions and those of theme and rheme. Therefore, locatives in marked thematic position at the front of any written sentence can take on directional significance, so communicating perspective to the reader, who must nonetheless know how to take or read the cue given by marked word order. Although Prague School theorists do not designate word order as an especially significant means of creating marked or contrastive meaning in written English, it is clear that variation of word order to achieve marked meaning is a strategy that is more favoured by written speech than oral speech and that, as such, it requires interpretive understanding on the part of any reader.

Thematic focusing also distinguishes the written text from the oral as is the case in two of Starret's narratives. Whereas the oral process description is essentially linear in structure and so presents all stages in the process with equal weight, a dialectical structure is imposed on the written description. Thematic attention is given to the last and most problematic stage of the process. Contrapuntally, once the problem is defined, the solution is then described. The written description becomes, by such structural focusing, an analysis of a problem and its solution. Moreover, the written description, because it imposes a problem-solving frame on its content, ignores certain other frames, such as that prescribing description of entrances before exits, which have primary salience for both readers and listeners. The reader must adopt an interpretive stance toward what is being read and so accommodate to this less salient and more analytic frame in the written description.

Conversely, in the oral description Starret first sets the scene and assigns perspective for his interviewer, Imbert Orchard. He then deals sequentially with the first, middle and last stages of the cattle drive. Each stage in the process is given equal attention and equal weight. The listener somewhat synaethestically watches the action as if seeing it on film. Spatial sequence is adhered to just as temporal sequence is adhered to in oral narration.

Differences in media and thus means of information processing affect differences in structure, treatment of topic, and perspective between the two process descriptions. To the extent that oral speech relies on unmarked svo syntax with unmarked animate agency, the oral production of description leans to narrative, while the written production, able to exploit contrastive and marked syntactic order more fully, leans to analytic exposition. These differences in orientation give rise to very different ideals of description. The "tellability" and specificity of the oral process description contrasts sharply with the approximation of archetypal generalization in written process description. Conceptualizing the process as a whole from the outset, the written description can attend to selected specifics requiring particular attention; rendering the process in balanced sequence, the oral description can "narrate" each stage as a distinct and exciting event in space and time where all participants, including the involved listener, play their assigned roles. The media not only structure and convey description differently but also determine different concepts of what description and descriptive adequacy are. Written description better captures and conceptualizes a series of actions as a defined and integrated process, whereas oral description better captures or renders a series of actions as a specific though habitual event. One appeals to the illusion of direct experience and observation, while the other appeals to the illusion that actions can be understood as generalized phenomena. Both achieve descriptive "adequacy" according to two very different ideals governed by media constraints.

4

Oral and Written Exposition

Exposition as a genre is normally associated with writing and, primarily, with the writing of academics. The concept of modern exposition comes into being as an outgrowth of the scientific revolution and in particular as a response to the needs of the Royal Society of London. In his *Essay Concerning Human Understanding*, Locke sets out for the Society a general theory of language which takes exposition as its principle aim:

To conclude this Consideration of the Imperfection, and Abuse of Language; the *ends of Language in our Discourse with others*, being chiefly these three: *First, To make known* one Man's thoughts or *Ideas* to another. *Secondly*, To do it *with* as much ease and *quickness*, as is possible; and *Thirdly*, Thereby *to convey* the *Knowledge* of Things. Language is either abused, or deficient, when it fails in any of these Three.[1]

Locke and other advocates of the "new philosophy" or science of the time rejected Ciceronian rhetoric as the principal methodology for both discovering and explicating content (Howell 1971:498-500). They embraced inductive rather than deductive reasoning and in so doing rejected a system of thought based on collectively held premises or beliefs. In asserting what is now called the "Scientific Method," they asserted also a principle of scepticism by which all beliefs or premises were subject to scrutiny and examination. Knowledge, then, did not derive from generally held beliefs or first premises but instead required discovery through induction and the empirical collection of data.

This "Scientific Revolution" involved a revolution in both methodology and the concept of knowledge itself. After the scientific revolution, knowledge was no longer socially or communally based, but was rather the outcome of the efforts of a particular group in the community, that is, the "new philosophers" or scientists. Descendants of the humanists, they conceived of themselves as "individuals" with individual perceptive powers. According to Locke's great essay with its fundamental argument for empiricism, perception itself was derived from one's own senses or sensory mechanism. As a sensate individual, a new philosopher was required to "communicate" individual observations, thoughts, ideas, and views, since only through such communication could one's special and individual knowledge be transmitted to others.

Locke's definition of language contains the principal elements of the new rhetoric of the eighteenth century. For Locke, language is primarily a means of transmitting concepts or ideas concisely or perspicuously in such a way that new knowledge "of things" is conveyed. The influence of this view can be seen in the language theories of a modern language philosopher, Paul Grice. According to Grice's maxims, which support his Co-Operative Principle of Conversation, communication of thought should also be efficient and perspicacious. In his four maxims, Grice asserts that a speaker should "make [his/her] contribution as informative as required," but not more so, speak the truth, "be relevant," and ultimately "be perspicuous" (1975:45–46). This stress on relevant and truthful information presented concisely is entirely in keeping with Locke's theory of language as exposition.

The pervasiveness of this Lockean definition of exposition is evident in the discourse theories of others, including modern rhetoricians and reading theorists. In *A Theory of Discourse*, James Kinneavy defines exposition as "reference discourse" (39), while the reading-theorists Arthur Graesser and Sharon Goodman distinguish exposition from narrative in eight principal ways:

(1) exposition concerns the transmission of that which is true
(2) exposition employs generic or universal time reference
(3) exposition is associated with written rather than oral speech
(4) exposition fosters descriptive conceptualization of states and features
(5) exposition relies little on inferences supplied by a reader
(6) exposition has as its general purpose "to inform the reader about truths in the world"
(7) exposition exploits a "pyramid development"
(8) exposition exploits logical connectives (1985: 144)

In their breakdown of features for exposition, as distinct from narrative, Graesser and Goodman incorporate narrative with fiction in their first criterion and so arrive at the common view that only expository discourse concerns the transmission of that which is true. But exposition is not distinguished from narrative on the basis of factuality. As a speech act, the direction of word-fit for exposition is exactly that for narration: word to world. What distinguishes exposition from other genres is its orientation to concepts. Werlich (1976) and Longacre (1968) both focus on this orientation in their respective definitions of exposition. Werlich defines exposition as focusing on the composition or decomposition of concepts. His definition thus embraces what would be termed "reference discourse" as well as analysis. In Longacre's treatment, exposition would be both deagentive and without contingent temporal succession but with prominent orientation to subject matter.

This orientation not to agents or to objects or actions in space but to subject matter explains the other features of exposition detailed by Graesser and Goodman. An orientation to conceptual composition or decomposition promotes the use of the generic or state present tense[2] and so the view that exposition concerns the transmission of "truths in the world." "Descriptive conceptualization" equally reflects such use. Such discourse also concerns the transmission of new information and therefore lacks the exploitation of inference found in readers of narrative. Pyramid organization and use of logical connectives are explained by the fact that exposition focuses on the transmission of new information. Pyramid organization allows new generalizations to be easily illustrated and supported by specifics, while logical connectives promote connection between conceptual features or elements rather than events in time and space. The association of exposition to written speech is understandable in a culture which codes and stores its knowledge in journals and texts rather than in epic poetry. As Eric Havelock (1963) points out, the epic poem is the "encyclopedia" of oral culture.[3]

One major problem in the definition of exposition is the distinction between exposition and instruction, since both concern the transmission of new information. Rhetoricians in the eighteenth century (e.g., Adam Smith) commonly collapsed the two making no real distinction between them. Failure to distinguish the two genres is also common in modern rhetorics or handbooks. These two genres can only be distinguished if instruction is thought of quite specifically as a speech act where the direction of fit is world to word. Exposition or lecturing is commonplace in the behaviour of teachers, but instruction requires that students be able to duplicate what has been explained to them. The speech act is not complete unless the student is able to reiterate the teacher's exposition. In contrast, "pure" exposition does not have a requirement of effectiveness. The reader of *Scientific American* reads to learn or to be informed but without any need or desire to master the new information as a student would. Ultimately, then, we must define exposition as discourse primarily concerned with the explication of new concepts, ideas, or analyses for a receptive reading or listening audience. This prototype of exposition is often confused with written discourse itself, which is characterized as explicit in contrast to implicit oral discourse. The criterion of explicitness is here conceived of as a feature of genre, in specific, exposition, which has as its fundamental concern the communication of new conceptual knowledge to readers and listeners alike.

POPULAR EXPOSITION: THE DEFINITION OF A LOVER

Definition is a particularly common form of exposition, usually considered important or necessary in academic writing. The two parallel texts considered here are examples of oral and written definition and concern the topic of love. The oral text is taken from a lecture, *The Politics of Love*, given by Leo Buscaglia, while the written text is a chapter taken from Buscaglia's book, *Loving Each Other*. Although Buscaglia is an academic, he is primarily known as a popularizer of his academic work on human relations. Both as a speaker and as a writer Buscaglia is enormously successful; his lectures and his books "sell out." We are looking, then, at exposition geared not to a specific academic audience but to the general public.

Both the oral and written parallel texts taken from Buscaglia are examples of "planned" discourse. Ochs has defined planned discourse as discourse which "has been thought out and organized (designed) prior to its expression" (1979:55). Ochs distinguishes planned from unplanned discourse more specifically by the following criteria:

Feature 1: Speakers in planned discourse do not rely on the immediate context to express propositions.

Feature 2: Planned discourse makes use of morphosyntactic structures (passive voice and verb tense) that are relatively late to emerge in language.

Feature 3: There is little repetition of lexical items in planned discourse.

Feature 4: There is less repetition of form and content in planned discourse.

In her discussion of planned and unplanned discourse, Ochs consistently parallels the language of children with unplanned discourse and that of adults with planned discourse. There is also an implied correlation of oral speech with unplanned discourse and of written speech with planned discourse. In fact, many of the features Ochs ascribes to planned discourse do correlate with those of written speech. Theoretically, there is less repetition of lexemes, phrases and clauses in writing which ideally promotes "integration" and "elegant variation." The passive voice is also a feature of written speech. The correlation between children's speech and unplanned discourse is understandable in light of certain correspondences to Ochs' planned discourse and written speech, for adults generally have access to written speech while children do not. Although Ochs does not explicitly make the connection between planned discourse and written speech, others do.

Chafe (1982) in particular has argued that because written speech is planned, it manifests features of integration (participles, nominalizations, attributive adjectives, conjoined phrases, items in a series, sequential prepositional phrases, complement clauses, and relative clauses). Chafe contrasts oral and written speech with regard to planning in this way:

In speaking, we normally produce one idea unit at a time. That is apparently about all we have the capacity to pay attention to, and if we try to think about much more than that we are likely to get into trouble (cf. the 'one-clause-at-a-time hypothesis' suggested by Frances Syder and Andrew Pawley). In writing we have time to mold a succession of ideas into a more complex, coherent, integrated whole, making use of devices we seldom use in speaking.(37)

In this analysis, written speech is what it is by virtue of being planned rather than unplanned. However, both Buscaglia's oral text and his written one are planned texts. Buscaglia uses notes and quotations written on small cards to give his lecture, but he composes it orally. What classical rhetoricians refer to as "invention" or planning precedes the delivery of his speech. There should, then, be marked similarities in the syntax of Buscaglia's two texts. In the oral as well as the written text we expect to see present both the features of planned speech identified by Ochs and the features of integration ascribed to written speech by virtue of its planned nature.

If we examine a syntactic profile of the two parallel texts we can see that there are significant syntactic similarities as well as significant syntactic contrasts between them, as shown in Table 6. With regard to sentence type, similarity occurs only in the almost equiva-

TABLE 6
Syntactic Profile/The Definition of a Lover

Sentences	Oral 92 (1434wds)	Written 137(2494wds)
Simple	42 (46%)	64 (47%)
Compound	06 (06%)	02 (01%)
Complex	13 (14%)	64 (47%)
Compound/complex	30 (33%)	07 (05%)
Embedded	01 (01%)	00 (00%)
Relative clauses	15	24
Adverbial clauses	18	28
Noun clauses	27	54
Co-ordinate clauses	44	09
Conjoining phrases	08	60
Participle phrases	06	16
Gerund	03	14
Infinitives	49	64
Passives	01	20
Exist. *There*/clefts	07	08
Attributive adjs.	71	150
(participles)	04	11
Nouns in apposition	00	06

lent percentage of simple sentences in the oral and written texts, a consistent finding in this study which indicates that simple sentences are preferred in both oral and written speech. A radical contrast occurs in the percentages for complex sentences, the oral text having only 14 per cent while the written text has a high 47 per cent. However, complexity is nonetheless favoured in the oral text by virtue of a very high percentage (33%) of compound/complex sentences.

Interestingly, there is an almost complete reversal of numbers and percentages in the two texts depending upon whether clauses or phrases are examined. There are 44 co-ordinate clauses in the 92 sentences of the oral text. These clauses feature in approximately 49 per cent of the sentences of the oral text.[4] In contrast, co-ordinate clauses feature in only 6.5 per cent of the sentences in the written text. The difference in percentages is striking, as it is if we compare conjoined phrases in the two texts. There are 8 conjoined phrases in the 92 sentences of the oral text. Conjoined phrases thus feature in only 9 per cent of the oral sentences. However, there are 60 conjoined phrases in the 137 sentences of the written text. These phrases appear in 44 per cent of the written sentences. These percentages indicate that despite planning, oral speech still favours compounding as a means of syntactic cohesion, while written speech prefers conjoined phrases, which produce synthetic syntactic structures in each sentence. Planning, then, does not seem to be a factor in the characteristic properties of either form of speech.

However, there does seem to be some indication that planning affects syntax. With regard to relative clauses, so important for syntactic integration, there is virtual equivalence in their percentages in each text. Relative clauses appear in 16 per cent of the oral sentences and in 17.5 per cent of the written sentences. A similar equivalence occurs for adverbial clauses. Adverbial clauses appear in 19.5 per cent of the oral sentences and in 20 per cent of the written sentences. Only in the noun clauses, which appear in 29 per cent of the oral sentences and 39 per cent of the written sentences, is there a more marked contrast favouring the written sentence in complexity over the oral.

What is noteworthy with regard to clause types in the two texts, however, is not the percentile equivalences in the relative and the adverbial clauses, but the very small percentages for relative clauses in both the oral and the written texts. On average, adverbial clauses appear with similar or equivalent percentages in oral and written texts. Relative clauses, however, are generally favoured in written texts. As embedded constructions, they allow nominal information in any sentence to be directly modified in sequence rather than as an afterthought. It is not unusual for an oral text to have only 16 per cent relative clauses in its sentences; a spread between 10 and 16 per cent is common. However, it is more common for relative clauses to occur in 20 to 30 per cent of the sentences of a written text. A percentage of 17.5 is very low.

In exploring reasons for the low percentage of relative clauses in the written text, we need to examine the much higher percentage of noun clauses in both the oral and written expositions. Noun clauses as complements are defined by Chafe as integrators in written speech (1982:44). However, their appearance in written or oral discourse is variable. They occur in either processing sub-variety as complements when speech or thought is reported. In the narrative or descriptive texts examined so far, they do not necessarily correlate with either written or oral speech. Yet noun clause complements appear frequently in both of Buscaglia's expository texts because exposition, having to do with the explication of concepts, fosters clause structures adjoined to assertions, opinions and thoughts. Conversely, exposition does not foster extensive identificatory or explanatory description of physical items in space. Exposition in Graesser and Goodman's view may be descriptive of conceptual states, but it is not descriptive of animate and inanimate entities or events. Its conceptual purpose promotes adjoined clauses of thought or opinion relating to what Werlich refers to as the composition or decomposition of concepts, but it does not promote structures such as relative clauses, which supply new descriptive information or old identificatory information. The percentage for relative clauses in the written text, then, may be equivalent to that in the oral, not because of planning, but because of genre constraints which have minimalized relative clauses considerably in the written text while greatly expanding the number of noun clauses in both the oral and written texts.

The difference of 10 per cent between the noun clauses in the oral text and those in the written text may suggest that planning facilitates greater use of noun complements in the written text, but since in general planning does not affect the characteristic syntactic structures of oral and written speech, it is unlikely that planning as such promotes the greater number of noun clauses per sentence in the written text.

Though planning does not markedly affect syntax in either of the two texts, it most certainly affects content. Buscaglia exploits much of the same material in both texts, using the same examples or quotations in many cases. The two texts are "parallel" precisely because they present comparable content and because they share a similar purpose.

As stated, both texts concern the definition of a "lover." The oral text is taken from a much larger discourse in which Buscaglia first introduces his research and then the concept of love as active and political before proceeding to define "lover" as he understands the term.[5] He begins his definition by characterizing the lover as a human being with a sense of humour. The written text, which constitutes one chapter from Buscaglia's book *Loving Each Other*, appears later in his overall discussion of the features of a lover because humour was rated by Buscaglia's informants in seventh place as a necessary feature for a loving person. In the written text, then, Buscaglia iconically treats each feature in the order in which it is ranked in importance by his informants.

Why Buscaglia treats humour much more prominently as a first or basic feature in the oral text needs to be considered. Humour as central to love is basic to his own vision or definition of love. The oral situation, which almost parallels that of a teacher addressing an audience of disciples, allows Buscaglia to assert his own ranking rather than to function more academically as a reporter of data as he does in the written text. Buscaglia, then, structures the two larger texts along different lines. To foster an ethos of himself as a responsible researcher and reporter of the facts, in the written text Buscaglia parallels his overall organizational structure to his findings. Conversely, in the oral text the role as the teacher, whose aim is motivation, overlaps frequently with that of the lecturer, whose aim is pure definition. The difference in approach is evident if we compare Buscaglia's introduction of the subtopic of humour in both texts:

But the **first** thing that we're going to have to do if we're going to decide we're going to be **lovers** is you're going to have to develop your sense of **humour**, because my goodness people are going to treat you strangely and you're going to have to learn to **accept** it with a good **laugh**. (Oral exposition)

It seems to me that deep relating without joy, laughter, and a sense of humor is an impossibility. (Written exposition)

In both topic introductions humour is a definitional feature, a *sine qua non*, for loving or being a lover. In the oral text, however, humour is presented as a means of coping with a new state, while in the written text it is a necessary feature of "deep relating" or love. While both definitions posit humour as a necessary feature, the oral definition asserts humour as primary, thus adding a motivational element to the definition for the audience. An *if-then* structure is employed in the subordinating syntax of the oral sentence which effectively sets conditions on the definition and transforms it from a definition pure and simple into a goal for which the audience must strive.

Structurally, the two introductory sentences exhibit the differences Halliday has remarked on in oral and written speech. The oral sentence is "choreographic" by virtue of its extensive use of dependent adverbial clauses, while the written sentence is "crystalline" because of its lexically dense syntax and abstract vocabulary. Both sentences, however, employ a copula or equative syntax as a main structure. An equative syntax is extensively used in exposition where definition is required or is the focus of discourse. The first main clause in the oral sentence is procedural: "the first **thing** that we're going to have to do." This main clause is then equated with a second main clause, "you're going to have to develop your sense of **humour**." In the first clause Buscaglia incorporates the idea of collective necessity into that of the "first **thing**." He presents both himself and his audience as actors with a future purpose. Simultaneously, he creates identification between himself and his audience through use of the collective pronoun "we" and involves that audience in a common, though unstated, purpose. In the second clause, which presents new information, identification with the audience is abandoned and Buscaglia, speaking as a teacher, supplies the specific purpose: "*you're* [my italics] going to have to develop your sense of **humour**." The syntax in this sentence is dramatic in that it creates an expectation which it must later fulfil. The vagueness of "**thing**," which Buscaglia stresses because he is introducing a new concept as topic in his sentence, is complemented by the specificity of "**humour**," also stressed because it conveys crucial new information.

In the oral sentence, Buscaglia presents his definition as a story in which his audience is an actor in the quest for a particular goal. The subordinate clause "if we're going to decide we're going to be **lovers**" presents a condition to the audience which must be fulfilled before the second part of the equation can be revealed. The audience must embrace its role before getting to step one in the quest Buscaglia lays before it. The causal clause "because my goodness people are going to treat you strangely and you're going to have to learn to **accept** it with a good **laugh**" logically explains why humour has been evaluated as a necessity in the main clause through use of the modal "have."

Through the use of conditionals, modals conveying the idea of necessity, and periphrastic phrases conveying futurity, all of which suggest difficulty and the need of commitment for the lover, Buscaglia evaluates as well as defines the lover. He also uses identificatory expressions such as "we" to create involvement in the definition for his audience. The definition Buscaglia presents is in this way romanticized for his audience, which is made to participate in the definition as an agent or role-player rather than as a critical consumer of new information.

In the written sentence there is greater appeal to abstract conceptualization and consideration. The sentence begins, like others in the chapter, with a qualifying statement: "*It seems to me* [my italics] that deep relating without joy, laughter, and a sense of humor is an impossibility." Buscaglia topicalizes his own view or opinion concerning the ideational content he is presenting. The effect is to make the reader aware of Buscaglia as the source of content or thesis. However, an impersonal construction such as "it seems to me" is also a weak expressor of personal view or opinion. A stylistically stronger statement would simply eliminate the qualifying expression. To avoid "weakness," composition students are thus taught to avoid qualifiers such as *I think* or *it seems to me*. Nevertheless, Buscaglia's use of such qualifiers in his written text, although less strong as a means of assertion, is also less threatening to a reading audience. Buscaglia approaches his readers on very different terms than he does his listeners. There are no expressions of necessity, "we're going to have to," "you're going to have to," but rather there are expressions of opinion and fact which are presented for the reader's consideration. The consistently moderate stand Buscaglia takes in his written text encourages a different form of involvement for the reader, who reads the text as a critic or judge. This moderate stand also explains why there are 10 per cent more noun clauses in the written text than in the oral, for use of these qualifiers or expressions of modality entails use of noun clause complements in their syntactic structure.

The noun clause complement of the qualifier "It seems to me" is also structured to advance a moderate or non-confrontational stand on the part of the writer. The copula structure it employs allows the nominal concept "deep relating," presented as subject in the sentence, to be evaluated. Like a qualifier, the subjective complement of the copula, "impossibility," expresses Buscaglia's intrusion on the ideational content. Yet where "it seems to me" is an expression of weak modality designed as a cue to the reader of respective interpersonal relations in the text, "impossibility" is an expression of strong opinion. As subjective complement "impossibility" also constitutes new information in the sentence. Thus, Buscaglia both constructs his definition as an evaluation and embeds his own view as new information in his introductory sentence. The effect of this very sophisticated embedding of evaluation or strong opinion, however, is not to undermine the weaker qualifier, but, in fact, to support its usage. In contrast to the low rating (seventh) given to humour as a characteristic of the lover by his informants, Buscaglia's embedded and focused evaluation asserts his own view that humour and love are strongly related or bound together, but it does so without seeming to express opinion at all. The Latinate "impossibility" is both formal and abstract; the syntax is equative and thus factual in its reading. Buscaglia's expression of strong opinion is camouflaged by his use of both qualifiers and factual equative syntax with a nominal abstraction as subjective complement.

In the presentation of new ideas or concepts to an audience, both the speaker and the writer must address the precepts of that audience. Although the expositor is neither a teacher nor a rhetorician, there are elements of motivation and persuasion in all expository texts, since new information tends to be resisted unless considerable groundwork is laid by a writer or speaker of expository discourse. In the two strategies discussed above, one oral and the other literate, Buscaglia creates two different personae for his respective listeners and readers. While the listeners participate emotionally in the oral definition, in the written definition he involves his readers in a factual exchange. The appeal, then, is not to the reader's emotional identification with the concept of a lover but with a view of the reader as a rational being concerned to know, as Graesser and Goodman put it, "about truths in the world." Written speech itself clearly fosters this contemplative ethos on the part of the reader, for the reader comes to the written text as a communication from a considerably distanced writer. Buscaglia does nothing initially to alter this rational ethos, but exploits it fully, thus employing impersonal and deagentized constructions to suggest simple factuality and lack of bias (while nonetheless covertly asserting his own strong opinion). Conversely, in his oral definition he makes agentive that which is abstract. His audience, to which he is physically near, is made to identify with a definition of lover which becomes, for it, a personal goal.

Buscaglia's success as a popularizer of his academic findings results from his understanding of the interpersonal dimensions of the two media he employs. The pseudo-factuality he achieves in his written text would have little impact on his listening audience, while the inspirational quality of his oral definition would serve only to alienate a reader as a single party at some remove physically or emotionally from others in the world. In the two texts, then, we see not only different ways of conceptualizing and addressing the respective audiences but also different ways of involving those two audiences and structuring content so that the new information is communicated.

Although there is greater interpersonal involvement of the speaker and listener in the oral text, involvement is a feature of both texts. To communicate new information, a speaker in oral or written speech must accommodate that information to his or her audience. In the oral text Buscaglia does so by relying heavily on narrative as a means of explicating his points as well as by presenting his new information as shared knowledge. To this end he consistently employs the construction *you know* as a form of address. In the written text Buscaglia exploits narrative only on two occasions, but he does involve his reader interpersonally in discussion of the humour of the lover through the extensive use of *we*, which marks information as shared.

The most pervasive expression of address used by Buscaglia in the oral text is *you know*. Chafe (1982) identifies this usage as a device of what he terms "involvement," which serves primarily to monitor information flow. Chafe states that "The speaker may do things to reassure him- or herself that the listener is assimilating what he or she is saying, or to prod the listener into noticing and acknowledging the flow of information"(47). *You know* does function as a monitoring device in certain contexts in oral speech. Placed at the end of a clause or sentence, it can be read as a request for confirmation: *Things are not what they used to be, you know.* In this position *you know* can be glossed as a question meaning essentially "do you understand?" or "do you agree?" If there is no comment from the listener to the effect that "no, I don't know," the speaker continues on with his or her turn. In Buscaglia's oral expository text, virtually all of the *you know*'s are in fronted position. Speaking to an audience of thousands in monologue, he has little opportunity to check audience comprehension where there might be some dispute over what is shared and what is not. The expression, then, serves two purposes for Buscaglia. It functions as a topic shifter by which he alerts his audience that a new topic is to be taken up in discourse, and it functions also as an expression of communality. At almost every point where Buscaglia introduces new information to his listening audience, he presents this new information as already known by the audience:

And you know there is nothing so contagious as **laughter**.

You know Saint Teresa of Avila had a wonderful philosophy.

You know for **years** and **years** and **years** I was told "Now Buscaglia, you must be serious. You must go you must **plant** your two feet **firmly** on the ground if you're ever going to get anywhere." Well, you know, with my feet firmly pa planted on the ground I couldn't get my **pants** on. Flying in the air I could get them on **anytime** in **any** position.

In the first statement, "And you know there is nothing so contagious as **laughter**," the audience is likely to know already Buscaglia's new proposition. In such an assertion he is reminding them of what they know, but may have forgotten or disregarded. The use of *you know*, then, has literal meaning, although such a usage would be an instance of an indirect speech act where reminding rather than asserting is the true act. In the following two examples *you know* has no literal meaning, although some members of Buscaglia's audience may have been familiar with the writings of Saint Teresa of Avila. The expression *you know*, however, is used in precisely the same way as in the first example. Use of *you know* indicates, as a paragraph indentation does in written speech, that a new topic will be taken up. It functions equally to focus attention on a special point made by the speaker: "Well, you know, with my feet firmly pa planted on the ground I couldn't get my **pants** on." More rhetorically, it presents new information as shared or given information. The effect of such presentation of new information is to create identification between the speaker and the audience. What the speaker knows the audience also knows, and through such an explicit sharing of knowledge the audience acquires not only new information but also a new bond or level of identification with the speaker.

Buscaglia's very sophisticated, though commonplace, use of *you know* appeals to a similar conception of knowledge in his audience. Buscaglia addresses his audience not as an informer or expositor presenting radically new ideas but as a speaker who is merely jogging its memory. In keeping with this identificatory usage, Buscaglia directly tells his audience at one point: "Everybody in this audience could conceivably develop a beautiful definition of what it means to be a lover. You **know** what it is." In the latter statement "you **know**" functions literally. Buscaglia stresses the verb *know* as a way of forcing recognition of this knowledge on the audience. The illusion of knowledge he affords his audience is more explicitly articulated by him, but as a strategy for communication of new information, it is characteristically used by oral speakers. To suggest that you know before I have even told you is, sociolinguistically, to grant you, the listener, equality with me, the speaker. With this illusion in place, the oral speaker can consistently introduce new information to a receptive audience confident of its own stature in what then becomes a collaborative activity.

In the written situation, Buscaglia cannot exploit a direct address such as *you know*, nor in the case of new topic marking does he need to, for he can indent his text spatially. To diminish the threat of new ideas to his audience and thus to facilitate their accommodation by his readers, Buscaglia employs other strategies which derive from the written situation. One strategy that I have already identified is to employ introductory qualifiers and then to embed strong opinions dramatically as new information in a sentence. The qualifiers such as *it seems to me, I'm certain, still*, which Buscaglia uses in his written exposition, supply a speaker ethos which is moderate rather than absolute. Another strategy comparable to the use of *you know* in oral exposition is the use of *we* as a form of involvement. Buscaglia uses *we* in his oral exposition, but very seldom. His preference is to address his audience directly as "you" and to accord his listening audience equal status with himself in the expression *you know*. Direct address to the reader, however, is entirely absent in the written exposition. There is nothing comparable to Fielding's address in *Tom Jones*: "We are now, reader, arrived at the last stage of our long journey." The collective *we*, however, is extensively used by Buscaglia in his written text. Where *I* and *you* function in contrast in the oral text, *I* and *we* are employed in the written exposition. Yet *we* does not function in precisely the same way as *you know*. Collective *we* marks information as shared, but it is also used by Buscaglia as a means of creating awareness of shared behaviour which in turn is evaluated negatively:

It is a common belief that there must be something wrong with contented people. *We* look at them as either fools, frivolous, or totally lacking in ordinary common sense. They are suspect. *Most of us* actually feel guilty when *we're* happy! *We're* convinced that *we* will either be punished for it or that gloom will not be too far behind. (my italics)

It is rare that *we* hear spontaneous, uproarious laughter. If *we* do, *we* are certain that the revelers must be ne'er-do-wells or drunk. *We* pay large amounts of money to get professional comics to make *us* laugh. *We* tumble over with laughter when they mimic *our* "sane" behaviours and in this way reveal *our* follies. *We* love clowns. . . . In a very real sense, *we* are all of *us* clowns—some more fearful and inhibited than others—but, nonetheless, potential clowns. (my italics)

In this usage Buscaglia not only identifies himself with the behaviour he wishes to analyse, but he also identifies that behaviour with his reader and so engages the reader in a form of indirect self-examination. Such a strategy is very different from the direct commands which appear in the oral text:

You know, don't expect **others** to make you happy. **You** create the joy and watch what happens. **You'll** be the **one** who is dancing through life and laughing through life.

The use of *we* in the written exposition does not negate the role of distanced critic which Buscaglia has assigned to the reader, but rather requires the reader to become a critic of his or her own behaviour in the process of examining human behaviour generally. The reader is simultaneously distanced from and involved in the text. The theoretical impersonality of written speech is not well illustrated by Buscaglia's strategic use of *we* in written exposition. As in all other genres, ideational meaning interacts with interpersonal meaning, simply because information is directed at real readers who must process it.

Concerning ideational meaning rather than interpersonal meaning, theorists analysing exposition have concentrated on concerns such as clarity, order, and organization. Graesser and Goodman refer specifically to the use of logical connectives and "pyramid development" in their definition of exposition. Clearly, information which is primarily new to a reader or listener must be presented and connected with care if communication is to be effected. However, Frank Smith has argued in the case of reading that, cognitively, more than decoding is involved for the reader. Reading requires that a reader participate in the creation of meaning in the text:

Reading is not primarily a visual process. Two kinds of information are involved in reading, one that comes from in front of the eyeball, from the printed page, that I call *visual information*, and one that derives from behind the eyeball, from the brain, that I call *nonvisual information*. Nonvisual information is what we already know about reading, about language, and about the world in general. (1973:6)

Smith's theory of reading can be extended to a theory of comprehension in general. His main point is that in communication, information explicitly supplied by a speaker interacts with world and contextual information possessed by a reader (or listener). Yet, in a genre such as exposition, an audience is expected to supply little if any information to effect meaning in the text. What Smith terms "visual information" and what might be termed "oral information" are the dominant sources of information. With regard particularly to written exposition, Olson (1977) and Kay (1977) have both argued that all meaning is "in" the text. Graesser and Goodman also observe that the "audience" in narration brings more inferential knowledge to narrative texts than it does to expository discourse. But in Smith's view such an analysis of exposition would constitute a rejection of his theory of reading since it would reduce the reader to a mere decoder of information already supplied. Smith argues that a reader cannot process information in any text unless sufficient nonvisual information is present:

The second major psycholinguistic contribution to reading is that there is a severe limit to the amount of information coming through the eye that the visual system can process. In other words, the trade-off between visual and nonvisual information is critical. The reader who relies primarily on visual information will simply overload his visual system; he will be unable to get as much information as he needs. He will read as if he were in the half-dark. (7)

Smith is saying that even in the case of a genre such as exposition, whose purpose is the communication of new information, reliance must be made on "nonvisual" information if a reader, or in an oral situation a listener, is to be informed in any legitimate sense. There is a quite marked limitation on the amount of new information which can be presented to a reader or listener in exposition. There is also a considerable value to be placed on redundancy, which facilitates processing of new information for both reader and listener. Ochs' feature analysis of planned discourse, in which she stipulates that planned discourse is less lexically repetitious and less repetitious of form and content, needs examination. Planned discourse, if expository, must exploit repetition to communicate new information.

Repetition and elaboration are strongly in evidence in both Buscaglia's oral and written expository texts. In the oral context of situation Buscaglia has an hour in which to explicate his findings and make his points; in the written situation he has the "space" of a book, somewhere between 200 and 300 pages, "in" which to do the same work. What is classically called "elaboration" or copiousness, however, is more obvious in the oral text. For example, at the beginning of his oral exposition Buscaglia notifies his listeners that he is about to commence the exposition proper:

And there is **so** much **material** to **cover** if you're going to be a lover. In fact there's **so** much material it reminds me of ah ah a mosquito in a **nudist** colony. There's so much tempting **stuff** to talk about.

The term "elaboration" rather than "repetition" is appropriately used for such stretches of talk. The second sentence expands upon the first in taking up the intensifier "**so**" and supplying a grammatical complement to it. Out of that complement Buscaglia delivers his punchline, which metaphorically compares the nude body seen from the perspective of a mosquito to subject matter or material seen from the perspective of the speaker. The purpose of this elaboration is to evaluate the topic positively and thus in another way motivate the audience to listen.

Elaboration is also the principal technique Buscaglia employs to present his points:

Humour is a **wonderful** antidote to cruelty and to rejection and to distrust and to condescension. You know, the comedian, Victor Borge, says that the closest distance between two people is a good **laugh**. I **love** that. And you know **Mama** taught that to us early. She laughed **all** the time. She used to drive Papa **crazy**. He' d come home with all kinds of **despairing** things and she'd get the **giggles**.

The paragraph above is characteristic of the majority in Buscaglia's oral text. It begins with a definition in the first sentence employing a state present which conveys a meaning of universal truth to the utterance. Within the sentence is a series of prepositional phrases connected by *and*. Buscaglia retains the formal parallelism not only to preserve the rhythm of his speech but also to allow full accent to be placed on each of the prepositional objects. They are given full semantic weight as they would not be if they were items in a series. Buscaglia then expands upon his point that humour overcomes the distance between people by citing an authority who presents the same idea as a paradox: "the closest distance between two people is a good **laugh**." The definition is supplied twice in two forms, one humourously paradoxical. A personal evaluation follows upon the evaluation supplied by the paradox. Finally, Buscaglia engages in a narrative which supplies specificity to the generalization.

This pattern or formula is employed again and again by Buscaglia in his oral exposition. Definition is followed by redefinition, which is then followed by a narrative which explicates the main concept or point. Like an oral bard, Buscaglia has at his disposal a compositional principle which allows him to explicate his findings and ideas in sequence. Alton Becker (1966) has identified a similar pattern in the expository paragraph. Viewing the expository paragraph from a tagmemic perspective, Becker analyses it in terms of functional slots which permit entry by "substitutable forms." Of the two major patterns Becker identifies, the first "has three functional slots, which can be labelled **T** (topic), **R** (restriction), and **I** (illustration)" (34). The three slots can be filled by a number of variant forms to allow a range of interactions:

For instance, the **T** slot can be filled by a simple proposition, or a proposition implying a contrast, comparison, partition, etc. The **R** slot is frequently a restatement of **T** at a lower level of generality, a definition of **T** or a term in **T**, a metaphoric restatement of **T**, etc. The **I** slot can be filled by one or more examples (often in a narrative or descriptive pattern), an extended analogy, a series of specific comparisons, etc. (35)

The other major pattern identified by Becker is that with two slots, the first of which is a **P** (problem) slot and the second of which is a **S** (solution) slot. The **P** slot, as implied, states a problem or effect which requires explanation, while the **S** slot supplies an analysis of a solution or cause. This second pattern is not employed by Buscaglia in his oral exposition.

From Becker's analysis of the first of the two major expository paragraphs, we can see the degree to which elaboration is built into this paragraph type. Redefinition or restatement in the second functional slot allows the reader or listener a second exposure to the main point or proposition. This is clearly crucial for a reader or listener trying to understand a new idea or concept. Exemplification in the **I** slot further elaborates the main proposition of the paragraph rendering it concrete rather than abstract.

Becker's tagmemic analysis of the expository paragraph is important in understanding how Buscaglia uses this pattern as a formula in oral discourse. Like the oral formulae employed by Anglo-Saxon bards, a given slot can be filled by a number of readily-accessible fillers. For example, the Old English "X-dagum" formula first identified by Magoun (1980) permits a range of possible fillers in the X slot before "dagum": "gear," "ear," "eald," or "fyrn." Together with "dagum," the four fillers compose a system available to the bard in oral composition. It is difficult for speakers in the modern period, unaccustomed to oral composition, to understand how speakers in other periods could speak for two or three hours successively. Such extended speaking was possible because bards employed oral formulae. Buscaglia uses written notes, but by and large they merely contain the exact quotations he draws on to support his points. By using the formulas above, however, Buscaglia simply composes orally until all the points he wishes to make are exhausted. There is, consequently, a high degree of formal repetition in Buscaglia's text. In three successive paragraphs copula structures supporting definition are used. In each case redefinition follows and then a narrative. Buscaglia then varies the pattern by using the **T** slot to assert a proposition, sometimes expressed in his own words and in other cases expressed through the words of an authority (e.g., Abraham Lincoln). But the overall pattern remains intact: definition/assertion, redefinition/restatement, narrative.

Buscaglia's oral exposition is coherent in a fundamentally different way from his written exposition. The written text exploits an overall dialectic structure of problem and solution; the oral text written down seems to be only a collection of points. What is termed "development" seems absent. This is so because in the act of oral composition Buscaglia is stringing his points together by association. As in oral narration, Buscaglia uses a rhapsodic technique. He knows where he wants to begin and he knows where and how he wants to end as well as the specific points he wishes to make, but apart from that he lets the text structure itself. He first defines humour as an antidote, which he then illustrates through a narrative about his mother, who responded to her husband's despair with laughter. His mother had the ability to see what was funny in what everyone else perceived to be tragic and so transform, like an antidote, an unhealthy state into a healthy state. Buscaglia's next point is that humour is contagious, and after that that each one of us is in some way quite ridiculous. These points all pertain to humour, but they do not develop one from the other in strict logical sequence. A good written exposition would stick closely to Buscaglia's statement that humour is an antidote "to cruelty and to rejection and to distrust and to condescension" and so take up each sub-topic and illustrate it. The idea of humour's antidotal qualities would control the entire text. However, in the oral exposition, the statement that humour is contagious arises associationally from Buscaglia's account of how his mother " 'd get the **giggles**." This brings to mind that everyone in the family would then get the giggles. The narrative in the **I** slot in the first expository paragraph supplies the topic for the **T** slot in the next expository paragraph.

Lexical cohesion in the oral exposition is often a key to how this associative principle works in the oral text. In the narrative illustration of the second expository paragraph Buscaglia recounts that "We were on the floor wondering what Mama was laughing at. **She** didn't know. It was just the **whole** thing was just funny." This proposition in the narrative that "the **whole** thing was just funny" takes Buscaglia to his next proposition which is "that **life** is a **great big wondrous** *joke* and you're at the **centre** of it. **You're** the **funniest** thing of all." Lexical cohesion is evident in the obvious repetition of the "funny" and in the semantic overlap of "funny" with "joke." The lexeme *funny* calls to mind for Buscaglia the idea of a joke, while "the **whole** thing" is subsequently specified as "**life**," both of which are stressed as important new information. Repetition of *funny* in the superlative "**funniest**" completes the process by which what the tagmemists would call a sememe or kernel idea is transferred from the narrative illustration to topic slot of the succeeding expository paragraph. This transfer is facilitated by Buscaglia's continued use of copula structures: "the **whole** thing was just funny," "**life** is a **great big wondrous** *joke*," "you're at the **centre** of it," "**You're** the **funniest** thing of all." Not only is there repetition of an equative structure (x=y), but there is also repetition of the same syntactic structure in the last two clauses (you = x) supplying semantic as well as formal repetition in the guise of copiousness or elaboration.

Coherence differs greatly in Buscaglia's written definition, but repetition is still in dominant use, although there is little semantic repetition as elaboration. The text as a whole is structured dialectically into two sections, the first stating and explicating a problem and the second stating and explicating a solution. Structured explicitly as an analysis, the text uses both expository paragraph types identified by Becker, but most especially the second **PS** type which, like the structure of the discourse as a whole, states a problem to which it then offers a solution. This pattern is used also by Martin Starret in his written process description of cattle driving and his written narrative about Gunninute the Outlaw, and it is clearly a preferred pattern in written discourse.

The first of the body paragraphs in the written exposition after that introducing topic is of the **PS** type, and within it we see the outline in minuscule of the discourse as a whole, or, to use a term from narrative discourse, its "abstract":

I'm certain that we have all been reminded many times that life is not to be taken casually, that "it's damn serious business!" To a certain degree, this may be true. But, that seems to me to be all the more reason to maintain and develop a keen sense of humour. In fact, I know that I have been saved, again and again, by my ability to see the humorous side of a situation, especially to laugh at myself and my imperfections. I know it takes courage, and a degree of borderline insanity, to smile and laugh in a world where, since the beginning of recorded history, we have continued to kill, rape, desert and hurt each other. We've been, until now, unable to find reason for all of this. Perhaps the giving up of reason and the acceptance of our humanness as the ultimate joke may offer us another alternative.

The problem stated in this paragraph is that life is a serious matter and thus that it requires serious response and participation. Buscaglia presents this problem as that supplied by an unstated "they" (he uses a deagentized passive for this purpose) to whom he can counterrespond. The problem, then, is a generally assumed one, having no specific source, but out there and powerful nonetheless. Rhetorically, Buscaglia agrees in part, but then he goes on to challenge not the initial proposition but its corollary stating his own better suggestion: "But, that seems to me to be all the more reason to maintain and develop a keen sense of humor." The real problem is not that life is a serious business but that we take life seriously.

Having identified the real problem in the first part of the paragraph, Buscaglia explores a solution in the second half. He begins inductively by citing his own experiences, presenting them as factual evidence: "In fact, I know that I have been saved, again and again, by my ability to see the humorous side of a situation, especially to laugh at myself and my imperfections." In the oral exposition this evidence is supplied in a narrative about Buscaglia's mother, but in the written exposition narrative is largely avoided and replaced by personal testimony or by appeal to authority. Buscaglia next asserts that laughter itself requires courage and nonconformity: "I know it takes courage, and a degree of borderline insanity, to smile and laugh in a world where, since the beginning of recorded history, we have continued to kill, rape, desert and hurt each other." He then evaluates this human situation and again poses another problem: "We've been, until now, unable to find reason for all of this." Finally, he states his solution: "Perhaps the giving up of reason and the acceptance of our humanness as the ultimate joke may offer us another alternative."

What first needs to be noted about this paragraph is the degree to which inductive development is employed. Contrary to the conclusion from Graesser and Goodman's feature analysis of exposition, it appears that written exposition does not necessarily exploit "pyramid development." Pyramid development is much more in evidence, indeed almost exclusively in evidence, in the oral text with its reliance on **TRI** expository paragraphs. In both problem and solution sections of his first expository paragraph Buscaglia leads into first a statement of the "real" problem and second a statement of a solution, which is expressed in the last sentence of the paragraph. Inductive development has the advantage of not seeming to be repetitive.

In the first sentence of the paragraph Buscaglia presents a generalization to his reader which is commonly expressed and therefore clearly old information: "we have all been reminded many times that life is not be taken casually." He even repeats this old information as elaboration: "that it's damn serious business." Starting with old information, which he knows he shares with his reader, he then proceeds to modify that information and present it as new in his own formulation of the problem. Such a strategy is very different from that used in the oral text, where new information is presented as definition or proposition and is then restated and illustrated. In the written text Buscaglia more frequently works from shared old information to unshared new information exploiting induction rather than deduction as a means of ideational development. Thus, in his written exposition Buscaglia has no need of a topic-introducing device such as *you know* because he employs a strategy in the development of his ideas whereby old information genuinely does precede new (which he nonetheless marks as shared through use of *we*). The preference oral exposition has for a deductive pattern of development has consequences not only for imbalance in the interpersonal relations of the speaker and listener, which must be modified, but also for the presence of semantic, lexical and formal repetition in the text. Conversely, written exposition can seemingly avoid repetitiousness of content and structure by exploiting inductive ideational development.

However, repetition does function in Buscaglia's written exposition. The very fact that he provides an abstract in his first expository paragraph is an indication that he intends to rely on repetition. As in narration, the reader is given a brief overview of what the text is about. With this outline in place as both an abstract and orientation for the reader, Buscaglia can expand on both the problem as he has defined it and the solution as he has defined it.The remaining text does precisely this.

Concentrating on the problem as defined in the text, Buscaglia exploits again a contrapuntal structure in the following paragraphs. In three of these paragraphs he cites authorities, all of whom state that tragedy must be met with laughter rather than despair. He even cites the constitution of the United States with its articulation of "the pursuit of happiness" as a constitutional right. This wealth of authority is then countered by factual evidence: "Still, in our time, there is pitifully little joy demonstrated." Over four paragraphs Buscaglia employs the same formal inductive pattern he uses at the commencement of his first expository paragraph, except that he reverses the ordering of the content. In the first expository paragraph an unstated "they" state that life is "a damn serious business" which should be taken seriously, to which Buscaglia counters, "*But* [my italics], that seems to me all the more reason to maintain and develop a keen sense of humor." In the next block of text, an extensively cited "they" reiterate Buscaglia, to which he counters, "*Still* [my italics], in our time, there is pitifully little joy demonstrated. There seems to be something not quite right about those who are happy." Although there is little formal syntactic repetition, there is formal structural repetition in the use of a contrapuntal pattern which leads the reader into a point or idea, and there is extensive semantic repetition. The gist of the chapter is stated in the first expository paragraph; the reader is reintroduced to the same points again and again with variation, as above, only in their explicit ordering.

Once Buscaglia has restated the proposition that we take life too seriously via a second presentation of this proposition as "new" information, he then amasses evidence to support this proposition in a series of seven paragraphs, two of which supply personal narratives. Whole paragraphs, then, serve the function of illustration, just as whole paragraphs can serve the function of statement of problem and solution. Buscaglia combines an inductive development with a deductive development by using extensive chunks of his text to illustrate the problem once it is introduced.

In the remaining text, Buscaglia offers his solution, but in the form of a dialectic of problem/solution. If, rather than taking life too seriously, we must then "pursue happiness," the question or problem becomes how to do so. Again inductively Buscaglia takes a paragraph to "arrive" at this restatement of the problem and to suggest a solution. In the next paragraph problem and solution are reiterated, except that their ordering is reversed, recalling the same strategy of repetition Buscaglia uses in his development of the initial problem that we take life too seriously. He next illustrates his solution with personal testimony and then reiterates the problem and solution in the original order stated. Finally, he reiterates the solution restating the proposition which occurs originally in the first paragraph:

Perhaps the giving up of reason and the acceptance of our humanness as the ultimate joke may offer us another alternative. (1st expository paragraph)

We are far too rational in our relationships, far too ordered, organized and predictable. We need to find a place, just this side of madness and irrationality, where we can, from time to time, leave the mundane and move into spontaneity and serendipity, a level that includes a greater sense of freedom and risk—an active environment full of surprises, which encourages a sense of wonder.

To the extent that this written exposition is planned, Buscaglia has built a high degree of repetition into his text. Where the written exposition differs from the oral is not in the degree of repetition, but in the kind. Semantic repetition or elaboration is seldom sequential, as it is in the oral text. Buscaglia frequently varies the ordering of restated propositions while using an inductive means of presentation which affords to one restated proposition the status of being new. Thus, there is little sense in the written text that ideas are being repeated. Only at the very end of the written text is there a degree of sequential repetition in which Buscaglia develops the idea that joy once found has a continuing, self-perpetuating, salutary effect.

Formal repetition is also less noticeable in the written exposition.

Further, there is less lexical repetition because words are not used associationally to compose the text in sequence. Lastly, there is some reliance on deductive as well as inductive development in the written text rather than a virtually exclusive reliance on deductive paragraph structures only. In the written exposition, Buscaglia tends to repeat in each paragraph a problem/solution pattern, but some paragraphs are devoted solely to setting up the statement of problem or illustrating a solution. Thus, there is a greater degree of functional specialization of paragraphs in the discourse as a whole, which itself is structured dialectically into problem and solution slots. Conversely, the oral exposition tends to replicate the **TRI** pattern in each paragraph, lending to the oral discourse a property of strong formal repetitiveness. Both texts, however, heavily rely on repetition for the benefit of the speaker/writer and for the listener/reader. Semantic repetition is necessary, as Smith argues, for the listener/reader in each discourse respectively, while formal repetition facilitates composition and planning for the speaker/writer. Where the texts differ along media lines is in the preference each has for different patterns and types of repetition which create coherence and cohesion.

CONCLUSION

Exposition and written speech are frequently associated, and often identified with each other. Such an association is understandable in a culture which stores its knowledge in books rather than in epic poetry. However, the two varieties need to be clearly differentiated, the one as a genre and the other as a medium. Co-identification of these two different types of variety has caused many linguists to ascribe the features of exposition to written speech itself, thus characterizing written speech as "intellectual" or "explicit" in nature. Explicitness is at best an ideal property of exposition in keeping with what Grice would call the Maxim of Quantity in his Co-operative Principle of conversation. Written speech fosters analysis to the extent that it fosters problem/solution discourse structures as well as a phenomenal view of events, but it is exposition as a genre which is concerned with what Werlich calls "the composition and decomposition of concepts." An oral philosopher such as Socrates, who thought of writing as dangerous to the mind, would not understand a characterization of written speech as "intellectual" and oral speech as "emotional."

Just as written speech should not be identified with exposition, it should also not be identified with planned speech. Planning does not affect the characteristic structures of oral or written speech in exposition. The additive syntax of oral speech remains as a feature of Buscaglia's oral exposition, while his written exposition favours more complex and conjoined structures as well as an abstract Latinate vocabulary. The distinctive features of oral and written speech need to be explained by another phenomenon other than planning time.

In distinguishing written speech from exposition, we must define exposition in terms of its principal purpose. Exposition as a genre has as its special purpose to convey new information. In every utterance, speakers must juggle information about topic and comment with information about what is shared and unshared between speaker and audience. Each genre achieves its own balance of these elements, but exposition especially concentrates its attention on new information and so places severe constraints on any writer/speaker. In expository discourse the listener or reader is in a position to bring very little "nonvisual information" to bear; therefore, a high degree of repetition must be built into expository discourse to permit comprehension to occur for the listener/reader.

Rhetorical considerations must be made on the part of the speaker if a listener/reader is to be open to the new information in the text. Buscaglia motivates his listeners emotionally to identify with the definition of a lover derived from his findings. Rhetorically, he also presents new information as old for his listeners by means of the frequent use of the address *you know*, which creates not only identification between speaker and listener but also an illusion of equality between them. In his written exposition Buscaglia simultaneously establishes the reader in the role of critic and participant in the subject matter with Buscaglia himself. Collective *we* in the written text is used when Buscaglia presents explicitly shared information, and when he wishes to involve the reader in a deeper, less detached consideration of human relations. *We*, then, is used whenever Buscaglia wishes to discuss negative new information that the reader might reject because of identification.

Apart from modes of address, repetition is the chief means by which an expositor can create access to new information for a listener or reader. Oral and written expository texts differ in their use of formal repetition. Oral expository texts prefer deductive structures which in themselves build repetition into their overall structure. Buscaglia uses the deductive **TRI** expository paragraph formulaicly over and over until he exhausts his material on the function of humour in the lover. Two of the function slots, the second or **R** (restriction) slot and the third or **I** (illustration) slot, in the **TRI** expository paragraph are functionally allocated to semantic repetition of the definition or proposition in the **T** (topic) slot. The second limits and restates the topic, while the third reiterates through illustration. Topic shifts are marked by use of *you know, well,* or other topic markers, while cohesion is supplied by topic transference from the **I** slot of one paragraph to the **T** slot of the next. Use of narrative in the **I** slot also provides a facile means of both interesting an audience and maintaining the formulaic use of the **TRI** paragraph as a whole.

Formal repetition in Buscaglia's written exposition is at the same time simpler and more complex than in the oral text. Formal repetition is simpler in the written exposition because Buscaglia superimposes a dual structure on his discourse as a whole, while also employing a dual structure in many of his paragraphs. The dualistic problem/solution structure greatly facilitates the sorting of material since it must fit one slot or the other. However, the degree to which there is specialization of paragraphs in the text as a whole is an indication of the greater complexity of the written exposition. Because the exposition as a discourse is divided into problem and solution slots repeating the formal pattern in the first expository paragraph, within the broad groupings of problem slot or solution slot there can be some degree of specialization as well as further formal repetition. There is thus a block of three paragraphs in the problem section of the written text entirely allocated to the citing of authorities whose ideals Buscaglia will contrast with facts. Another block of seven paragraphs is used to illustrate the restated problem once Buscaglia has reintroduced it a second time in the text (as new information since he employs an inductive development). Generally, where there is specialization, there is repetition. The space of the book or chapter allows Buscaglia to luxuriate in detail. Where statement of topic, restatement, and illustration are confined in one paragraph in the oral text, the written text may use one or more paragraphs for each of these functions. The controlling problem and solution slots are highly expandable into subfunction slots, if not infinitely expandable.

As in Buscaglia's oral exposition, semantic repetition derives from formal repetition. Both the oral and written exposition employ abstracts, but the written abstract, more like a true narrative abstract, provides an outline of the main ideas in the text. The problem and solution slots of the remaining text are therefore reiterative. With regard to the written expository text as a whole, there is what Graesser and Goodman call "pyramid development," since the more explicit abstract serves as a semantic base for the remaining text.

Associational cohesion is not possible in such a text because all propositions must relate back to those initially stated in the first expository paragraph.

The view that planned discourse is not formally and semantically repetitive is clearly incorrect. Repetition in an expository text signifies planning. In Buscaglia's oral exposition the definitions or propositions he asserts in the T slot are elaborated upon by quotations from authorities and narratives which he has prepared well in advance of his lecture. Equally, in the written text Buscaglia reiterates most of his propositions by citing whole sets of authorities. Narratives, personal testimony, and quotations are all used to illustrate the problem or solution defined or redefined. Planning, therefore, explains the presence of a high degree of repetition in either expository text.

Differentiation in pattern type in each discourse can be explained by constraints on the speaker or writer in the two situations. Just as oral speech relies primarily on an additive syntax, so for a monologic speaker in the construction of text, it is easier to string propositions together, connecting them associationally, than it would be to provide a conceptual abstract and refer back to the propositions made in it. Moreover, continued use of and reliance on a pattern of statement, restatement, and illustration in sequence allows the speaker to concentrate on content. Presentation of information in sequence also facilitates processing for a listener, who would have great difficulty keeping in mind an abstract to which other material is then related. Developing one proposition at a time and relating it associationally to another allows the listener to take new information in with efficiency, which the presentation of a gestalt would not.

In contrast, an abstract in written exposition not only facilitates planning for the writer, who embeds an outline into his or her text, but also serves as an aid to a reader, who, with the conceptual plot in mind, can better follow elaboration upon it. The reader, of course, can take information in at a much slower rate than a listener, who must follow speech at its normal rate of output. Reading is achieved in what are termed "saccades" or jerks of the eye over text. If information is not successfully processed in a saccade, the reader will regress and reread text until processing is achieved. Presentation of an abstract for a reader is useful, since he or she is then in possession of a gestalt to which to refer conceptually in the continued processing of the text. Even the construct of a problem/solution format in the text provides the reader with a useful gestalt which can facilitate processing.

Despite content (new information) in common, oral and written varieties of exposition differ in composition and structure. While the strategy of repetition is exploited in the composition of both sub-varieties, written exposition achieves repetition through contrapuntal organization of ideas, whereas oral exposition does so formulaicly. The oblique use of repetition in written exposition creates an illusion of explicit representation, but both written and oral exposition are explicit or as fully explicit as required to introduce and predispose readers and listeners alike to new information.

5

Oral and Written Instruction

Werlich (1976) has defined instruction as a genre which focuses on the composition of future behaviour. Longacre (1968) does not designate instruction as a separate genre or text type in his typology, but he does distinguish two forms of procedural discourse, "how-to-do-it" and "how-it-was-done," on the basis of [+/- projection], that is, on a distinction between past and future orientation. "How-to-do-it" or instruction is thus also designated as being future oriented by Longacre. A conception of instruction as focusing on the composition of future behaviour is equally consistent with a speech-act view of instruction as having a direction of fit which is world to word. Like the speech-act direction in argument, instruction requires that the world replicate the word.

Instruction is likewise comparable to the speech-act verb group of "directives." As in such clauses, a high degree of agent and patient interaction is evident since change in a patient's behaviour or state of knowledge is the primary purpose of instruction. However, the greater the degree of predictive power ("do x, and y will occur"), the greater the degree of agency for a given instructor. Thus the imperative mood and the "future" tense serve to mark the genre in the predicate.

Longacre's designation of instruction as a form of procedural discourse is an important insight into the nature of this genre. The attention to "how" or method in instruction, combined with an orientation to process and consideration of future time, marks the genre as being particularly sensitive to both analysis and sequence, which in effect are equated. The sequence in which directives are given is crucial. Just as Labov defines a minimal narrative "as a sequence of two clauses which are *temporally ordered*" where a change in order "result[s] in a change in the temporal sequence of the original semantic interpretation" (1972b:360), so we must also define a minimal instruction as a sequence of two clauses which are temporally ordered. A specific temporal order of directives constitutes the "how" or methodology of a given instruction. Clarity of sequence is fundamental to instruction, and the unstated rule would be that the simpler the sequence, the better the instruction.

As discussed in the last chapter, instruction is also distinguished from exposition in its patient orientation. New information is transmitted to a hearer or reader in both exposition and instruction, but in instruction constraint is placed on the patient to reduplicate or "know" what has been transmitted. Mnemonics, then, is of major importance to instruction, and as such it explains the concern with process and sequence.

POPULAR INSTRUCTION:
HOW TO MAKE YOGURT AND YOGURT CHEESE

The two parallel texts under discussion in this chapter concern the making of yogurt and yogurt cheese. The oral text is taken from a television cooking program *The Frugal Gourmet*, while the written text is taken from a complementary cookbook with the same title. The "Frugal Gourmet," Jeff Smith, is a cooking expert whose program on the PBS television network was so successful that a text of his recipes was prepared to be sold independently in bookstores. The written text can be read independently as other cookbooks are, or it can function as a complement to the half-hour television programs themselves.

Jeff Smith, like many teachers, exploits not only the media of oral and written speech but also that of television. As a medium, television is well adapted to orality, although much of the oral speech on television is scripted. Still, television likes talk, and so there are any number of talk and interview shows thriving within it. Many news programs now incorporate live interviews into their format. However, to use Marshall McLuhan's terms, television is a cool medium, while instruction is a hot medium. McLuhan (1964) defined media in terms of their promotion or non-promotion of involvement for a listener or reader in the creation of information: television is a cool medium in that it allows the listener to participate in the creation of meaning or the construction of information, while instruction is hot because only one participant supplies all the information.

On the basis of McLuhan's analysis, television and instruction should not mix well, and yet there is a great deal of oral instruction on television, the abundance of cooking shows being an outstanding illustration. In fact, to the extent that television is a cool medium promoting informational participation, hot instruction is often well modified and cooled down; consequently, instructional programs such as Julia Child's or Jeff Smith's are very successful indeed. The strong other- or patient-orientation of instruction is well suited to a cool medium like television, which itself promotes involvement by the watcher/listener. In particular, television does not supply good visual information as, for example, film does; thus, information is almost exclusively supplied by the human voice. The viewer, then, is in the odd position of sitting at home (usually) watching a human voice. Television focuses attention on the voice in a way that normal conversation between two parties or an oral lecture does not. It involves the watcher/listener in the voice in very much the way oral bardic verse involves the listener, leaving it open to the same criticisms Plato levelled at the poets, that is, that it is hypnotic in its effect.[1] It helps, then, as is the case with both Child and Smith, to have an unusual voice or marked vocal mannerisms which promote attention to the voice itself.

Taken independently, both texts transmit almost entirely new information to their respective audiences. The problem for each is to be sufficiently clear and mnemonic so that the listener or reader is able first to grasp the method and second to replicate it. The particular constraint of this genre is the second criterion; the listener/reader must be able to duplicate the method or instruction has not taken place. Thus, the patient must be able to remember the process depicted and the individual steps within it. The written text, in particular, can function both as an instruction and as an aid to memory. The recipe not only communicates a list of ingredients and a particular methodology but also preserves that list and method graphically on a highly transportable and generally durable medium, paper. Oral instruction must develop other purely linguistic strategies to achieve the same level of mnemonic effect. In this genre, as Plato himself would argue, memory and knowledge are synonymous.

Of all the sets of parallel texts examined in this study, none are so markedly contrastive as the set comprising oral and written instruction. The oral text is almost four times the length of the written, and it is also one of the longest texts collected.[2] Such length is remarkable because Smith has only a half-hour in which to teach seven recipes, and as usual in his cooking programs, he feels pressed for time. The written text, in comparison, is one of the shortest texts collected. Of course, it has been argued by Chafe (1982) and others that all oral texts should be long, while written texts should be short because syntactic integration is a feature of written texts. However, syntactic integration is not a factor in the shortness of the written instruction. The written text, like the oral, relies almost entirely on simple sentence structures. Moreover, the written text does not express the same information more briefly than the oral text; it relies heavily on the reader and on the context of situation which it creates to supply information. The written instruction is an example of a minimalist text, elliptical in the analysis of Brown and Yule (1983:201–4). Where the oral text is long owing to the speaker's need to make information memorable in language, the written text is short because it employs highly elliptical structures and because much of the burden of memory has been taken from the written medium by its preservation in another medium, paper.

In general, the features characteristic of oral and written speech predominate in each parallel text. The additive syntax of oral speech is revealed by the dominance of simple sentences as well as by a high number of co-ordinate clauses in the oral text. The written text, however, is highly constrained by genre, since there is a much higher percentage (69%) of simple sentences in the written text than is common is most written discourse. This percentage is explained by the fact that the written text is largely composed of a mnemonic list. Nonetheless, the syntax of the written text is largely attributive, having the usual dominance in adjectival structures such as participial phrases and attributive adjectives, with a slight dominance in relative clauses (relative clauses are present in 13 per cent of written sentences and 10 per cent of oral sentences). Still, relative clauses feature little in these instructional texts in comparison to the preceding expository parallel texts (see Chapter 4).

The oral text evidences a much higher use of noun clauses and infinitive phrases than does the written text, while, typically, adverb clauses are essentially equivalent in number in both texts. The presence of a greater number of noun clauses is explained by the fact that thought and opinion are much more extensively reported in the oral text, which is not constructed largely as a list. The dominance of infinitive phrases in the oral text indicates, however, that purpose is being explicitly marked in the text. The relative absence of infinitives in the written text indicates the implicit character of this written discourse, which more generally relies on visual gesture and shared frames of reference than does the oral, which is far more explicit (see Table 7).

The implicitness in the written text, in contrast to explicitness in the oral, corresponds not only to differences in length but also to differences in interpersonal relations. The media of oral and written

TABLE 7
Syntactic Profile/How to Make Yogurt

Sentences	Oral 325 (3784wds)	Written 73 (804wds)
Simple	191 (59%)	50 (69%)
Compound	35 (11%)	01 (01%)
Complex	55 (17%)	19 (26%)
Compound/complex	30 (09%)	00 (00%)
Embedded	15 (04%)	03 (04%)
Relative clauses	33	10
Adverbial clauses	35	09
Noun clauses	27	02
Co-ordinate clauses	113	03
Conjoining phrases	51	29
Participle phrases	01	06
Gerund	14	05
Infinitives	83	06
Passives	14	04
Exist. *There*/clefts	05	00
Attributive adjs.	243	111
(participles)	11	08
Nouns in apposition	12	01

speech significantly alter interpersonal relations in this genre and thus mnemonic constraints and length. However, the authoritarian interpersonal relations characteristic of this genre are most evident in the written text. The imperative which we see even in the title of the written text, "Yogurt and Cheese: Make Your Own," governs the interpersonal relations between the writer and the reader. The lexeme *recipe* derives from the appropriately imperative form of the Latin "recipere" and was originally a written command given by Roman physicians to their patients in the form of a prescription. The literal translation of the Latin "recipe" would be "receive!"

Conventionally, recipe books comprise three major slots: a title slot, an ingredient slot, and an instruction slot which tells the reader what to do with the ingredients he or she has collected. With the exception of the title or topic, the text is made up almost entirely of indirect and direct commands, the first set telling the reader what ingredients to get and the second what to do with what has been collected. In cookbooks such as Smith's *The Frugal Gourmet*, this highly authoritarian relationship is modified only by the inclusion of an orientation.

In contrast, Smith greatly modifies the imbalance of power between himself and his listeners in his oral instruction, although he fully acknowledges the fact of his very extended turn in the conversation:

Let me check the eggs. I think they're **done**. For **sure**. I bet I've overcooked them because we're busy talking. And you say oo with **me** busy talking. Yes, I know. I'm doing all the talking.

In the oral situation Smith promotes the involving illusion that "we're busy talking," only to acknowledge the truth determined by the monologic nature of the genre that "Yes, I know. I'm doing all the talking." Smith's success as a teacher is in large part the result of the illusion of intimacy and sharing he creates for his audience because such an illusion creates emotional and intellectual involvement in the information he is transmitting.

Both texts commence by introducing a topic and providing an orientation, thus preparing their respective audiences for specific instruction and anticipating lack of knowledge. However, topic introduction and orientation are treated very differently in the two texts. To introduce his topic, Smith uses a chapter title in his written text, while he uses a commissive speech act in his oral instruction. In the oral text Smith can first directly address his audience and then indirectly indicate his topic via a conventionalized commissive speech act or promise. "Hi and welcome to my **cheese** factory. Today, I'm gonna make **cheese** for you outa **yogurt**." In this commissive speech act, which in variant forms is conventionally used to open many cooking programs, topic is announced as a goal. Smith also grammatically marks himself as agent and the audience as patient. "**Cheese**" here is grammatically the goal, and thus, logically, we also have a future periphrastic form "gonna" combined with an infinitive of purpose. The enterprise Smith envisions is highly directive in nature and with all other features marks the text as instructional. "**Cheese**" is also stressed as new information in the sentence, as is "**yogurt**." Conventionally, this new information is understood as a new topic in the discourse since it is also the new goal undertaken on behalf of the audience by Smith. What the program is about in general terms is "making"; on the specific occasion "Today," what the program is about is making "**cheese**."

In the written text a title is employed: "Yogurt and Cheese: Make Your Own." If we read this title as a sentence, what Smith does is to topicalize "Yogurt and Cheese" by fronting it. He then physically separates off the rest of the sentence with a dash and adds the imperative "Make Your Own." Use of a directive in the title marks the written text as instructional. A new topic is juxtaposed with a marker of genre to indicate specific purpose within a larger one.

The syntactic differences that we see in the two conventionalized means of introducing the topic exist throughout the remainder of the two texts. The written text consistently exploits the imperative mood, while the oral text consistently exploits the future periphrastic form *is going to* in conjunction with the infinitive of purpose. The 69 per cent of simple sentences in the written text is largely explained by the dominant use of the imperative in its instructional body, while the much larger number of infinitives in the oral text (83 to 6 in the written) is explained by the predominant use of the periphrastic future as well as by the grammatical conception of making cheese as a goal.

However, as stated, Smith does provide an orientation in his written text to enable the reader to follow better the instructions he later gives in the text. This orientation provides a means not only of modifying the authoritarian personal relations in the main body of the text, but also of supplying sufficient background information about yogurt so that the nature of the process of making it is entirely clear. Like all speakers, Smith has made an assumption about the general state of his reader's knowledge. Assuming the reader knows nothing about yogurt, Smith provides conceptual orientation before launching into the specifics of instruction, as a good teacher does. Recipe books, unlike cookbooks, are not written with wholly ignorant readers in mind; they are read and used by cooks who already know something about cooking. In recipe books, for example, if a reader does not already know how to "fold" eggs in, or to "sauté" onions, he or she has no recourse but to buy a cookbook or go to a cooking class.

In both instructional texts, Smith supplies background about the origins of yogurt and in turn information about where the reader can go to purchase a yogurt starter. These two background texts are structurally very different and indicate different processing constraints on Smith as he conveys new information to his students in each medium:

In the old days when they began ah taking **care** of **herds** of **goat** and **cattle** and they would milk these creatures you see. When they'd leave the milk set about **natural** yeasts in the air, bacteria in the air in the desert, would land in the milk and cause it to to ah **ferment** as ah **yogurt** . . . (Oral instruction)

Yogurt is probably the oldest cheese that we know. Originally *it* was discovered by nomads in the desert when natural yeasts that were present in the air landed in their milk products and preserved them. *The yeasts or yogurts were saved and used to thicken and preserve more batches of milk. Milk* was also stored in bags made of the stomach of an animal, thus providing a natural rennet that would turn the milk to a curd.(my italics) (Written instruction)

In his oral instruction, Jeff Smith provides background information by means of a pseudo-narrative, while in his written instruction, Smith's discourse is topically focused with the goal yogurt or a referring expression as grammatical subject of each sentence. In the oral pseudo-narrative, Smith begins with a time frame and then marks agency, "they," cataphorically referring to "desert peoples," in a series of transitive structures: "began ah taking **care** of **herds** of **goats** and **cattle**," "milk these creatures," "leave the milk." Through transition from a subordinate clause to a main clause, "bacteria" then becomes the new topic of the narrative, but it is equally agentive: "would land," "and cause it to to ah **ferment**." The fact of taking care of goats and cattle results in their being milked, which further results in the exposed milk attracting bacteria and the subsequent fermentation of the milk. The actions of human agents have inadvertently resulted in the discovery of yogurt, and so the oral orientation is presented as a story about these agents and their actions. Primary new information in this orientation is supplied by transitive verbs in the predicate.

In his written orientation Smith uses his first sentence to introduce the topic yogurt. He does not begin with a narrative temporal reference, but with a topically focused definition: "Yogurt is probably the oldest cheese that we know." The reader of his written text has already been introduced to the topic of yogurt by a title in the text, "Yogurt and Cheese—Make Your Own." Rather than discussing the actions of agents in a situated time period, Smith retains yogurt as an abstracted topic and through a copula verb structure evaluates this topic as one of interest for the reader. The copula structure allows Smith to topicalize yogurt, define it as a cheese, and in turn evaluate this topic through use of an attributive adjective, "oldest," modifying "cheese," and a restrictive relative clause "that we know," also modifying "cheese." In the written text, then, Smith employs a nominal attributive syntax which extensively exploits adjectival information and permits the introduction and definition of a term.

While in the first sentence of the written orientation, "yogurt" is topicalized and evaluated ("the oldest cheese") through an attributive copula syntax, in the second sentence, cohesion between sentences is provided by retaining yogurt as the sentential subject through the referring expression "it." More importantly, syntax as equally attributive as that employed in the first sentence of the text is used in the second. Structurally, a clause in the passive voice is comparable to a copula construction. Where *to be* is a main verb in a copula construction, it functions as an auxiliary in the passive voice. Use of a passive construction allows further new information to be ascribed to the defined topic yogurt: "discovered." Significantly, through the use of this passive construction, the agents (nomads) which are foregrounded in the oral text are backgrounded in the written (though marked as new information through the *by* phrase of the passive voice). The third sentence is also in the passive voice (with deletion of the *by* phrase), thus allowing more new information to be ascribed to the topic yogurt: "saved," "used." The topic yogurt then is progressively "discovered," "saved," and "used." The left-directional attributive syntax of written speech facilitates not only topic focusing and so ease of visual processing but also the abstraction of process from action.

Use of the passive voice in the written orientation is one means by which written speech as a variety can promote recall for a reader. The passive acts first to introduce yogurt as a new topic, but the repeated use of "yogurt" or a comparable referring expression in the subject slot of a series of passive constructions transforms "yogurt" as topic from new to old information while simultaneously allowing new information to accrue to the now old topic. Such syntactic means, which are available primarily to written speech, facilitate the processing and retention of the background information Smith provides for the reader. With topic in left-hand position in each clause, the reader's eye is confronted by new information only in right-hand position, and since topic is identical in all left-hand positions, new information in right-hand position is even more easily taken in. Rhetorically, the structures Smith employs are perfectly suited to the mnemonic needs of the reader he is addressing.

The oral text does not appeal to the processing needs of a reader but to those of a listener and the speaker himself. Background information is presented in story form, which enhances processing and interest for a listener. Indeed, a listener would have difficulty processing the written text, although information proceeds from left to right, because, as well as a syntax that attracts the listener's attention to new information, there must also be a high degree of redundancy in oral texts. Once the new concept of yeasts is introduced into the oral text, Smith employs elaboration to reintroduce the concept to the listener: "When they'd leave the milk set about **natu-ral** yeasts in the air, *bacteria in the air in the desert* [my italics], would land." Such elaboration is entirely functional and adds to the coherence of the oral text. Moreover, in keeping with the needs of a listening audience, Smith is also more explicit about the actual process of discovery in his oral text. Presenting new information to his listeners, he organizes it temporally and subdivides events into discrete stages. He informs his listeners first that nomads began to domesticate and use herd animals, specifically cattle and goats. Second, he explains that these animals were milked. Third, he explains (*when* is used to convey conditional rather than temporal meaning in the third sentence) that the milk taken from these animals was left exposed to the air. This information is entirely implicit in the written text where the reader is informed only that nomads had "milk products." Processing the written text, a reader must construct for him- or herself the information that is explicitly supplied in the oral text. In effect, the reader must interpret the expression "milk products" as representing semantically a stage of completion after milking has occurred and so conceptually supply the specific activities of the preceding stages, thus bringing what might be termed a "milking frame" to the written text in the process of reading it. Not only is there greater topical focus in the written text, but in keeping with focus on the topic yogurt, there is also greater focus on the last stage, fermentation. Such topical focus or emphasis requires that the reader actively participate in the creation of the written text by bringing a "milking frame" to bear on overall interpretation of the information supplied.

The oral and written orientations which Jeff Smith provides are parallel texts, but they do not "mean" the same. In the oral text, the listener can easily follow the stages of herding, milking, and leaving of milk which are not explicitly indicated in the written text. The oral orientation allows the listener to process information in logical resultative sequence. Deletion of any stage, such as milking, would undermine the understanding of the listener and thus the very function of the orientation to supply new background information. Also, by beginning at the beginning, the speaker has a strategic means of conveying information. Conversely, it makes sense for Smith to delete certain information in his written text, where he focuses on the goal yogurt as his principal topic. Smith can background preliminary stages where human agents are focal and create further thematic focus on the very last stage of fermentation. The implicit nature of the written text also fosters brevity, while the explicit quality of the oral, which relies exclusively on narrative sequence, fosters length.[3]

The problem of memory becomes even more focal in the main instructional body of each parallel text. Not only do we see different strategies employed by the same speaker but, in turn, very different structures resulting overall in two very different texts. In the main body of Smith's written instruction, he provides some further orientation to the series of directives he gives, but he no longer assumes little or no knowledge on the part of the reader. Throughout the remainder of the text the reader becomes co-participant with the writer in the creation of meaning. Using the physicality of the written page, Smith commences the body of his instruction by setting it off on the page from his orientation. A centred asterisk is used to set off the orientation physically from the yogurt recipes. Where transition has to be sententially marked in oral speech ("Well today I'm going I'm ready to fly with you here. Lots of **marvelous** things that we can make with **yogurt**"), the written text marks off space on the page to "announce" the beginning of a new section or stage. The centralized asterisk is followed by a left-margined title, "Yogurt," which specifies the subtopic. The reader, however, must know that, capitalized and left-margined, the word "Yogurt" is a title and, as such, indicates the topic of the new physical section and that, more specifically, the title is a title of a recipe or set of directions. Capitalization accompanied by centred or left-margined placement cues the reader to the fact that a new topic has been announced, but these cues are entirely implicit and conventional and must be known beforehand or understanding cannot occur.

Use of physical space in a written text is one means by which such texts perform indirect speech acts such as announcing or shifting topic, but such use of space must be conventional or the implicature they provide would not be supplied by the reader. Although Smith is also at some physical remove from his audience in his oral instruction, he knows his audience can both see and hear him, and so he must explicitly announce any shifts in topic or new topics. Conversely, in the written situation the reader cannot see and hear, and so speech acts such as topic shifting or announcing are performed through visual reading cues such as marked placement of topic on the page. Just as the passive creates topic focusing, so centring and bolding a word on a page uses the strategy of physical positioning of a word to convey topicality.

Further orientation is supplied in the next segment of the text where Smith first evaluates the recipe he will supply and then addresses his reader's attention to a potential problem in the yogurt-making process:

The rules here are simple. Just remember that you can kill the yogurt by getting it too hot. On the other hand, the yogurt will not grow if you do not keep it warm enough. So use the old heating pad method.

In the first sentence of this orientation Smith evaluates "the rules" as "simple." The question, of course, is "what rules?" Moreover, where is "here" in this first sentence? The rules that Smith is referring to in further relation to "here" are the rules in the recipe for yogurt which he will shortly supply. But there has been no prior mention of a recipe in this section of the text, only an asterisk and a left-located title, "**Yogurt**." The concept of a recipe is brought to the text by the reader, who interprets the asterisk and the title together to mean that the writer intends to commence actual instruction or, in the written situation, to provide a recipe. Although the lexeme *recipe* is never used, the reader brings a recipe frame to the text and thus accurately locates the rules in the recipe itself. Moreover, because the recipe frame or concept is provided by the reader, there is no need to announce explicitly the commencement of yogurt making itself as Smith does in his oral text: "So here we go. I've thrown I'm *making* [my italics] a gallon at a time. **Easy** to do."

In the second sentence of his orientation to the yogurt recipe, Smith supplies more conventional orientation. The evaluation of rules is designed to modify the reader's concerns about making yogurt for the first time. Smith also positively evaluates the recipe in his oral instruction: "**Easy** to do." He then dialectically juxtaposes this statement of ease with a warning of difficulty: "Just remember that you can kill the yogurt by getting it too hot. On the other hand, the yogurt will not grow if you do not keep it warm enough." Smith brings a problem/solution framework or structure which is commonly used in written discourse to the written text. In keeping with this framework, Smith's next and last sentence in the orientation to the yogurt recipe is presented as a solution: "So use the old heating pad method." The actual recipe which follows is in this way presented as a solution to the problem announced in the orientation. Use of such a dualistic structure as that of problem/solution is helpful both for the writer and the reader. This structure facilitates organization of the text for the writer and processing for the reader who has a conceptual framework with which to accommodate new information in the text. Seeing the recipe as a means of solving a problem, the reader is made to read the recipe actively. Associated with such a frame, information in the recipe takes on greater salience for the reader and so is read with greater attention and care.

In the list of ingredients which precedes the actual directions given in the written text, the reader is required to bring another frame of reference to the written text. Again, a left-margined title, "EQUIPMENT," is employed to announce a new subtopic. The title is also fully capitalized as a graphic means of expressing significance. A list of ingredients and supplies is set off beside the title:

6- to 8-quart stainless steel or enamel kettle
Cheese or yeast thermometer (needs to go from about 100 degrees to 220 degrees Fahrenheit)
Heat diffuser or flame tamer
4 quarts fresh milk
4 1-quart widemouthed canning jars with lids, sterilized
Heating pad

The list is the most basic written form since writing was invented as a memory device to keep records and accounts.[4] The records associated with Minoan (also termed Mycenaean) Linear B, for example, have been characterized as "grocery lists."[5] Above, in this list of ingredients, we also have a grocery list, but, again, one that has to be read as such. There is no explicit statement to the effect that these items are required to make yogurt. The reader must bring another frame to the text, that of the grocery list, which is simultaneously an aid to the memory and a set of instructions to purchase certain items. In contrast, Smith orally makes the purpose of the ingredients explicit and adds further evaluation in the form of information about cost and accessibility of the items:

When you make your own yogurt, the equipment is very simple. You need a **stainless steel** pan. You can't do it in aluminum or enamel see. Put it into a stainless steel kettle. And you need a **thermometer**, a **good** cheese thermometer. These are not hard to find. One that will go from what does mine go from? from ah from about 20 degrees centigrade to about 250 degrees you see. You want to be able to control this **very very** carefully. Then I want you to buy a **heat diffuser**. These are very simple to find. It's ah a **cheap** gadget, but a **marvelous** thing that ah will on the burner, you see, it functions as a **double boiler**. It makes the heat **very very** even. And you want to put that under your pot because stainless steel is **generally too thin** to use ah for normal cooking. For me, everything burns, but use a heat diffuser and it won't.

Through a series of assertions which function as indirect directives and through the imperative mood and more subtle commands marked as expressives, such as "Then I want you to buy a **heat diffuser**," Smith explicitly supplies a "grocery list" while also evaluating the ease with which certain supplies can be acquired and the expense they will entail. He also explains the purpose or reason for buying this equipment, employing causative conjunctions ("because"), causative verbs ("makes," "functions"), and five infinitives of purpose. Smith also explicitly assigns the listener a new role of agent ("When *you make* [my italics] your own yogurt") with a specific goal for which acquisition of equipment is a partial fulfilment.

Smith's frequent use of the directive *see* or *you see* in the passage above compares functionally to his capitalization of *equipment* in the written instruction: "EQUIPMENT." Unlike *you know*, *you see* is seldom fronted in a given utterance: "You need a **stainless steel** pan. You can't do it in aluminum or enamel see." *You see* functions not as a monitoring device to determine if an audience has understood but as a verbal emphatic which stresses the information it follows. It is another form of directive to the audience to note certain information especially. The "see" in this utterance is related to the command form used in everyday speech, *see that you do/don't*, which as an idiom conveys that something must be "seen to" or effected. However, *you see* is also an explicit directive, a command that you "see" or note a particular point, while capitalization as a visual cue implicitly and conventionally implies significance when not functionally marking the beginning of a written sentence.

The written recipe itself commences immediately with a directive: "Heat the milk to 180 degrees Fahrenheit in a stainless steel or enamel kettle." Smith follows this with orientation clauses which specify different possibilities for the use of milk products: "You may use skim, low-fat, or whole milk." "May" in this sentence is used to signal deontic modality where permission is granted by an agent to a patient. Smith maintains his status as authority through use of such a modality. Orientation is next followed by external evaluation. Smith indicates his own preferences, using, nonetheless, an imperative in the first evaluative sentence: "Remember that flavour is not terribly affected by butterfat. I prefer using low-fat milk for yogurt so that the final product can be used in low-fat/low-salt dishes." This evaluation becomes thematic as a concern in the remaining text. What follows, however, are more directives: "Cool ... Add ... Blend ... Place ... and cap." Only one orientation clause stipulating the amount of one ingredient intervenes. The idea of a recipe as a command is central to its meaning, for the recipe is in fact a conventionalized series of commands which instruct a reader.

Instruction in the body of the written text is facilitated by minimizing information. Smith makes use, via written or visual cues on the page, of frames of reference which he shares with the reader. Thus, he makes use of a recipe and grocery list frame as well as a problem and solution frame. In the case of the first two frames, information can be minimized on the actual page by such cognitive shorthand, while in the case of the third frame, a problem/solution frame for the recipe facilitates recall by producing thematic focus and salience. The visual cues available to written speech as well as a dualistic problem/solution structure in the main text serve to keep the written instruction simple and, in turn, to make the written text linguistically accessible and easy to recall.

Brown and Yule have examined the particularly elliptical nature of this written form of instruction, noting specifically that "recipes involve particularly rapid and obvious changes of state" (1983:202). However, information in the written recipe above seldom accounts for changes of state in the yogurt being prepared. Once a referring expression such as "the milk" has been provided for a given referent, the expression is seldom altered or modified despite the fact that the referent in question may have undergone a given change in state. Looking at Smith's instructions for making yogurt in his written text, we can see that uniformity of reference is quite evident:

Heat *the milk* [my italics] to 180 degrees Fahrenheit . . .

Cool *the milk* [my italics] to 115 degrees. Add starter to yogurt from your last batch. You generally need about 1/2 cup of a previous yogurt to 1 quart of new milk. Blend it in carefully so that the yogurt will be smooth. Place the mixture in a sterile jar, and cap with lid.

In another kettle (any kind will do), place water that is 115 degrees, right on the button! Put the jars of new yogurt into the water, which should come up about three-fourths of the way to the lid of the jar. Cover the kettle, and place it on a heating pad set for medium heat. Eight hours later you will have fine yogurt. Refrigerate before using.

In the first instructional paragraph the recipe directs the reader to "Heat the milk." "The milk," of course, is referential to that in the list of ingredients. The "4 quarts fresh milk" listed in the ingredients logically connect to "the milk" in the instructions. The article "the" marks the information as old and there is lexical repetition of "milk" so that the connection seems plausible for the reader. However, in the instructional text, Smith does not always present information which he has introduced in the list of ingredients as old information. "Heating pad" is introduced as new information in the third instructional paragraph: "Cover the kettle, and place it on *a* [my italics] heating pad set for medium heat." In assigning new or old status to a referring expression, Smith employs a principle of proximity. If a referring expression is physically close on the page to an earlier reference, the expression will be marked appropriately as old, but if there is a marked distance between the two referring expressions, straining the reader's memory or requiring saccadic jerking of the eye back over read text, old information will be reintroduced as new.

Concerns for reading ease are the most likely reasons Smith retains the construction "the milk" in the second instructive clause, although the "milk" in the second clause in no longer the same milk as that in the first or in the list of ingredients. "The milk" in the second instructional clause is milk which has been heated to 180 degrees. The reader, then, must supply a new conceptual referent for the term "the milk" in the second instructional clause. Indeed, the reader must supply a great deal of other information. For example, the reader must know that the instructions are given in the order that they should be carried out. Between the sentences "Cool the milk to 115" and "Add starter to yogurt from your last batch," there are no connectives such as *then, and after, next, now, first, second* to mark explicit sequence. Sequence, so important for the methodology of recipes, is not explicitly marked except iconically in the sequence of the sentences as they occur in the text. But lack of explicit marking of changes of state or of sequence is not necessarily a hardship for the reader, for the situation created by the text also supplies information.

It would be quite possible for the written text to be composed in such a way so as to mark changes of state and sequence:

To begin making yogurt first heat 4 quarts fresh milk to 180 degrees Fahrenheit in a stainless steel or enamel kettle. . . . After heating the milk to pasteurize it then cool the heated milk to 115 degrees and then add a commercial starter which you can get at your local health food store to your cooled milk for your first batch and your own starter for all other subsequent batches.

A text such as that which I have composed above is more or less fully explicit, but it is also hard to follow as an instructional text. It would serve better as a process description detailing the actual steps in making yogurt. The directives alone would identify it as instructional. Within the text are the features of integration Chafe cites as those characterizing written speech, but such features mar the written instruction, because far too much information is embedded in the text. Where the reader can supply information him- or herself explicitness of reference only undermines text processing.

Although "the milk" in the yogurt recipe changes state from step to step, the reader can see the transition in the process of following the recipe. Thus, reference is appropriately as simple and unvaried as possible for both the first time user relying on the recipe as an instruction and for the ongoing user relying on the recipe to aid memory. There is no advantage to an explicit directive such as *Cool the 4 quarts of heated fresh milk* over "Cool the milk" since the reader already knows that 4 quarts of fresh milk have been heated; presumably he or she has just heated them. Unnecessary information concerning changes of state are, therefore, eliminated from written recipes.

Certain changes of state are marked in a written recipe, however. In the third instructional clause of the written instruction, the reader is commanded to "Add starter to yogurt from your last batch." Technically, this sentence is badly written; there is an error in modification. What Smith wishes to say is *Add starter from your last batch to yogurt.* Smith and his editors have failed to notice not only the error in modification but also the incorrect presupposition that the reader has already made yogurt and thus has a "last batch." What has been forgotten in the main body of the instructional text, which relies so heavily on reader information, is what is clearly understood in the orientation, that the reader is a first-time maker of yogurt. Smith has momentarily forgotten his audience and is thinking of the recipe as it would be used by someone like himself.

The use of "yogurt" rather than "milk" is also interesting. At this stage the heated and cooled milk is not yet yogurt, yet Smith uses "yogurt" as the referring expression for the goal in this sentence: "Add starter to yogurt." In using the term "yogurt," Smith is unconsciously anticipating the major change in state that addition of the starter will produce in the readied milk. Smith marks this change of state in his written text by simply and unconsciously employing a new referring expression, "yogurt," which in itself entails a new result or alteration.

Reading a written recipe is largely a matter of following it in sequence. Although readers of recipes do first read over a recipe, recipes are usually read in discrete bits. Thus, a directive is first read and then performed, after which the next directive is read and performed. A more explicit text providing information about changes of state or specific sequence would serve only to make the text difficult to process since what the reader wants to do is to get to the next directive or instruction. For this reason most sentences in written recipes commence with a directive: "Cool the milk ... Add the starter ... Blend it in carefully ... Place the mixture." The new topic as action is appropriately fronted as it would not be if information about sequence were supplied: *Then you cool the milk.* In fronted position, stripped of sequential information, the directives also have the advantage of being capitalized in a written text, so making them easy for the eye to locate in a text from which the eye darts back and forth. Only orientation clauses providing information about amounts or variation in preparation intervene between the specific directives which are given in the sequence they must be taken. The written text expunges all other information, which would only distract a reader who is simultaneously a performer. The reader must know the conventions involved in reading such a text, but the elliptical simplicity of the text as well as its formal syntactic repetition in the form of a repetition of directives in sequence also aid the reader to process the text while attempting to duplicate its instructions. The text is fully explicit, given its own particular contextual constraints. In keeping with Grice's Maxim of Quantity, based on his Co-operative Principle of conversation, the written recipe is only as informative as it needs to be. As constructed, the written recipe facilitates mimesis just as the oral text does, but, of course, it is direct mimesis in actual performance.

The oral instruction differs maximally from the written in its main body as well as in its overall structure. The oral text is structured first as a demonstration or illustration and then as an explicit instruction, while the written text, having no illustration slot, immediately instructs through a series of direct commands. In the oral situation the student/listener is told how to mimic the illustrated behaviour of the instructor, whereas in the written situation the reader actually "follows" the text which replaces the instructor.

Differences are most evident if we examine how each text commences and proceeds with instructions:

So here we go. I've thrown I'm making a gallon at a time.   **Easy** to do. Put a **gallon** in my stainless steel pot, brought it to a 180 degrees and I cooled, let it cool to 115 degrees. Got that. That's **very** important,the 115 degrees. Bring it to a 180 because you are going to **pasteurize** it. That was the number that ah Louis Pasteur decided on, remember. And then you bring it down to a 115, because then it's **just** warm enough to excite the starter, that is say the yogurt bug that we're going to add to this, and it is a **bug**, it is a bacteria.

Marvelous creature. So I have some yogurt left over from my last batch and at this point I'm going to add oh a **good cup** to my gallon here, previously made yogurt. (Oral instruction)

Heat the milk to 180 degrees Fahrenheit in a stainless steel or enamel kettle. You may use skim, low-fat, or whole milk. Remember that flavour is not terribly affected by butterfat. I prefer using low-fat milk for yogurt so that the final product can be used in low-fat/low-salt dishes.

Cool the milk to 115 degrees. Add starter to yogurt from your last batch. You generally need about 1/2 cup of a previous yogurt to 1 quart of new milk. (Written instruction)

In his oral instruction Smith explicitly marks the commencement of the actual instruction for the listener: "So here we go." He next introduces the specific topic or subtopic of this segment of the discourse using a syntactic construction, the present progressive, similar to that used to introduce his specific topic of the lesson: "I've thrown I'm making a gallon at a time." The present progressive indicates that Smith's activity is a process engaged in over time. He is also an agent with a goal, to make a gallon at a time. He then evaluates the activity for the audience: "**Easy** to do." The evaluation serves to involve and motivate the audience since Smith offers the evaluation as a generalization rather than as something specific to himself. Via the evaluation Smith shifts attention from his own actual agency to the potential agency of his audience, for after the evaluation he reviews his actions, in effect reviewing the principal stages in the yogurt-making process, and then requests confirmation on the part of the audience that it comprehends: "[I] Put a **gallon** in my stainless steel pot, brought it to a 180 degrees and I cooled, let it cool to 115 degrees. Got it?" He again stresses "**gallon**" since, although not new, the information is important as the cornerstone of his instruction.

To this point in his discourse Smith has explicitly marked the commencement of his instruction and indicated that the specific topic of the immediate lesson is yogurt making. He has also supplied an abstract of the process he is teaching. The listener who is hearing this lesson for the first time has been fully oriented to the nature of the speech act and its specific concern and has been given a general overview of the process to be learned. Smith continues by reiterating and elaborating on each of the stages of the defined process. This strategy is comparable to that used in oral exposition in that both oral exposition and instruction begin with a statement of a generalization or, in the case of instruction, a statement of a general process.

However, Smith does not end a paragraph with illustration supplied by narrative as does Buscaglia in oral exposition, but begins with illustration supplied by narrative: "Put a **gallon** in my stainless steel pot, brought it to a 180 degrees and I cooled, let it cool to 115 degrees. Got that?" Smith uses a narrative in the initial illustration slot of the oral discourse as a means of introducing the new information to his audience. Deletion of agency in two of the clauses puts topical emphasis on verbs carrying information about the specific process to be learned. As well, formal repetition of sentence pattern facilitates ease of processing for the listener, who is then asked if processing has been successful.

Not content that processing has been fully successful, Smith repeats information about the cooling temperature. Since Smith is in the particular situation of teaching an audience physically removed from him, he employs repetition and evaluative stress to compensate for distance, although most likely these mnemonic strategies are basic to all oral instruction. Smith uses vocal stress literally to mark information he deems important, or he combines stress with evaluation as in the elaboration which follows information about cooling the yogurt: "That's **very** important, the 115 degrees." By using the deictic "that," which directs attention to the cooling temperature, itself right-located in the text and so marked emphatically in terms of word order, and stressing the emphatic adverb "**very**" to produce doubled emphasis, Smith ensures the mnemonic value of this stage in the process. The use of explicit evaluation, stressing, deixis, and marked word order all combine to mark the information as memorable for the listener.

Having repeated and stressed information about the cooling temperature, Smith next reiterates the entire process, adding further explanatory commentary which, like emphasis, serves to give the information salience:

Bring it to a 180 because you are going to **pasteurize** it. That was the number that ah Louis Pasteur decided on, remember? And then you bring it down to a 115, because then it's just warm enough to excite the starter, that is say the yogurt bug that we're going to add to this, and it is a **bug**, it is a bacteria. **Marvelous** creature.

In this block of his oral instructional discourse, Smith has repeated the instructions for a second time, except that he has shifted from the past tense denoting his own actions to the imperative mood which directs the actions of the audience. The purpose of repetition in the text at this point is to facilitate memory of the specific steps for the listening audience. In oral discourse there is no means by which the speaker can physically preserve information except in language, and so repetition is a principal means by which the text is made mnemonic for a listener. The very strategy of first providing an illustration and then directing the listener to duplicate each step already illustrated is simultaneously mimetic and mnemonic. Indeed, the strategy of mimesis governs the structure of the oral text, determining the consistent pronominal alteration of "I" and "you" in the agent slot or of Smith in the role of commissive agent, doing for, and of Smith in the role of directive agent, telling "you" to do.

The supportive causal information in the first directive clause also facilitates memorization for the listener. By giving the student/listener sufficient reasons for each major step, in effect characterizing each step, Smith aids the recall process for the listener. For example, in the first direct command, "Bring it to a 180 because you are going to **pasteurize** it," Smith stresses the infinitive "**pasteurize**" which denotes a specific process in itself. This stressing, of course, acts to mark the process and so make it salient in memory. However, the purpose of stressing the concept in the first place is to facilitate association of the general concept of pasteurization, which is easy to remember, being a concept available generally in the culture, with the specific number, "180," which has no such general accessibility and which is still new information for the listener. Thus, the strategy Smith employs here is not repetition or marked word order or explicit evaluation but stress in conjunction with general or known information. New information is made familiar for the listener trying to learn the recipe. This mnemonic strategy is commonly used when we have to remember new names or phone numbers and so forth. The letters of the new name can be directly associated with something familiar or known to us. A common medieval method of memory retrieval was to conceptualize certain information in certain rooms of an imaginary house. Equally, the causal information Smith provides is a form of explanatory elaboration which serves to give the number "180" a larger reference and so both disambiguate it from other numbers and make it memorable.

Smith further and more directly encourages association of the number with pasteurization by adding more elaboration: "That was the number that ah Louis Pasteur decided on, remember?" Although Smith uses the demonstrative "That" as subject, much as he does to point to and evaluate the cooling temperature, the construction he employs in this sentences is for all intents and purposes a cleft which, of course, further acts to focus attention on "the number," modified in turn by a restrictive clause "that ah Louis Pasteur decided on." The cleft focuses attention on the number as topic and further associates it with pasteurization by lexical repetition of the noun "Pasteur." Twice Smith associates old or known information with focused new information so that the association is absolutely clear and entirely memorable. As well, he requests confirmation of association from the listener: "remember?" This last speech act can be interpreted both as a monitoring device meaning "do you remember; is that association clear in your mind?" and as a command or reminder to remember.

This same strategy is employed with the temperature 115 degrees. Smith explicitly marks sequence, "And then," and again correlates a new idea, the number "115" with a concept of warming which is familiar and known. Emphasis, however, is here placed on new information, specifically, the adverb "**just**," which specifies the degree of warmth as the number itself does. The idea of a degree of warmth is thus twice indicated, once as a number and second as a concept based on human empirical knowledge. The adjective "warm" is further modified conceptually by an infinitive of purpose, "to excite the starter," which a third time specifies the concept of a degree of warmth, although on the third occasion characterizing that degree in terms of a specific goal or purpose, exciting the starter. Smith has explained the concept of a starter in his narrative orientation ("So they began to **save** the starters you see, save the yogurt and pass it on among generations"), but although he designates "starters" as old information through attachment to the article "the," he nonetheless further elaborates on this concept in the body of the instruction to ensure association of the starter with warming the milk to 115 degrees: "that is say the yogurt that we're going to add to this, and it is a **bug**, it is a bacteria. **Marvelous** creature." Ongoing elaboration of yogurt as "**bug**," "bacteria," "creature" also focuses attention on the yogurt itself as agentive and so capable of creating changes in state. Through such elaboration Smith makes explicit the fact that recipes are fundamentally about changes in state and that changes in temperature, warming and cooling, result in changes in the food being prepared. Smith even etymologically makes this point a second time later in the text:

You know what the term for yogurt is ah in Lebanese? The word is "**leben**" L E B E N which is connected with the **German** term for some reason, we don't know, for life, "leben" 'life' "leben" in German. **Why** would they use such a word? Well, **because** this milk is now **alive**. It has a **bug** in it. And the bug will keep the milk alive and ah literally preserve it. A **marvelous marvelous** concept.

Here again a chain of associations is supplied for the listener: Lebanese "leben" to German "leben" to English "alive" back to "bug." Just as the temperature "180" is explicitly associated with the process pasteurization to facilitate recall, so the temperature "115" is explicitly associated with the bug that agentively transforms milk into yogurt in the process of preservation. Yogurt, life and preservation are all bound together in associational relationship. Each stage in the process of yogurt making is laden with associational references that allow a new idea to be associated and, indeed, incorporated into an old or known idea. Smith uses lexical and syntactic repetition, elaboration, stress, deixis, focusing, and cognitive association extensively to ensure both understanding and recall for the listener, for whom knowledge means memory.

Typically, Smith ends his oral instruction on yogurt making with one last reiteration of the process:

Did you get the recipe? 180 in in the kettle. Cool it down to 115. Add your starter. Put it in jars. Put it in a kettle of water that is at exactly 115 degrees on a heating pad overnight. You've got it. Alright.

This last reiteration alone compares syntactically to the written instructional text. Here all extraneous information is removed and the text appears only as a series of commands in the order in which they must be effected. However, such a minimalized text can serve in the oral situation only as a last reminder or aid to the memory, while in the written situation such a text serves as basic instruction.

CONCLUSION

The oral and written instructive texts examined in this chapter solve the problem of memory for their respective audiences in markedly different ways. Where solution to the problem adds length to the oral text because the solution must be entirely linguistic, it minimizes length in the written text because written speech itself can create context as well as foster the use of inference and association, specifically in a reader. In a superficial sense, the oral text appears to be much more explicit than the written. Topics are announced through explicit speech acts and not one-word titles. Shifts are announced equally through verbal assertions of commencement and not through asterisks. The discourse cues used by oral speech are almost always lexical and sentential, while written speech exploits visual cues whereby words set off or apart from others on the page conventionally carry topic or topic-shifting meaning. In this way, written speech exploits a form of symbolic representation closer to that of gesture, where a particular gesture has a particular meaning. The ability of written speech to exploit the physical properties of the printed page allows for uniquely visual gestures which oral speech cannot command. The benefit to written speech is that through such visual marking, texts can be briefer and thus potentially more readable for the eye.

Written cues alone, however, do not explain the brevity of written instruction and the greater length of oral. Structurally, the oral text is divided into an illustration and application slot. The student/ listener is first told what the instructor has done, is then directed to replicate each step, and is finally provided a summary of the main steps to reinforce remembrance of the process. The text, then, is structurally mimetic and so linguistically mnemonic for the listener. In contrast, the written text has no illustration slot. There is no way that the written text, which replaces the instructor, can provide illustration. Instead, the written text employs a problem/solution frame and by so doing adds salience to the recipe now conceptualized as providing a solution to a problem. The structural properties of each text promote memorability, but in using repetition as a linguistic strategy, the oral text is necessarily elongated.

The oral text is elongated also by its use of right-located structures, emphatic phrases, stress, deixis, and elaboration and by its greater use of cognitive association whereby new information is incorporated through association with known general concepts. The written text uses none of these means with the exception of cognitive association, which it nonetheless uses only in the orientation where it is concerned to introduce new information to the reader. In the main body of instruction, the written text relies on the reader's ability to bring referential frames to bear and on the context of situation which the text itself creates. Where the written text can signal conventionally on a page through capitalization and left-location of *equipment* that a grocery list is being provided, it states little more. If the reader can observe changes of state in the foods he or she is preparing, no information is provided in the text to represent these changes unless, as with the referring expression "yogurt," a final change or result is marked. The written text also visually cues the reader to each step in the instructional process by eliminating information about sequence so that the eye is drawn easily to a capitalized command which marks a specific step in the overall process.

The written text concerns itself with ease of processing for the eye, while the oral text concerns itself with ease of processing for the ear. For the ear there is repetition, stress, deixis, and right-location; for the eye there is marked visual placement, capitalization, fronted capitals, and topic-focusing in an uncluttered visual context where all extraneous information is eliminated, in particular that which is provided by the context of situation and that provided by conventional implicature on the part of the reader. The eye is able to dart back and forth easily from the text; the ear can learn the recipe in the process of continuing familiarity with its basic stages and elements.

Both texts accomplish instruction, but each appeals to very different senses and so presents information for processing differently. These empirical facts determine in large part the differences in the structures of the two texts. Visual cues and visual stress (capitalization) as well as the visual simplicity of the written instruction aid the reader trying to follow and so learn it, especially for the first time, while inbuilt structural repetition and elaboration in the oral text aid the listener trying to remember and so know it.

6

Oral and Written Argument

Through language we can alter the world or others' perception of it. When we do so, we engage in argument, which, like instruction, has a speech-act direction of fit which is world to word. Linguistically, argument is marked not through tense, as in narration (simple past), description (simple present), or exposition (simple present), but through mood or speaker modality (*might, may, could, would,* and so forth). Thus, if I say *Swimming improves health,* I am asserting a fact and engaged in exposition. If I say *Swim to improve your health,* I am uttering a directive and engaged in teaching or instruction. However, if I state, using the subjunctive, *Were you to swim, your health would improve,* I would be forwarding an argument. If the hearer to whom I have addressed this argument actually goes out and swims because I have related swimming with health, then my argument has also been persuasive. To the extent that there may be weak or strong argument, different levels of speaker modality can be expressed. *Pit bull terriers could be muzzled* is weaker as an argument than *Pit bull terriers must be muzzled.* Through markers of modality such as *may, might, would, should,* and *could* speakers can indicate the extent to which the world correlates with or should accommodate to the word.

Argument, unlike instruction and persuasion, is also reciprocal. The dialogic nature of argument requires that it be governed by rules of order and procedure of the kind investigated by discourse analysts and ethnomethodologists in their analysis of everyday conversation. Sacks et al. point out that argument is a variant of everyday conversation on a continuum between conversation and formal debate (ceremony):

It appears likely that conversation should be considered the basic form of speech-exchange system, with other systems on the array representing a variety of transformations of conversation's turn-taking system, to achieve other types of turn-taking systems. In this light, debate or ceremony would not be an independent polar type, but rather the most extreme transformation of conversation—most extreme in fully fixing the most important (and perhaps nearly all) of the parameters which conversation allows to vary. (1974:730-1)

In Longacre's (1983) definition of argument as "behavioural discourse" both agent orientation and addressee orientation co-exist in this genre, marking its basic dialogic quality. No party to an argument gives up his or her right to the floor, as is the case in narrative or instruction and, more subtly, persuasion. Turns in argument may be much more choreographed than those in everyday conversation, but there are clear rules which give each party an opportunity to speak. Nonetheless, argument, even at its democratic best, is highly constrained socially.

In her work on argument, Anita Pomerantz (1984) demonstrates that disagreement in conversation has dispreferred status, except in a specific circumstance where a prior speaker has proffered a self-deprecation. Generally, however, agreement with a prior assessment has preferred status, while disagreement has dispreferred status. Pomerantz' analysis is not really very surprising. Talk, even between equals, is social. We do not readily disagree with co-conversationalists because we value the social bonds which are created by commonly shared values and perspectives. When disagreement is greatly feared by a society, it may exploit extreme formality in oratory to offset completely any possibility of verbal conflict, as in the case of Merina oratory: "Not only is the orator strictly limited in what he can say, but freedom of intonation and loudness *which he would have in ordinary conversation* [my italics] is almost totally non-existent . . . Merina speech acts can be seen as a continuum from polite to impolite speaking and oratory is so 'polite' that the choice of what can be said and how it can be said has largely disappeared" (Block 1975:8).

Such means, however, are very extreme because disagreement itself is not a favoured means of social interaction. Formal debate is physically as well as linguistically constrained in most societies. The law courts are one official and ceremonial location in which debate is guaranteed preferred social status. The special dress of lawyers and judges in such socially prescribed places set aside for debate "announces" the legitimate separation of such behaviour from that in the everyday community. Debates between political opponents are equally formalized by use of special locations such as parliaments, explicit and formal rules of behaviour, and so forth. Potential conflict, although only verbal, is thus extensively controlled by the society which simultaneously permits but limits disagreement.

In everyday speech there are also clear limits to what socially competent speakers will and will not say. Seldom do speakers bluntly disagree with other speakers. Pomerantz cites a number of strategies employed by speakers in disagreement with other speakers (1984:70–4). A speaker may simply delay assessment by offering no comment. This is a common tactic used by politicians who do not wish to incriminate themselves. But it is not a popular strategy since social interaction stops momentarily. Other strategies are thus more common and more successful. "Repair initiators," which are used to request clarification (*what?*, *hm?*), are often employed to delay possible disagreement. Even more common and more successful is a "yes, but" strategy. The speaker first agrees or acknowledges the prior speaker's point and then counters with a disagreement. Pomerantz states that "An apparent puzzle regarding the agreement-plus-disagreement turn shape is *why* recipients agree with assessments when they will shortly disagree with them" (72). But, of course, the "yes, but" strategy does exactly what a courtroom or parliament does physically; it contextualizes disagreement. The affirmative slot in this linguistic strategy reaffirms the social bond between the two disputants. Only once the social bond is established and acknowledged can argument commence.

Concerning the interaction of this genre and the media of oral and written speech, Michael Mulkay has observed that "there is some indication that strong disagreement is easier to declare in writing than face to face" (1985:201). Mulkay examined a set of eighty letters written by thirteen biochemists arguing about fundamental needs within their discipline and found that although an agreement or "yes" slot preceded each disagreement or "but" slot, disagreement was actually fostered by the distanced communication characteristic of writing. This observation is consistent with findings in this chapter. To a certain extent, the written context of situation frees a speaker from the strong social constraints of face-to-face interaction. A writer may also employ a third-party strategy by addressing the reader not as an antagonist but as a judge or supporter. This strategy is available to oral debaters equally if a judge is present, but it is not a possibility in conversational argument or debate. The written situation may also allow a writer to express emotion more forcefully and thus use passion and sarcasm to underscore his or her position. The strong sociality of oral argumentation is contrasted with the greater degree of individualism permitted in written texts. Overall, interpersonal and ideational meaning are differently balanced and achieved in oral and written varieties of argument.

SOCIO-POLITICAL ARGUMENT: THE NEW COLD WAR

The arguments under examination in this chapter concern the hypothesized causes of the New Cold War between the East and the West. The oral text is taken from a British television programme, *Voices* (June 1985), where two experts in modern political science, Fred Halliday and Noam Chomsky, argued the question of cause with regard to the New Cold War of the 1970s and 1980s. The written texts are taken from Fred Halliday's analysis of the New Cold War, *The Making of the Second Cold War* (1983), and Noam Chomsky's earlier analysis, "Towards a New Cold War" (1980).

Halliday's argument can be characterized as a difference hypothesis. He argues that there is a new Cold War because the social, political and economic differences between the two major world rivals, the USA and the USSR, make such conflict inevitable. The New Cold War, then, is an aspect of what he terms "The Great Contest" between these two superpowers. Chomsky argues a very different position: the New Cold War, like the old Cold War (1950s), is a product of American rhetoric; that is, the USA has manufactured and fostered hostility between itself and the USSR as a means of engendering nationalism in the United States which in turn serves to maintain support for imperialist "Grand Area" (world economic empire) planning and control. As in his earlier linguistic analysis, Chomsky sees a form of political deep structure which is obscured by a given surface structure. For Halliday, the conflict is real and inevitable, while for Chomsky, it is a form of political means to a given political end, American economic control of its "Grand Area."

The two political scientists come to their argument on television after each has written on the topic of a new Cold War. Chomsky's written text is as much an analysis of the cause of the New Cold War as it is an attack on those in his country who have obscured that cause and so promoted lack of understanding of the war's sociopolitical implications. Halliday's book is a counter to other analysts, including Chomsky, who he feels have not correctly dealt with or acknowledged key facts, that both the USA and the USSR have promoted the rivalry between them and that they are thus equally culpable. Each of these written texts, then, exists "conversationally" in the context of others. One has to be familiar with the general discussion to understand the theses of these two political scientists fully. These texts exist as conversational turns in a much longer conversation which occurs not so much in time but over time.

Despite considerable stylistic differences between these two speakers, in both their oral texts an additive syntax predominates while an attributive syntax is dominant in their written arguments.[1] The oral texts display a virtual equivalence in the percentages of simple sentences structures (41%/Chomsky, 43%/Halliday) as well as dominance in co-ordinate clause formation. However, in Chomsky's oral text there is an almost equivalent percentage of relative clauses to that in his written text (33%/oral, 35%/written). It is unusual to find such a high percentage of relative clauses in an oral text. Eight of the nine relative clauses in Chomsky's oral text are used to convey new information, while five of the seven used in the written text convey new information. Chomsky would seem to favour use of relative clauses as a means of embedding and conveying new information in both oral and written texts.

In the two written texts there is typical dominance of adjectival structures (relative clauses, participles, and attributive adjectives) as well as the passive voice, although variation occurs in preferences for specific clause types. Stylistically, it would appear that Chomsky favours a nominal style in both oral and written speech. Where noun clauses are favoured in the oral text, there are gerunds in the written. Moreover, there are no adverb clauses in the oral text and only two in the written sample. (See Tables 8 and 9).

In the oral argument, the problem of representing disagreement as disagreement is handled very differently than it is in its written counterpart. A "yes, but" strategy is pervasive in the oral argument and largely structures it. Conversely, a reader-oriented strategy is more dominant in the written arguments, which nonetheless incorporate "yes" and "but" slots into their general structures.

In the oral argument between Halliday and Chomsky, Halliday, who is also the moderator, asserts agreement both as a means of commencing argument and as a means of ending it. Argument cannot continue if genuine agreement has been established between two parties. If there is genuine agreement or agreement "to disagree," argument ceases. The purpose of the first assertion of agreement, by which Halliday opens the oral argument, however, is to establish background to the discussion in his role of presenter or moderator and also a sense of communality between himself and Chomsky:

Halliday: Noam, both you and I have written books on what we call the New Cold War and we seem to **agree** on the fact there is a new Cold War, a

TABLE 8
Syntactic Profile/Chomsky

Sentences	Oral 27 (579wds)	Written 20 (508wds)
Simple	11 (41%)	10 (50%)
Compound	04 (15%)	00 (00%)
Complex	06 (22%)	09 (45%)
Compound/complex	04 (15%)	01 (05%)
Embedded	02 (07%)	00 (00%)
Relative clauses	09	07
Adverbial clauses	00	02
Noun clauses	07	02
Co-ordinate clauses	14	02
Conjoining phrases	15	10
Participle phrases	06	09
Gerund	01	12
Infinitives	06	05
Passives	03	05
Exist. *There*/clefts	07	01
Attributive adjs.	47	71
(participles)	03	05
Nouns in apposition	05	02

TABLE 9
Syntactic Profile/Halliday

Sentences	Oral 33 (797wds)	Written 40 (1184wds)
Simple	14 (43%)	13 (32.5%)
Compound	01 (03%)	00 (00%)
Complex	08 (24%)	18 (45%)
Compound/complex	09 (27%)	09 (22.5%)
Embedded	01 (03%)	00 (00%)
Relative clauses	12	27
Adverbial clauses	07	07
Noun clauses	17	11
Co-ordinate clauses	23	11
Conjoining phrases	16	37
Participle phrases	05	10
Gerund	02	04
Infinitives	11	14
Passives	06	17
Exist. *There*/clefts	07	07
Attributive adjs.	55	192
(participles)	01	11
Nouns in apposition	05	05

worsening of East/West relations and particularly us/Soviet relations since the late Seventies. . . . So we **agree** that just as there was a Cold War in the late Forties and early Fifties so there seems to be a **new** Cold War **now**.

But I also get a sense that there's some **disagreement** between us, that you lay greater, more stress on control **within** the domains of each power. You say the United States and Soviet Union are **losing** influence, have been losing influence over their respective allies since the Sixties or since the great days of the Fifties for both of them and that in a way they're **using** the Cold War rhetoric, they're **using** the idea of conflict between them I think **not** to prosecute a conflict against each other which I think in **your** view is largely mythical or not so substantial but to **control** the people who are subordinate to them. And I think you've even said that the **real** enemies of the United States is not the Soviet Union so much as Japan, Western Europe that they are seeking seeking they're seeking to control those things, whereas in **my** view there is of course, there is this **element** of controlling the situation at home, of Britain controlling its own population, United States controlling its population, controlling the weaker allies in the Third World, but I give I think a much more **weight** to the **reality** of the East West conflict. I **do** think the United States and the Soviet Union have a **lot** to conflict about and that you can't understand this New Cold War if you **don't** see that the conflict has in fact got a lot of substance to it.

I have reproduced this long passage to examine more closely the contours of argument within it. The use of pronouns and the use of stress in this introduction indicate the structural properties of the argument. Halliday begins by pronominally uniting himself with Chomsky in a state of agreement. In the first sentence concord is stated three times through pronominal use: "both you and I," "we," "we." Agreement is also marked explicitly through the verb "**agree**" which he stresses. The friendliness conveyed by Halliday informally addressing Chomsky as "Noam" establishes conviviality and concord between the two co-conversationalists, as does "both," which as an adjective has partitive meaning since it suggests that the nouns or pronouns it modifies share a common state or relationship: *Both my friends are Canadians*. Moreover, as well as strongly establishing concord in the opening of his introduction through pronouns, adjectives, explicit lexemes, and stress, Halliday ends his first introductory oral paragraph with a resultative assessment of agreement: "So we **agree** that just as there was a Cold War in the late Forties and early Fifties so there seems to be a **new** Cold War **now**.

In the first introductory paragraph Halliday has characterized the New Cold War as both he and Chomsky view it. As a result of his sharing similar analyses or conclusions with Chomsky, Halliday continues to maintain that they "**agree**," with stress on this positively connoted lexeme emphasizing further that there is strong sharing, concord, friendliness and participation in social values. The affirmative slot in Halliday's "yes, but" strategy has been extensively fulfilled, taking an entire paragraph to be linguistically achieved.

Mulkay notes this combination of strong agreement with strong disagreement and perceives it as an exclusively written strategy (1985:210), but in oral as in written argument, a speaker can combine strong agreement with strong disagreement. More to the point, strong agreement must be asserted in any argument where strong disagreement will follow. The strategy is not an example of "blatant inconsistency" needing strategies to obscure it as Mulkay argues (221). Rather, it is an enabling mechanism, allowing disagreement to occur and proceed.

Having established through numerous linguistic devices a state of strong agreement between himself and Chomsky, Halliday turns to the "but" slot in his introduction. Appropriately, he commences this slot with *but*: "But I also get a sense that there's some **disagreement** between us, that you lay greater, more stress on control **within** the domains of each power." Halliday's strategy is to distance himself from the fact of disagreement as well as to place responsibility for that disagreement on Chomsky. Using here a composite verb of experience, "get a sense," which is resultative, Halliday places himself in the role of experiencer rather than agent of disagreement, which he would be were he to use the verb *agree* as he does in his initial "yes," slot. Use of the noun *disagreement*, instead of the verb *agree*, distances Halliday from the potential dispute. Disagreement is something Halliday experiences, not something he actively does. Thus, Halliday stresses "**disagreement**" as a means of marking important new information in the text, not as a form of emphasis. He subsequently elaborates upon that new information, further defining it in a noun clause which explicitly places Chomsky in the role of agent and therefore defining him as the source of the disagreement Halliday experiences: "that you lay greater, more stress on control **within** the domains of each power." Although this statement constitutes the first sally in the verbal debate between Chomsky and Halliday, Chomsky is in fact portrayed as the actor causing a rift between the two "friends." Halliday further stresses "**within**" since the preposition, as such, characterizes the main difference between their two stances. Where Halliday stresses conflicts **between** the two superpowers, Chomsky stresses conflicts **within** each empire, especially those within the United States. Stress on the preposition focuses attention on crucial, distinguishing new information, specifically, that which distinguishes Chomsky's position from Halliday's.

What Chomsky can do and say has been limited by Halliday's respective linguistic assignment of the roles of experiencer and agent, and, indeed, it is at all times limited by the need to preserve a social bond between the speakers while they are in the act of disagreement. There can be little appeal to an outside party or offence will be taken by one's co-participant, nor can there be much very strong articulation of disagreement without extensive preparation. At the commencement of his argument with Chomsky, Halliday chooses confrontation by selecting grammatical roles. He also employs stressed pronouns to indicate further the fact of a new separation between the disputants initially designated in conjunction as "you and I" or collectively as "we": "which I think in **your** view is largely mythical . . . whereas in **my** view there is of course there is this **element**." The two speakers are expressly distinguished rather than being one as before. Halliday has countered agreement with disagreement, but he has done so subtly through grammatical markers of interpersonal status rather than through use of any explicit and potentially disruptive lexemes. The disagreement between the two co-conversationalists is therefore free to continue.

As the assigned agent of disagreement, Chomsky is put in the position where he can do little except articulate his own thesis. He cannot at this point in the argument counterattack; he can only defend himself by stating his position as calmly and rationally as he is able. His main strategy is to adopt a very cool, rational persona as a means of counteracting the aggressive agentive role Halliday has given him. Chomsky commences the defence of his position by asserting and expressing his thesis in his own terms: "I think what the Soviet Union has wanted is essentially to be able to run their own dungeon without internal interference ah and to compete for influence in the Third World at targets of opportunity." Given that Halliday has characterized Chomsky grammatically as the source of the disagreement between them, Chomsky counters by using another experiential verb, "think," which serves also to convey rationality to its experiencer.

It is important to note that Chomsky also employs no semantic stress in the sentence cited above. He could easily have stressed the pronoun "I" as a means of distinguishing his position from Halliday's, or he could have stressed new information such as "dungeon" in the verb phrase "to run their own dungeon," but he does not. The complete absence of contrastive stress of any kind in this sentence speaks to Chomsky's use of a very modulated tone of voice, which in turn conveys cool, impartial rationality. Just as Halliday subtly establishes an agentive persona for Chomsky, no doubt hoping that Chomsky will fulfil it to the letter and be seen to be aggressive and over-defensive, Chomsky subtly establishes a new persona for himself, that of the impartial thinker. Moreover, not only does he recharacterize himself, but also he recharacterizes the Soviet Union, personifying the superpower through verb constructions as a jailer and not as an aggressor.

Chomsky maintains this rational persona by continuing to use experiential *I think* structures and by citing sources:

The United States is an **extremely** open society ah nothing like it in the world. We have **tons** and **tons** of documentary evidence and it's very very **explicit** the there was very careful and very explicit planning for the postwar world and it **didn't** in it it was supposed to be a world which was going to be **open** to penetration and exploitation uh by uh American-based uh ultimately international uh uh uh uh corporations.

Exploiting the additive syntax of oral speech, Chomsky argues that the openness of American society has resulted in the availability of data, which in turn indicates that there was an American master plan for world exploitation. His thought, therefore, is not subjective, but rationally governed by his exposure to "**tons** and **tons** of documentary evidence." He counters with a social fact, the openness of American society, against Halliday's personification of him as initiating argument, and through resultative relation of one clause to another, demonstrates that his thinking is socially governed and socially justified rather than aberrant. The openness of American society results in his knowledge of its "Grand Area" planning and, in turn, his view of events as he thinks/experiences them. Such a resultative analysis determined by oral speech undermines completely any assignment to Chomsky of the role of prime mover or first disputant in the argument. Moreover, since result clauses focus on concluding events or results rather than initial events, Chomsky is in fact deflecting responsibility from anyone and anything. He is not an agent actively challenging another authority but merely a recipient or beneficiary of an open society.

In conversation Chomsky is free to debate genuinely with Halliday only after he establishes a new role for himself through the grammatical and intonational means indicated above. The remainder of his turn is structured into characteristic "yes" and "but" slots. In his "yes" slot, he grants a weak agentive role to the Soviet Union by characterizing it as an **"impediment"** to American Grand Area planning. With Halliday he agrees that the Soviet Union has gotten in the way in the Third World. In keeping with such weak agreement Chomsky follows with a very moderate, non-adversarial statement of disagreement. Again he cannot afford to appear aggressive:

Uh uh but **what** *I think* **has happened** over the years is that the Cold War has increasingly come to serve have a certain functional utility for the superpowers. They can **use** it. It's useful for them and *I think* that's a **major** reason for its persistence. It's not a zero-sum game. It's not a competition in which one gains where the other loses. And *I think* you can see that by looking at the incidents of the Cold War. (my italics)

Chomsky commences his "but" slot with "but" as does Halliday; he then proceeds to recount his own experience of disagreement between Halliday and himself. Struggling initially to maintain the floor against Halliday's potential incursion into the discussion so that he can fulfil this slot and thus fully articulate where he differs from Halliday and not simply defend himself, Chomsky stresses the floor holders, **"Uh uh,"** marks the commencement of a new "con" topic through "but," and then states his own experience through an *I think* structure and its noun clause complement.

Having established his rights, Chomsky then articulates disagreement non-aggressively through use of the experiential construction *I think*, which takes as its noun complement what could be termed an analytic narrative: "but **what** I think **has happened** over the years is that the Cold War has increasingly come to serve, have a certain functional utility for the superpowers." Narrative interpenetrates oral argumentation just as it interpenetrates all other oral discourse forms and, of course, some written genres as well, though never as extensively. Chomsky marks the fact that he will embark on a narrative through stress on the noun clause **"what . . . has happened"** which as a speech act announces its commencement. Rather than be seen to disagree with Halliday, Chomsky chooses to tell a story. Of course, the study of history is precisely this kind of analytic storytelling. In argumentation, however, such storytelling has the strategic advantage of not appearing confrontational while simultaneously advancing a thesis and the persona of the speaker as that of one attentive to the facts.

In the narrative abstract which Chomsky provides for Halliday's benefit, he evaluates the past events he is about to recount, and in so doing, advances a thesis: "the Cold War has increasingly come to serve, have a certain functional utility for the superpowers." The analysis is resultative rather than causative. Result is marked in the present perfect form of the main verb *come*, which denotes a resultative state of recent completion. This resultative state marked by "has come" is complemented by the infinitive of purpose "to serve," which characterizes the state. Chomsky elaborates on this concept of service, "have a certain functional utility for the superpowers," and then proceeds to elaborate the thesis itself: "It's useful for them and I think that's a **major** reason for its persistence. It's not a zero-sum game. It's not a competition in which one gains where the other loses." In this elaboration upon his thesis, what is interesting argumentatively is Chomsky's transition from elaboration stated affirmatively to elaboration stated negatively. Thrice Chomsky conveys the affirmative point that the Cold War is advantageous to the superpowers; first through the infinitive "to serve," then through the noun "utility," and lastly through the adjective "useful." This elaboration serves to establish his thesis clearly in positive, non-confrontational terms. For purposes of non-confrontation Chomsky again employs an *I think* structure which is resultatively linked with his last affirmative evaluation: "It's useful for them and I think that's a **major** reason for its persistence." As a result that the Cold War is useful to the superpowers Chomsky experiences/thinks this reason "**major**." Stating his own experience of the facts, Chomsky is not explicitly disagreeing with anyone, but he is nonetheless strongly asserting his own evaluation, and so he places intonational stress on the adjective "**major**," which positively evaluates "reason."

This strong assertion of his own narrative thesis reinforced by repetition, intonational stress, and positively connoted evaluation is followed by implicit rejection of Halliday's thesis: "It's not a zero-sum game. It's not a competition in which one gains where the other loses. And I think you can see that by looking at the **incidents** of the Cold War." Chomsky follows a positive evaluation of his own thesis, stated resultatively, with an equally resultative rejection of Halliday's thesis that the Cold War is a "zero-sum game" and "a competition in which one gains where the other loses." Chomsky does not commence his "but" slot with any articulation of disagreement between himself and Halliday but logically and rationally *arrives at* implicit disagreement with Halliday through a series of result constructions. Importantly, the additive syntax of oral speech fosters such logical resultative argumentation.

Chomsky ends his analytic rejection of Halliday's thesis with a further *and* of result, which explicitly links this thesis to Halliday's, and he asserts through another use of experiential *think* that Halliday will change his mind as a result of Chomsky's narrative: "And I think you can see that by looking at the **incidents** of the Cold War." Chomsky ends his narrative abstract by asserting agreement since his narrative will logically result in a new vision of events for Halliday and thus an end to their disagreement and the argument at hand. Chomsky's promotion of agreement between himself and Halliday further undermines Halliday's representation of Chomsky as an agent who has initiated disagreement, for Chomsky now casts himself in the role of one who is prepared agentively through narrative to resolve disagreement.

Although oral argument permits and facilitates strong disagreement between parties, the social constraints of such debate do limit the possibilities of strong evaluation and so strong disagreement. Strong disagreement, then, is cautiously choreographed in oral speech, where it must be embedded in expressions of agreement both strong and weak. At any stage in the oral argument where personal meanings threaten to take centre stage entirely, both speakers back down from positions of strong disagreement. For example, at the commencement of one argument turn Chomsky states bluntly: "Well you see I think pa part of what you say is true but part of it in my view is simply **mystical**. The talk about about alternative social systems and **values** and so on I think is really mysticism." Only Chomsky's continuing use of experiential *I think* clauses modifies his strong negative evaluation of Halliday's analysis. Nonetheless, so struck by this evaluation is Halliday, that to halt the argument momentarily, he asks for clarification: "You say it's mystical to say the Soviet Union and United States?" Halliday is unable to complete his sentence, but the effect of this request for clarification is to make Chomsky modify the extreme negativity of his evaluation: "They're **different** but that's **not** the problem." Rather than directly evaluate Halliday's thesis, Chomsky reverts to a "yes, but" structure, which first acknowledges agreement and then asserts a counterposition: "that's **not** the problem." To assert that something is "**not** the problem" is much more moderate than to evaluate an argument as "**mystical**," for in doing so, one is not directly attacking the analytic competence of another speaker, but simply rejecting an analysis.

Having in a sense gone too far and thus momentarily halted debate, Chomsky continues to modify the negativity of his "but" debate slots by asserting stronger agreement with Halliday, reinforcing the social bond between them and permitting the continuation of the debate: "Um well, I agree with everything you've said and I think it's exactly half the story. And now let's turn to the other half." Chomsky creates for himself and Halliday two new personae, the professor and the student. Professorially, Chomsky portrays this telling of the other half of the story as a collective enterprise: Chomsky asks Halliday to let the two of them "turn to the other half." The request is rhetorical but nonetheless a social overture. Strategically, Chomsky continues to include Halliday as a partner in his analysis throughout the rest of his turn: "Here *we* have to ask what the American **goals** were. And those *we* know very well from the documentary record [my italics]." By including Halliday grammatically as a partner in his narrative analysis, Chomsky attempts to deflect the centrality of personal meanings in the debate and so more effectively argue his own position or present his own narrative of events. Pronominal reference in oral argument, then, has a key role to play for it consistently marks the degree of sociality between any two speakers, or, at least, the degree of desired sociality.

The oral debate ends when both parties assert agreement between themselves on one main point:

Chomsky: And what is the rivalry over?
Halliday: And and and
Chomsky: And **what** is the rivalry over?
Halliday: Not . . . the rivalry is over Soviet power and the increase of Soviet power.
Chomsky: Well the the
Halliday: **Both both** in terms of its geographical extension in the Third World and **also** in terms of this symbolic element
Chomsky: Hold it
Halliday: Of how strong is the Soviet Union.
Chomsky : But notice that this notice what we're **agreeing** on.
Halliday: **Yes.** Can can I go on to say that **what** we **do** agree on and this is where you and I would disagree with many of those in the peace movement is that the arms race while it does have an irrational element and while it is extremely dangerous is also in part motivated by rational political concerns.
Chomsky: Absolutely.

One can see from the shortness of the turns above that argument is disintegrating between Chomsky and Halliday. Chomsky has become the teacher asking his student central questions to which the student must respond. In effect Chomsky ends the discussion by focusing attention on a point of agreement between himself and Halliday: "But notice that this notice what we're **agreeing** on." Halliday emphatically acknowledges this agreement between them:

"**Yes**." Moreover, after requesting that he keep the floor, he further emphasizes that agreement by bonding himself and Chomsky together in one social group against those in another, the peace movement, thus employing the only third-party strategy in the entire argument, largely as a means of ending it. Halliday ends the argument not only in agreement with Chomsky but in solidarity with him against other theorists.

In written speech the strong dialogic nature of argument is modified to a much greater extent by the simple presence of a reader. Not only is the reader supplied orientation to respective differences between co-disputants, but also the reader is subtly given the role of supporter, friend, or judge of the writer. In his analysis of a collection of bio-chemists' letters concerned with the status of research in their field, Mulkay found that two-thirds of the disagreement expressed was prefaced by agreement (1985:213). Full incorporation of a "yes, but" structure in the written letters is explained by the fact that these scientists were responding directly to one another where disagreements occurred. However, Mulkay also found that in their letters the scientists were inclined to incorporate a third party into their specific two-party arguments. Thus, Mulkay notes an elegant strategy whereby a writer establishes solidarity with an outside source, so placing responsibility for disagreement on the party he or she is addressing. This strategy, as such, is not employed by either Chomsky or Halliday in their written arguments, but a similar one is. Both Halliday and Chomsky incorporate a third party, the reader, into their debate, either as a judge who is directly addressed or as an assigned sympathizer who is encouraged to side or identify with the writer's position. The reader may be given the notion that he or she is afforded both sides of any question, but, in fact, the reader is actively encouraged to reject any counterposition and embrace the writer's.

In his examination of the relationship between readers and writers, Ong points out that "the writer's audience is always a fiction":

What do we mean by saying the audience is a fiction? First, that the writer must construct in his imagination, clearly or vaguely, an audience cast in some sort of role—entertainment seekers, reflective sharers of experience (as those who listen to Conrad's Marlow), inhabitants of a lost and remembered world of prepubertal latency (readers of Tolkien's hobbit stories), and so on. Second, we mean that the audience must correspondingly fictionalize itself. A reader has to play the role in which the author has cast him, which seldom coincides with his role in the rest of actual life. (1977:60-1)

In particular, Ong analyses Hemingway's fictionalization of his audience, noting that Hemingway uses the definite article "as a special kind of qualifier" as well as the demonstrative pronoun *that* to characterize introductory information as old rather than as new: "In the late summer of that year we lived in a house in a village that looked across the river and the plain to the mountains" (from *A Farewell to Arms*). As Ong points out, Hemingway expects his reader to know the year, river, plain, and mountains: "The reader—every reader—is being cast in the role of a close companion of the writer" (63). The writer is not presenting new information but encouraging recall. As the writer's "companion-in-arms" and later "confidant," the reader is assigned a most "flattering role." As Ong notes, "Hemingway readers are encouraged to cultivate high self-esteem" (63).

What Ong says about the readers of literary narratives is no less true of the readers of other genres and, in particular, written argument, where the reader is assigned a very specific role. Readers as judges or sympathizers also cultivate high self-esteem, since as judges they are by definition elevated and as sympathizers align themselves with the superior position as defined by the writer. Depersonalization of the main opponent, which is another strategy used in written argument, not only further encourages personal solidarity between the writer and the reader but also permits strong and overt attack by the writer. These strategies may not win over all readers, but their purpose is nonetheless to do so and so to convert readers to an already established position or thesis. Written argumentation, then, corresponds to active persuasion of a very subtle sort.

In written argument, the writer has complete control over the assignment of interpersonal roles. For example, Chomsky aligns his reader with him against the "intellectuals," who he feels have sided with "the Western propaganda system." Halliday's approach is to isolate eight distinct "schools of thought" that he can analyse as inadequate as a means of prefacing articulation of his own position. Halliday relies heavily on an impersonal attributive syntax and the incorporation of the reader as judge and commences immediately with an orientation slot addressed directly to the reader:[2]

It might, at first sight, appear fruitless to search for underlying factors which shape the course of international relations: a system involving over one hundred and sixty states, many non-governmental forces, and several levels of interaction allows of no simple explanation. But if it is intellectually implausible to reduce world politics to being the expression of some single cause, a Hegelian essence or a *primum mobile*, it may be less outrageous to suggest that there are certain theoretical approaches which can, without undue simplification, provide coherent explanations of recent world history by highlighting deep trends within it.

What we note first in Halliday's prose is the extent to which personal meanings are stated impersonally. Halliday uses a very impersonal style to distance himself from a dispreferred status of disagreement rather than the strategy of passive experience he uses in oral debate. What we might call "style," which would not be an individual style so much as a general academic style, is used in this passage much as a "yes" slot is used in interactive argument. In the "yes" slot of oral debate, the speaker first agrees with his or her opponent to facilitate disagreement, whereas in his written text Halliday uses impersonal style to mask disagreement, while in fact, he is initiating it even in his orientation. In his first sentence, "It might, at first sight, appear fruitless to search for underlying factors which shape the course of international relations," Halliday employs extraposition which creates focus on the evaluation "fruitless" in the sentence. The modal "might" marks the text as an argument since Halliday is presenting an hypothesis to his reader who must judge or weigh the possibility presented, in this case that something is fruitless. However, *might* is a marker of weak argumentative stance. Halliday is attempting to achieve a very balanced and so nonconfrontational tone in his argumentative text. The verb "appear" and the phrase "on first sight" covertly mark the reader's participation in evaluation and thus assigned status as a judge in the text. The sentence, then, primarily concerns Halliday's evaluation of the reader's evaluation, but the sentence does not read as if it is about the interpersonal relations between writer and reader. There are no explicit markers of interpersonal status, such as pronouns, as there are in the oral argument between Halliday and Chomsky. Halliday's assignment of the role of a judge to the reader is obliquely achieved through an attributive syntax characteristic of written speech.

Equally oblique is the second instance of extraposition, which Halliday uses as a means of focusing attention on new evaluative information: "But if it is intellectually implausible to reduce world politics to being the expression of some single cause, a Hegelian essence or a *primum mobile*, it may be less outrageous to suggest that there are certain theoretical approaches which can, without undue simplification, provide coherent explanations of recent world history by highlighting deep trends within it." Again, Halliday uses an attributive syntax, NP Cop Comp, further complemented by an infinitive of purpose. The infinitive is the delayed and so focused "true" subject of the sentence. First Halliday himself marks through the conditional "if" that the evaluation or argument which is to follow is mild, only a possibility. The modifiers "intellectually implausible" are next supplied and, like the infinitive, focused in the sentence. The exact source of this evaluation is not explicitly stated, but since the construction "it is intellectually implausible" denotes a general state, it also denotes a general evaluation incorporating Halliday and his reader in one grouping. The infinitive of purpose "to reduce" marks the speaker's own negative evaluation of other analyses. However, none of the sources of these analyses is provided since, of course, the verbal *to reduce* marks activity but deletes information about tense and agency. Thus, an activity is evaluated negatively through negative connotation without reference to any agent or source of the activity.

In the main clause of the sentence Halliday employs the same syntax a third time to articulate his own position or thesis. He uses "may" to mark again his argument as one which is only possible, and so he continues in his role as non-confrontational arguer merely putting possibilities before his reader. However, the modifiers "less outrageous" simultaneously evaluate the opposition negatively and Halliday's own position positively. The reader's explicit status as judge is marked by the adverb "less," which is explicitly contrastive. The reader is in the position of a judge before whom Halliday places a potential contrast between what is outrageous and what is "less outrageous." If it is a possibility that one position is less outrageous than the other, as it was a possibility that a given activity is "intellectually implausible," then these possibilities must be considered by the reader, who is very clearly being directed toward one possibility rather than another. Further, in contrast to the negatively connoted infinitive "to reduce," which characterizes Halliday's evaluation of other positions, Halliday moderately presents his thesis by means of the infinitive "to suggest": "it may be less outrageous to suggest that there are certain theoretical approaches."

Halliday employs adjectival modifiers and relatives extensively. He conforms to the general syntactic properties of written speech. Yet, strangely, Halliday's writing, which exploits a high degree of adjectival evaluation, seems impersonal and, indeed, objective. Speaking about Halliday's book, one reviewer states "Fred Halliday's writing on international affairs has always been cool, clear and free of prejudice, and his latest book is no exception."[3] The perception of Halliday's writing as "cool, clear and free of prejudice" is extremely important to the persona Halliday wishes to construct for himself and the leverage such a view of him by the reader gives to his argument. The use of extraposition, modals, and infinitives together with modifiers allows Halliday to denigrate any counterposition strongly while seeming to be above the fray himself. In the passages above the markers of weak argument or assertion, "might" and "may," as well as the conditional "if," strategically invite the judgment of the reader as does characterization of his activity of presenting a thesis as "suggest[ing]." The writer appears moderate or "cool," rather than assertive and therefore disagreeable. Also, by employing constructions such as infinitives which delete agency, Halliday appears not to be attacking anyone directly, although he is doing precisely this through an attributive syntax and his extensive use of evaluators. Most important of all is his assignment of the role of judge to the reader. If Halliday is only "suggest[ing] that there are certain theoretical approaches which can, without undue simplification, provide coherent explanations" or suggesting possibilities through markers of speaker modality, "might" and "may," and the marker of condition "if," then the reader and not Halliday himself must ultimately judge the other positions. The responsibility for disagreement is not Halliday's but the reader's. The attributive syntax of written speech allows Halliday simultaneously to correlate markers of weak argumentative stance (*may, might, if*) with strong evaluation ("intellectually implausible") and so effect strong argument or evaluation while appearing mild and objective.

As Halliday proceeds with his written argumentation, he progressively abandons his initial moderate persona for one which is much more overt in its rejection of other positions. In his actual introduction to the eight schools of thought that he identifies he commences directly with evaluation:

It is remarkable how many of those who practice or comment upon international politics do, in fact, make assumptions about what its constituent elements are. These assumptions may be presented explicitly, and justified by reference to recent events, history or what is said to be common sense. They may be implicit, but known to both exponent and audience. At the risk of some condensation of the argument, it is possible to identify at least eight major schools of thought, each of which purports to offer an explanation of contemporary world politics and hence of why Cold War II began.

Addressing the reader directly, Halliday commences his introduction of his eight schools with the evaluation "remarkable," which is focused in the sentence. The reader is being directed by this evaluation to attend to a given "fact." What is "remarkable" according to Halliday is that "those who practice or comment upon international politics do, in fact, make assumptions about what its constituent elements are." Halliday orients his reader to the counterpositions of his opponents through use of a relative clause: "those who practice or comment upon international politics." Use of the demonstrative plural "those" denotes distant exophoric referents. These distant referents are subsequently defined and evaluated through the relative clause which modifies the unspecific deictic, "those." Halliday evaluates these distant agents as belonging to two groups, that which "practice[s]" and that which "comment[s] upon" international political events. Verbs rather than adjectives in the relative clause do the work of evaluation. Chomsky would be included in the group which "comment[s] upon" international politics since he is not by university training a political scientist as Halliday is. By characterizing the analysis of certain of his opponents as that of comment, Halliday is negatively evaluating that analysis as being less professional than his own. Indirectly, then, he establishes his own authority by virtue of its absence in other disputants.

More crucial negative evaluation, however, is supplied by Halliday in the verb construction "make assumptions." The composite verb *make assumptions* is more pejorative than the simple verb *assume*. To *assume* is only to hold a belief that a given set of circumstances exists, but to *make assumptions* is to construct actively incorrect notions, literally to *make* assumptions. Through his choice of *to make assumptions* rather than *to assume* Halliday heightens the agency of those he is opposing only to characterize more strongly such agents in negative terms. Halliday ends his overtly negative evaluation of the "eight major schools of thought" in his introduction of their main premises by explicitly stating that these schools, through what M.A.K. Halliday terms "grammatical metaphor," "purport" to offer a legitimate analysis. The verb *to purport* is of course negative in connotation since *to purport* is to make false claims for oneself or one's views.

By specific linguistic means, Halliday negatively evaluates the arguments of other theorists. Through a *those who* relative structure, which first simply refers or points outside Halliday's text and then defines that which is pointed to, Halliday characterizes other theorists in his own terms rather than their own. In this way, the relative clause, which is a fundamental feature of written speech, is used to convey to the reader new information that is specificatory.[4] By classing and naming other theorists, Halliday gives himself extensive power over their material. His use of the nominal composite verb *to make assumptions* and the verb *to purport* also defines or evaluates negatively other theorists, or, less specifically, "those who." More importantly, however, by using a specificatory relative clause, Halliday can characterize his opponents without having to identify them. The degree to which Halliday depersonalizes his opponents, denying them nominal substance, is the degree to which he feels free to disagree with them. As in his assignment of the role of judge for the reader, Halliday is not seen to disagree with anyone, although he embeds strong negative evaluation of counterpositions into his orientation.

Like Halliday, Chomsky also employs an attributive syntax in written argument as a strategy to incorporate negative evaluation. He also incorporates his reader as a judge. However, unlike Halliday, Chomsky uses the device of direct address to the reader throughout his argument, specifically when he summarizes the thesis closest to that of Halliday:

If there is indeed a renewal of superpower confrontation, it is likely to resemble the Old Cold War in certain respects but to be crucially different in others. *Consider* (my italics) first some likely similarities. The Cold War is generally described as a "zero-sum game" in which the gains of one antagonist equal the losses of the other. But this is a highly questionable interpretation. It would be more realistic to regard the Cold War system as a macabre dance of death in which the rulers of the superpowers mobilize their own populations to support harsh and brutal measures directed against victims within what they take to be their respective domains, where they are "protecting their legitimate interests." Appeal to the alleged threat of the powerful global enemy has proven to be a useful device for this purpose. In this respect, the Cold War has proven highly functional for the superpowers, which is one reason why it persists despite the prospect of mutual incineration if the system misbehaves, as sooner or later it very likely will.

In the passage above, Chomsky involves his reader directly through the imperative "Consider." Chomsky's reader is commanded to weigh not evaluated possibilities but "some likely similarities" between the Old and the New Cold War. Such an address engages the reader actively in the analysis Chomsky provides. The view that only oral speech involves a speaker and an audience in interaction is not supported by Chomsky's use of a direct imperative to his reader or by Halliday's more subtle involvement of the reader in judgmental evaluation. Writers address and involve their readers consistently and, of course, strategically in written argument.

After his use of an authoritative command to the reader to consider certain similarities between the Old and the New Cold War, Chomsky, like Halliday, provides orientation for his reader: "The

Chomsky, like Halliday, provides orientation for his reader: "The Cold War is generally described as a 'zero-sum game' in which the gains of one antagonist equal the losses of the other." Chomsky here uses an attributive syntax to characterize the position of his opposition and so provide "background" for his reader. The adverb "generally," which does the work in this sentence that an agent marker would do, indicates that the position is held by a majority of theorists who have examined this phenomenon. Through a passive construction, "is generally described," Chomsky subtly characterizes the analysis of these unspecified theorists as that of description only. Chomsky's further rejection of their description or thesis marked by "but" provides his evaluation of this counterposition: "But this is a highly questionable interpretation." Use of "questionable" is comparable to Halliday's extensive use of evaluators or of a specificatory relative. As an adjective derived from a verb, *questionable* permits subtle negative connotation without marking agency. Of course, the chief questioner is Chomsky, who by using the deagentized adjective in conjunction with the state *be* presents his evaluation as a general assertion and so not specific to him alone. As in Halliday's written orientation, Chomsky is equally mild and objective for the reader "Consider[ing]" the arguments being made. However, continuing to use an attributive syntax, he follows up weak argument with strong by using the modal *would*, a marker of strong evaluation and thus stronger argumentative stance: "It would be more realistic to regard the Cold War system as a macabre dance of death in which the rulers of the superpowers mobilize their own populations to support harsh and brutal measures directed against victims within what they take to be their respective domains, where they are 'protecting their legitimate interests.' "

The extent to which an attributive syntax plays a role in fostering evaluation as argument in Chomsky's text, as in Halliday's, can be seen in the following paragraph:

1   *It is unrealistic* to suppose that the propaganda *campaign was planned or centrally orchestrated* (my italics).
2   Rather, *it was conducted* on the basis of perceived self-interest, with the willing cooperation of the secular priesthood in conformity with traditional and quite intelligible tendencies towards service to the state (my italics).
3.   *Opportunities were seized and exploited* as they arose (my italics).

What is noticeable is that although the first three sentences of the paragraph superficially employ two main structures, extraposed "it" and a "passive" structure, all share the same underlying attribu-

tive syntax (NP Cop Comp) which facilitates evaluation. Equally attributive phrases or clauses follow. Thus, in the second sentence
three prepositional phrases ("on the basis of perceived self-interest,"
"with the willing cooperation of the secular priesthood," "in conformity with traditional and quite intelligible tendencies towards
service to the state") follow in sequence, each adverbially modifying
the passive verb phrase "was conducted." Information is not linear
or sequential as in right-directional structures (*John hit the ball*) but,
rather, exclusively left-directional and recursive.

We have here a strongly phenomenological view of events since
agency is entirely backgrounded in these left-directional (or back-
attributing) structures. As he defines and redefines the "campaign,"
which is his topic, Chomsky identifies the cause of the American
campaign: "it was conducted on the basis of perceived self-interest."
The analysis he presents is abstract. In his written argument
Chomsky could not be more unlike the narrator he becomes in oral
argument. The past participle "perceived," serving as a modifier to
"self-interest," allows an event or experience to be abstracted from
its personal context and incorporated into a noun phrase, "self-interest." Rather than stating that the Americans responsible for foreign
policy acted when they saw that certain situations were advantageous to them, Chomsky has abstracted "perceived self-interest" as
a motive or cause which serves to explain the foreign policy he
disagrees with. Not having access to a syntax which permits such
abstraction, Chomsky would not be able to isolate motives apart
from the agents who act. Chomsky follows up this phenomenological view of cause with an equally deagentive representation of effect: "Opportunities were seized and exploited as they arose."

Chomsky largely ignores specific agency until he has provided an
analysis of cause. However, he does mark agency in his subsequent
written argument, although he stresses less the role of propagandists and more that of "the secular priesthood" or "docile intellectuals" who have failed to identify and see through state propaganda as
Chomsky himself has:

The taking of the American hostages in Iran was also exploited, not without
cynicism, as a target of opportunity in the process of overcoming the "Vietnam syndrome." Shortly after the crisis erupted, the *New York Times* ran a
front-page story by *Hedrick Smith* headlined "Iran is Helping the U.S. to
Shed Fear of Intervening Abroad." *Smith* reported "an important shift of
attitudes" in Washington "that, many believe, will have a significant long-
term impact on the willingness of the United States to project its power in
the third world and to develop greater military capacities for protecting its

interests there." "We are moving away from our post-Vietnam reticence," one policymaker said. *Democratic National Chairman John White* stated that "we may have reached a turning point in our attitude toward ourselves, and that is a feeling that we have a right to protect legitimate American interests anywhere in the world." *Senator Frank Church* indicated support for military intervention in the Middle East "if our interests were threatened." The "lesson of Vietnam," *Smith* reports, is that we must be "more selective" in the use of military power with a more careful calculation of the costs to us, as we consider intervention "in such regions of potential American influence as the Middle East and the Caribbean." *Consider* what must be intended if our influence in these regions is regarded as only "potential." (my italics)

In this passage, quotation is taken from very specific speakers to explicate the negative evaluation Chomsky supplies: "The taking of the American hostages in Iran was also exploited, not without cynicism." Quotation, or the incorporation of others' speech into text, is used strategically by Chomsky as illustration. Thus, Chomsky quotes speakers such as Hedrick Smith and the Democratic National Chairman John White. Such quotation gives Chomsky's discussion some flavour of dialogic argument, but it is still Chomsky and not his co-conversationalists who govern the use and placement of their speech. Moreover, directing the reader to "Consider" as he does, Chomsky in large part governs the reader's response to the quotations he supplies. The reader is not only proffered the disagreement Chomsky supplies, but also made to focus upon it and so be actively involved in Chomsky's stance or position.

Dialogism is also strategically employed by Chomsky in a more covert manner. He represents the inner thoughts of the intellectuals whom he attacks by portraying them much as a novelist might—by using interior dialogue to portray a character:

But such programs require a docile and obedient population. It has therefore been imperative to overcome what is now called the "Vietnam syndrome," that is, the reluctance on the part of large sectors of the populations of the West to tolerate the programs of aggression, subversion, massacre, and brutal exploitation that constitute the actual historical experience of much of the Third World, faced with "Western humanism." In part as a consequence of the Indochina wars, dangerous feelings of sympathy for oppressed and suffering people developed in Western society. These had to be reversed and the image of Western benevolence restored, a difficult task, but one that was forthrightly addressed and carried out with great skill by the Western propaganda system.

Chomsky's use of evaluation here is quite evident, but it is also complex. In *The Dialogic Imagination* Bahktin has pointed out the role-playing competence of literary writers. Similarly, in the passage above, Chomsky first "speaks" as a propagandist for the American government. His characterization of this position is itself a form of evaluation, what Labov would call internal evaluation. He represents the American state as requiring "a docile and obedient population." This use of evaluation penetrates the persona of the American state and represents the true thoughts of what Chomsky calls "the Western propaganda system." The fact of a requirement for a "docile and obedient population" is an indirect negative evaluation of the system on Chomsky's part, for this is not *his* representation of the American people but that of the system.

Chomsky continues to characterize the opposition by representing its inner thoughts. He uses extraposition which focuses attention on the evaluation of his co-disputants: "It has therefore been imperative to overcome what is now called the "Vietnam syndrome,' that is, the reluctance on the part of large sectors of the population of the West to tolerate the programs of aggression, subversion, massacre, and brutal exploitation that constitute the actual historical experience of much of the Third World, faced with 'Western humanism.' " Via the extraposition Chomsky employs, the evaluator "imperative," which represents the system's evaluation, is focused as new information for Chomsky's reader. The "true" subject in the sentence, "to overcome what is now called the 'Vietnam syndrome,' " also focused as new information, specifies its purpose.

The reader is progressively made aware of what Western propagandists think through structures which present their evaluation of events as new information. There are two levels of evaluation in Chomsky's text: his own, supplied indirectly through the portrait he paints, and that of the propagandists whom he opposes. This system of evaluation is complicated further when Chomsky himself provides direct external evaluation: "In part as a consequence of the Indochina wars, dangerous feelings of sympathy for oppressed and suffering people developed in Western society." In this sentence Chomsky is no longer covertly presenting the views and beliefs of the propagandists in the United States. Rather, he is explaining to the reader the principal effect of the Vietnam War on the American people. The modifier "dangerous" represents the evaluation of the system, while Chomsky's own direct external evaluation is provided by the modifiers "oppressed and suffering," which indicate with whom Chomsky's sympathies lie. In one sentence Chomsky employs three levels of evaluation, simultaneously representing his own perceptions externally and internally in conjunction with those of the propagandists with whom he disagrees.

Chomsky also employs sarcasm as a form of external evaluation. It is evident in Chomsky's use of the term "Western humanism" in relation to his characterization of American foreign policy as consisting of "programs of aggression, subversion, massacre, and brutal exploitation." Since the two evaluations are in conflict, Chomsky points again through evaluation to the phenomenon of exploitative foreign policy, which is misrepresented as "humanistic."

CONCLUSION

As processing varieties, oral and written speech do not prevent speakers from exerting their own styles, but they do clearly delimit possibilities for meaning. In contrast to the direct and often bluntly adversarial Chomsky of written argument, that of oral argument is highly constrained and falls back primarily on a strategy of narration, requesting to tell the "story" as he sees it, suggesting that it will serve to unite Halliday with him in agreement. Halliday too is not permitted to keep the power of role assignment which initially gives him the upper hand in the oral debate. However, his use of an impersonal style and a depersonalization strategy in written argument, in conjunction with an attributive syntax which facilitates strong negative evaluation, serves to create for him an objective and "cool" persona and in turn advances his own difference hypothesis.

Overall strong disagreement is promoted in written argument, more so than in oral argument. The tripartite structure of written argument, which incorporates a reader as judge or sympathizer, alters the basic dialogic and egalitarian relations in oral argument. Oral argument is affected to a much greater extent by politeness phenomena and thus the degree to which interpersonal meaning constrains or determines ideational meaning. Oral argument cannot proceed unless sufficient social bonding is present throughout conversation, and it ceases if a balance between agreement and disagreement is not maintained by the co-disputants or if agreement is reached. Typically, oral argument achieves a unified structure by commencing with agreement and ending with agreement, thus verbally containing the disagreement that is voiced. The presence of a triad in written argument alters its nature radically. Using the reader as a sympathizer or judge, the writer may either depersonalize or otherwise characterize his or her co-disputant as a means of facilitating strong disagreement in the orientation slot of written argument. Such depersonalization or characterization is itself a form of argumentation since a co-disputant's position may be attacked in the course of such representation to the reader.

Syntactic processing is also a powerful influence in both forms of argument. Where an additive syntax fosters resultative analysis and so logical examination of events in sequence, an attributive syntax fosters evaluation, especially that which can be negative, as well as a phenomenological causative analysis of effects. By using variant forms of a basic Noun Phrase + Copula + Complement structure, the writer can integrate new information into a given written sentence through a form of nominal modification. Such an attributive syntax encourages the use of adjectives, relative clauses, and verbals. In addition, it encourages causal analysis hy promoting attention to depersonalized motives ("perceived self-interest") rather than the actions of personal agents. Conversely, there is little discussion of cause in oral argument. Chomsky, for example, consistently exploits or incorporates narrative into his oral argumentation. He requests the floor to tell the "story" as he sees it. Narrative is less threatening to a co-disputant argumentatively, and it also facilitates deductive reasoning whereby a conclusion can be arrived at logically.

Quotation can also be strategically used in written argument. Use of quotation in written argument to some extent permits the incorporation of an oral argument structure into written debate. Writers can quote a co-disputant, indicate some area of agreement, and then disagree. The letter-writers in Michael Mulkay's data used an orientation slot to represent their co-disputant's position and then first indicated partial agreement, after which they disagreed. Chomsky uses quotation in this way also, although he uses it primarily as a form of illustration of his own points.

A writer's acquisition through quotation of another writer's words alters the interpersonal relations between co-disputants. Quotation can either allow the incorporation of another writer into one's text as an authority to support argument, or it can serve as a means of representing another's argument in preface to attack, but in both cases the speech of one writer is integrated and becomes one with that of another. Moreover, strong attack is facilitated by the command one writer has over another's speech. Nonetheless, quotation also allows writing to be multi-vocal. The intertextuality of all writing is a by-product of the use of quotation, which permits the re-representation of preserved speech and so the expansion of argument not only among speakers but also over time.

Oral and written argument share the quality of interactive speech and the problem of representing disagreement between speakers, but in each medium interaction and disagreement are presented differently. The syntax of written speech encourages evaluation of a very complex kind as well as analysis and abstraction via left-attributive constructions. The written situation also predetermines the writer's use of the reader as a moderator or judge to whom appeal is made. The writer's co-disputant can be depersonalized through specificatory relatives or other devices or characterized strategically to facilitate strong disagreement or attack. As well, the writer can integrate the thoughts and ideas of other writers in his or her argument for strategic purposes. In contrast, the syntax of oral speech disallows the phenomenological abstraction found in written argument and emphasizes the interpersonal relations between speakers, who mark their roles through the degree of transitivity in verbs or through use of pronouns. The additive syntax of oral speech promotes resultative analysis of events, which, in combination with a narrative strategy, promotes argument that is deductive and logical rather than causative and evaluative. Each medium strongly influences argument and requires different linguistic and intellectual strategies to effect social disagreement.

7

Conclusion

In this examination of the effects of media across five recognized genres, I have attempted to determine the presence of consistent differentiation and so provide an accurate description of these media. Media should interact with genre in quite recognizable ways for there to be linguistic categorization of media as processing varieties. Confusion over the relationship between media and genre has caused some theorists to place media on a continuum of language use rather than to identify oral and written speech as distinct varieties and, more specifically, as processing varieties. However, genre and media are two distinct forms of variation in language, although genre is highly influenced by processing. There is a also very strong correlation between oral speech and narrative. Narrative invades all other genres, but more so and more significantly in oral speech than in written speech.

The primary focus of attention has long concerned differences in syntax between oral and written speech. Taking all sentences from all texts used in this study, I found marked differentiation only in the percentages for complex sentences; 20 per cent of all oral sentences are complex, while the number is 35 per cent for written sentences. This finding would seem to confirm Chafe's view that written speech is "integrated," supporting more subordination than oral speech, and disconfirm Halliday's characterization of written speech as "crystalline," supporting primarily simple sentence structures. However, simple sentences appear with almost comparable frequency in all the oral and written texts (49% oral; 45% written), so that Halliday's argument for the simplicity of written syntax is equally validated. Both theorists are, in fact, correct in their respective analyses of written speech. What the data show is that both oral and written speech favour simple sentence structures, while written speech alone seems to favour complex structures.

However, it is necessary to have a closer look. Only by examining the numerical breakdown for clause and phrase types can we glimpse a real syntactic profile of oral or written speech. For example, in adverb clauses there is a 5 per cent difference of frequency between the oral and written texts, while in noun clauses a 4 per cent difference obtains. Momentarily excluding relative clauses after Halliday, who sees them as "embedding devices," these percentages do not support his view that oral speech is more "choreographic" than written, and equally they do not support Chafe's view that written speech is more "integrated" than oral. The differentiation between noun and adverb clauses is not so great that either position concerning either variety is well supported. Hypotaxis is favoured in both oral and written speech and therefore is a feature of both. Yet, when we examine relative and co-ordinate clauses, we do see significant variation.

Beaman (1985) has argued that written speech favours the use of relative clauses to convey new information. However, in the narratives she examined, she also found that relative clauses were dominant not in written speech but in oral speech, which nonetheless conveyed more identificatory information through its use of relative clauses. Thus, Beaman found more relative clauses in oral speech, but they were clauses which conveyed not new but old information. Yet, although Beaman found a 19 per cent difference between use of oral and written identificatory relatives (conveying old information) in her study, I found only a 5 per cent difference. As well, I included in my analysis specificatory relative clauses, which add twelve percentage points to the relatives in oral speech conveying new information. Beaman's data[1] may have relied too heavily on a set of texts which were produced in response to researcher's requirements that speakers retell a story seen on film. Given that the main character in the film was a pear-picker, the identifying relative clause, "the man who's picking pears," may have been used with greater frequency than such a construction would be by a natural narrator composing his or her own narrative. Such identifying relative clauses were used only nine times orally and seven times in writing in my data, suggesting a quite limited use in both oral and written speech and further suggesting the dominant use of relative clauses as a linguistic means of conveying new information in texts.

If specificatory relative clauses, a sub-variety of informative relative clause, are taken into consideration, as well as data from across genres, a very different profile of relative clause use in oral and written speech from that found by Beaman, who examined non-naturally occurring narratives only, is produced. The total of all relative clauses across genres in this study was 219. There were 180 informative relative clauses (82%), 16 identificatory relatives (07%), and 23 specificatory relatives (11%). Together informative and specificatory relative clauses made a total of 203 (93%). Relative clauses, then, are primarily used to convey new information in texts. They are also primarily used in written texts (with 15 per cent more frequency) and not in oral texts as Beaman maintains.

To determine why relative clauses are more dominant in written speech, we need to examine the other major clause type which revealed significant differentiation in the oral and written data: co-ordinate clauses. Why should relative and co ordinate clauses alone differentiate clause types in oral and written texts? What is the relation between them or, more precisely, what is the function each serves but marks differently in the two varieties? Pawley and Syder's "one-clause-at-a-time constraint" explains in large part the additive composition of clauses in oral texts, and so the very high percentage of co-ordinate clauses (48%) in the oral data. As I have argued, this is less a constraint and more a processing tendency in oral clause formation. However, it does explain the low percentage of relative clauses in oral speech. A dominant additive strategy of composition does not easily permit the synthetic incorporation of one clause into another to allow modification of a given NP; new information is simply "added on" and proceeds in sequence with the NP topic continuing in subject slot. Yet, this constraint does permit the adding on of other subordinate clause types such as adverb and noun clauses since they are not, as Halliday maintains, "embedding devices." Thus, there is no significant variation in the oral and written data between frequency of adverb and noun clauses, which can be positioned before or after a main clause but are not integrated. This is equally the case with infinitive phrases, which also exhibit only a 4 per cent difference between the oral and written data.

Clearly, very different processing strategies are employed in the composition of oral and written sentences. The high frequency of adjectival relative clauses is paralleled with dominance of other adjectival structures such as attributive adjectives and participles as well as a nominal structure in the gerund. Conjoining phrases in the written data contrast almost exactly with co-ordinate clauses in the oral (45% conjoining phrases; 48% co-ordinate clauses). The integration which Chafe refers to, or the "crystalline" quality defined by Halliday and which I define as "synthetic," since a very complex kind of synthesis of information takes places in the use of these structures, characterizes written speech. The other major contrast between oral and written speech in the data above, a 37 per cent difference in frequency in the use of the passive voice in written texts, suggests equally that marked differences exist between the processing strategy employed in oral speech and that employed in written speech.

Although a "one-clause-at-a-time constraint" or tendency explains in large part the processing constraints in oral speech, it is necessary to consider further the character or nature of processing in written speech. The use written speech makes of visual gesture and marked word order as well as integrators such as relatives, attributive adjectives, conjoining phrases, participles, and gerunds suggests a synoptic syntax adapted to rapid processing by the eye, rather than one which, as Chafe (1982) maintains, is a product of more time for planning on the part of writers. In the data examined in this study, planning had no major impact on syntax; planned oral speech retained the general syntactic features of oral speech rather than taking on those of written speech. Planning cannot be a significant explanation for the use of relatives and other integrators unless it could be demonstrated that structures such as relatives are generated initially as simple sentences by a writer and then are reprocessed and integrated into written clauses. This procedure might be followed in some instances, but it cannot explain a 15 per cent difference in relative clause frequency, a 20 per cent difference in participle frequency, or a 120 per cent difference in use of attributive adjectives. Chafe's argument for planning would suggest that we first write as we speak and then rewrite and so reprocess sentences to create integration. Moreover, it would suggest that there is equivalence in meaning between the original and the processed clauses. This suggestion, however, is not confirmed in this study, particularly with regard to participles. Ultimately, what Chafe is arguing for is another variant of the translation hypothesis put forward by Cook-Gumperz and Gumperz (1981) and earlier by Bloomfield and de Saussure. But, cognitively, writers cannot be engaged in such translation, for were this so, more intellectual effort would be given to syntactic transformation than to expression of meaning.

We can look briefly at two parallel sentences taken from the data to examine underlying processing differences between oral and written syntax:

But the **first** thing that we're going to have to do if we're going to decide we're going to be **lovers** is you're going to have to develop your sense of **humour**, because my goodness people are going to treat you strangely and you're going to have to learn to **accept** it with a good **laugh**. (Oral exposition)

It seems to me that deep relating without joy, laughter, and a sense of humor is an impossibility. (Written exposition)

Both sentences employ a copula or equative syntax as a main structure, which is consistent with the fact that definition is the focus of discourse. What is noticeable in the oral sentence is the extent to which it is story-like and procedural: "the first **thing** that we're going to have to do." This main clause is then equated with a second main clause, "you're going to have to develop your sense of **humour**." Causation, expressed in the third clause, "because my goodness people are going to treat you strangely," follows. This oral sentence, composed of five clauses, is highly "choreographic" in Halliday's terms, but it exhibits, despite two subordinate clauses, a fundamental heuristic of sequential processing.

In the written sentence Buscaglia goes about things very differently. The gerund "deep relating" replaces the clause "the **first** thing that we're going to have to do if we're going to decide we're going to be **lovers**," while the phrase "without joy, laughter, and a sense of humor" replaces "you're going to have to develop your sense of **humour**." Information in the written sentence is left-directional, while it is right-directional in the oral sentence. In the written sentence new information is consistently back-attributed to the topic "deep relating" and also focused by the extraposition "it seems to me."

The strategies underlying oral and written syntactic composition reveal very different means of organizing and conveying information. The strong heuristic orientation to right-directional structures exploiting procedure, sequence, and thus narrative in oral syntax contrasts maximally with the attributive, left-directional structures in a written syntax supported lexically by abstract nominal verbals or nominalizations.

Differences in processing also profoundly affect discourse. This is evident in a number of ways, but most obviously in the way pseudo-narrative structures invade non-narrative discourse types. For example, in another set of parallel texts, background information is presented as pseudo-narration in the oral text, while it is presented as topically focused in the written:

In the old days when they began ah taking **care** of **herds** of **goat** and **cattle** and they would milk these creatures you see. When they'd leave the milk set about, **natural** yeasts in the air, bacteria in the air in the desert, would land in the milk and cause it to to ah **ferment** as ah **yogurt**. (Oral instruction)

Yogurt is probably the oldest cheese that we know. Originally it was discovered by nomads in the desert when natural yeasts that were present in the air landed in their milk products and preserved them. The yeasts or yogurts were saved and used to thicken and preserve more batches of milk. (Written instruction)

The presence of a "pseudo-narrative" clearly derives from the exploitation of right-directional structures in the oral text. A story is told about an unspecified "they" whose doings explain how yogurt was discovered. New information is coded in active verb predicates, and action proceeds in sequence from milking and leaving aside to bacterial landing and transformation of milk into yogurt. Agency is altered only in the switch from "they" to "bacteria."

In contrast, the written instruction employs left-directional attributive structures which promote ease of visual processing for a reader. The syntax of the clauses in the written text is remarkably simple. In the left-hand position of each clause, the topic yogurt, a referring expression, or a semantically related expression is employed. New information in right-hand position is ascribed to it, linked by a copula or auxiliary verb. Old thematic information is in left-hand position of each clause, while new rhematic information is in right-hand position. Mathesius (1975) refers to such a syntax as "objective" because it takes the reader or hearer's processing needs into consideration.[2] In a certain sense, then, we have not only what Mathesius calls an "objective" syntax, but also another type of "additive" syntax in the written text, since by using copula and passive structures the writer can conveniently add on new information to any defined topic in left-hand position. This feature is particularly important for a language such as English where readers process written texts from the left to the right, and it may explain why readers in English process information in this direction.[3]

However, it is noteworthy that old and new information as well as theme and rheme are conventionally placed in the oral text also. New information marked in the predicate of each clause complements that in the theme slot and information follows in sequence rather than accumulating to an original topic as it does in the written text. What differentiates the two texts is not communicative dynamism or functional sentence perspective, but the predominant direction of information, either back- or left-directed in the case of the written text or right-directed in the case of the oral. It is also clear that the selection of topic is related to the selection of syntax.

Whatever the full explanation may be, strong processing differences exist, with the effect that abstraction and topic-focusing are strongly evident in written texts while pseudo-narrative is evident in oral texts.

Discourse is also affected by the means of achieving cohesion in the two media. In oral speech, *and* is employed more than any other conjunction. Through conventional implicature, this conjunction has approximately eleven forces in English (sequence, result, contrast, condition, parallelism, addition, comment, similarity, purpose, simultaneity, emphasis), although sequence and result are the two most dominant. In all uses of *and* the second of two events in sequence is foregrounded; however, where result is inferenced, the second of any two or last of a series of clauses iconically follows action or event as consequence or result.

In contrast, written speech prefers a synthetic organization of clauses. Moreover, in contrast to *and*, left-branching participles in written speech can function as syntactic conjunctions having simultaneous or causal semantic force: *Running fast, I tripped over a hidden wire.* What participles create syntactically is an analytic correlation of related events. Precise information about time is lost, while information about the relation of events is gained. Through syntax English can express varying degrees of relatedness between events. However, an oral syntax generally conveys a loose relation of result or sequence: *I was running fast and I tripped over a hidden wire.* The conjunction *and* signals that the two events, running and tripping, are literally connected, and by conventional implicature, one event, tripping, results from the other, running. But running has not caused tripping to occur in this oral syntax; that is, tripping is a result of running; it is not a derived effect of a predetermined cause. Yet were one event to be "subordinated" to or integrated into another syntactically by means of modification and so lose information about time, bound relation or causativity would be expressed: *Running fast, I tripped over a hidden wire.* When a verb is transformed into an adjective, it continues to denote a given action or activity, but it also syntactically becomes incorporated with another event and event-time and creates either a meaning of simultaneity between two distinct events or a meaning of bound relation or cause. However, the greater the degree of syntactic incorporation of one event into another, the greater the degree of bound relation or causativity expressed. In left-hand position a participle can conventionally mark a precipitating cause which has as its derived effect the event in the main clause. Cause iconically precedes effect, just as in the oral syntax above action precedes result.

Such a syntax is not only "synthetic" but also "synoptic." Through the use of fronted participles, which causally connect one event to another, the reader's eye can process in one saccade or jerk information relating to two events. There is heightened processing efficiency in such reading that would not occur were an additive syntax employed, where two distinct clauses would require two or more saccades. Moreover, the greater the degree of synthesis, the easier processing is for the reader. However, such synthesis also results in the generation of altered meaning where cause and order are favoured over sequence and result.

Oral and written speech are not neutral transmitters of meaning but creators or co-creators of meaning. Cognitively, human speakers and writers determine ideational and interpersonal meaning at the same time as textual meaning. Content does not precede form, but rather it is co-produced with it and so is influenced by form, or more specifically, the processing varieties of oral and written speech. This co-production would be equally the case for signing. Genres, then, are heavily influenced by media, as this study shows. The right-directional, narrative structures that characterize oral speech invade all non-narrative genres. In narrative itself, access to left-directional structures produces very different perspectives on events in the written versions examined. This characteristic is important for interpretation of events, as can be seen in the history of Gunninute, where use of the passive marks Gunninute as an agent in the *by* phrase where he is characterized as a "Murderer." Through the force of this construction Gunninute's killing of a second packer is conceptually accommodated to his first:

1. *Another horse haser* of another outfit *was shot and killed* dead that forenoon also *by apparently the same Murderer,*

2.*who* by these terrible acts *proved or appeared to prove* that both *deeds had been committed by the same crackshot ability* (my italics). (Written narrative)

In contrast to this interpretation, which collapses two distinct actions into one type, the oral version presents a very different picture:

And **it seems** that on his way back into **Hazelton** there was a a **drover** or a **pack train man** running in a bunch of horses just coming out of a **side** road to the one that **Gunninute** was travelling on on his escape toward Babine and he saw this cloud of dust and he saw the man behind it and he **shot** him by mistake.

The additive syntax of oral speech enforces the pristine nature of events, disallowing interpenetration of one event by another. In contrast, written speech actually fosters such contamination, not only through the passive but also through an attributive syntax where information is consistently back-attributed to a preceding topic. There is no question that an attributive syntax fosters analysis and abstraction as we can see very clearly from the respective versions of oral and written description, but there can be other more troubling semantic effects as well. Thus, it is important to realize that neutrality is not a feature of media and that each imposes a semantic potential on genre.

Recognition of the non-neutrality of media, however, should not entail favourable characterization of one over the other. The written Gunninute text above is disturbing because it indicates how very differently the same speaker renders the past in each medium. I am convinced that the oral version represents events more accurately than the written, but both versions are nonetheless interpretations mediated by processing. To assert, as does Halliday, that written speech is decontextualized speech and so "puts distance between the act of meaning and its counterpart in the real world" (1987:78) is to assume that there can be absolute correlation between meaning and the world and that oral speech is somehow closer to that correlation than is written speech. Oral and written speech provide different perspectives on the world to the extent that each semantically affects discourse. The ability to abstract agency from events or transfer agency to nonanimate entities such as gates permits an analysis of events as processes. The abstraction of the animate is potentially disturbing, but it is through such a linguistic process that events or experiences can be seen and understood in bound relation to other events.

Not only information as ideational content but also information structures are differently treated in the two varieties. Halliday has argued that in English "Information choices, those concerned with given-new, are realized phonologically, by intonation features" (1976:175). More recently, he has stated that "whereas in written language there is a tendency to proceed lineally from the known to the informative since there is no resource in the writing system for expressing this kind of meaning, in spoken language there is a great deal of variation, as the speakers exploit the potential of tonicity to its full rhetorical effect" (1985:56). However, the tendency to proceed from known to unknown is a cognitive and linguistic strategy for information processing fundamental to both oral and written speech. As Leonard Scinto has pointed out,

We observe that the information focus, i.e. new information, is usually (a) noninitial, (b) nonanaphoric, and (c) occurs within the Rheme component of a textual element. On the other hand known information is usually (a) initial, (b) anaphoric, (c) often deleted by ellipsis (this is especially true in the case of spoken discourse), and (d) occurs in the Theme component of a textual element. (1978:180)

Scinto further quotes Weltner with regard to information theory:

The more unexpected a sign the greater its information. Its information approaches zero when the receiver can expect the sign with near certainty. In the restricted sense of information theory, information is a measure of the novelty value of the sign for the receiver. One may also consider information as a measure of the uncertainty of a situation, which will be removed by the occurrence of an event from the field of possible events.(1971:8)

In English known information precedes unknown information. A linguistic context of shared knowledge is provided syntactically before unknown or unexpected information with news value is presented to a listener or reader. Stress and intonation in oral speech are employed to reinforce this linear transition from known to unknown, but they are not themselves the principal means by which new information is conveyed. In oral speech, where theme and new information coincide syntactically, a device such as new-*this* is employed, or a comment word such as *well* or *o.k.*, or commonly an existential construction such as *there is*. Stress alone seldom marks information as new in marked initial location in a clause or sentence: *This guy John is Fred's friend. My brother John is Fred's friend. Well, John is Fred's friend. There is John who's Fred's friend.* In the sentences cited, *John* would be stressed in oral speech and so marked as new information. However, *John* would also most often be embedded in structures which serve to introduce or, in effect, announce the coming of new information to the listener. Even sentence-initially new information is most often preceded by old information or a device such as new-*this*, which notifies the listener that what follows is new and thus unexpected.

Written speech can also exploit linear processing to convey new information: *It is physics which is difficult.* Such an attributive syntax is used to focus new information. However, written speech can also exploit the gestural properties available to it by being recorded on a durable, flat and usually rectangular surface to convey information implicitly. Textual space, in contrast to verbal stress, can be employed in the treatment of old and new information. For example, using the spatial properties of the recording medium, the poet George Herbert wrote "Easter-wings," which iconically or visually represents the wings of an angel in two stanzas. Twentieth-century concrete poets have also experimented with visual gesture in poetry. Yet, visual gesture is not a poetic device but a part of the repertoire of written speech itself. Martin Starret uses a marked syntactic construction to convey specialized meaning for his reader:

From the Hudson's Bay pasturefield or from Joe Bowes's feed lot probably the most activity of the season would occur.

In this construction a prepositional phrase has been fronted and so thematized. Such a construction is an indirect speech act on the writer's part effecting perspective for the reader. The writer uses word order itself as a means of conveying specialized meaning. Marked word order is not uncommon in oral speech, but to the extent that written speech allows both reader and writer to see language, visual cues, including marked word order, are predominant features.

Capitalization and the fronting of imperatives can also be used in a genre such as written instruction to facilitate ease of visual processing. Visual cues such as capitalization and word placement on the page serve gesturally to give certain topics salience and, in turn, cue the reader to bring certain frames to bear on the reading of a given text. As well, written speech can exploit the spatial properties of the page and so frequently uses gestural short-hand to convey information. For example, a recipe is a conventionalized list. No information to the effect that the reader needs to go out and buy the items in the list is provided as it is in oral cooking instruction, where a teacher may also add information about where it is best to get certain foods or items used in cooking. In this sense written speech is close to sign language, which also exploits gesture.

Titles in written speech further exploit conventionalized "frames" or conventionalized gestures already and necessarily known to the reader. A new topic is generally announced in oral speech through explicit performative verbs, while in written speech new topics are announced through titles. In oral speech a speaker may state explicitly, "Today I'm gonna make cheese for you outa yogurt," or "You want the InDian story how that was . . . how it happened to be there or how she was created?" or "And there is **so** much stuff to **cover** if you're going to be a lover . . . There's so much tempting **stuff** to talk about." In written equivalents titles are used: "Yogurt and Cheese— Make Your Own," "Astace the Indian," "Loving Each Other In Joy."

The title is a written convention which has as its purpose to announce topics. The written title exploits placement on the page in conjunction with capitalization or bolding to "announce" a new topic, and so it simultaneously exploits textual space and the reader's incorporation of conventionalized "frames" into the text. The greater explicitness of written speech over oral speech is a fiction, for written speech uses visual gesture extensively in numerous conventional ways to effect meaning. So unconscious are most readers of the exploitation of marked word order, spatial placement and conventional frames that written discourse does, in fact, seem at all times explicit. Yet the visual medium of written speech relies on implicit visual information, which requires that the reader actively bring information to a text.

In genres such as exposition and instruction, where new information is by definition given prominence, reading and listening require considerable processing skill. Such genres linguistically manifest their increased attention to new information through structures which facilitate processing and retention of new information. In oral exposition a TRI (Term, Restatement, Illustration) pattern is used formulaicly. New information, which places great processing demands on a listener, is conveyed in a structure which is maximally redundant. A dual problem/solution pattern is more commonly used in written exposition. The superimposition of a solution frame on new information gives it the salience it requires to be effectively processed by a reader. This pattern is also employed in "The Legend of Gunninute" and in Martin Starret's process description of cattle driving. The prevalence of this pattern suggests a strong predisposition to dual structuring in written texts in all genres to facilitate information processing.

In instruction, where new information must not only be processed and understood but reduplicated, complex linguistic strategies are employed in both oral and written speech. Where lexical and syntactic repetition, stress, deixis, topic focusing, and cognitive association are all employed, sometimes separately and sometimes in conjunction, as a means of giving new information strong salience and thus memorability in oral instruction, titles, frames, and an attributive syntax are employed in written instruction. The marked difference in strategy results in marked differences in each instructional text, one being maximally long to accommodate lexical, syntactic and structural repetition, and the other being short because verbal and syntactic visual cues permit synthesis of visual and "non-visual" information.

Unlike ideational meaning and information structures, treatment of interpersonal meaning does not differentiate oral and written speech. Conventionally, oral speech is thought to be more contextualized and thus more exploitative of interpersonal meanings between speakers. In contrast, written speech is thought to be decontextualized and so distanced and impersonal. Thus, Wallace Chafe characterizes oral speech as "involved" and written speech as "detached." Chafe defines "involvement" in oral speech in terms of six major features: first person reference, reference to speaker's mental processes, monitoring of information flow, emphatic particles (*really*), fuzziness (*sort of*), and direct quotations. Few of Chafe's features have to do with "A speaker's involvement with his or her audience" (46). Certain features are not exclusive or even dominant in oral speech. For example, quotation is primarily a mnemonic written device. It is common in conversation for speakers to report the speech of others, but only written speech has the resources to effect true quotation. Quotation is extensively used in written exposition and argument and, as a feature, permits the important intertextuality of written discourse.

Neither *you know* nor *you see* are monitoring devices; they are linguistic means by which speakers can direct the attention of, or maintain good interpersonal relations with, other speakers. Commonly, oral speakers employ the device of *you know* as a means of involving their listeners, while writers more often employ the pronoun *we* for the same or a similar purpose. In exposition, where new information is conveyed, *you know* has the effect of marking new information as old and, through such marking, conveying new information as a form of aid to the memory. *You know*, for example, is used by Leo Buscaglia extensively before an audience of many thousands of people. In this context of situation this feature of oral conversation is clearly not a way to see if a listener has understood or followed a point in discussion. As a device *you know* is used more to facilitate the transfer of information than to check on its transmission. It also keeps speaker relations on an equivalent plane since information is theoretically shared rather than transferred. *We* has a similar purpose in written exposition since it can mark experience or background as shared between reader and writer. Importantly, it also promotes critical self-examination.

A feature of "involvement" such as "fuzziness" (*sort of, kind of*) is also not a feature of speaker involvement with audience but rather an indication of ongoing processing of information by a speaker. Moreover, whether a usage such as *and so on* should be termed "fuzzy" needs consideration. Chafe cites the following example: "(29a) schemes for striking, lifting, pushing, pulling, *and so on*."

There is nothing semantically or functionally very different about the oral usage *and so on* and the written usage *etc.* The speaker in the cited construction provides a very explicit list of activities. He or she makes the decision to conclude this listing process by indicating that other "schemes" are comparable by means of the phrase *and so on*. A speaker in written speech would use *etc.* The speaker has not been "fuzzy" but very explicit and has in turn made the decision to bring listing to an end by use of this colloquial device.[4]

Features such as "emphasis" and markers of "speaker's mental processes" also need consideration as features of involvement. Again taking examples from Chafe, four of the five he cites are clearly from oral narratives and all mark forms of external speaker evaluation:

(26a) and I had no idea I had gotten there.

(26b) but . . . I can recall . . . uh . . . a big undergraduate class that I had.

(26c) and I thought . . . am I alive?

(28b) And he got . . . really furious.

In each of the above examples the speaker is engaged in a personal narrative. Were Chafe comparing these narratives with written narratives, he should have found the first person pronoun used very much as it is in an oral narrative. Natural narratives, oral or written, are conventionally told in the first person; indeed, literary theorists speak of "first person narrative" as a separate narrative type. Thus, in Martin Starret's personal narrative, "The Boy in the Mirror," there is no marked difference in the use of the first person in the written and oral versions. However, Starret uses the first person infrequently in his oral and written process description's of cattle driving, despite the fact that his oral version is a pseudo-narrative. First person usage is, therefore, a feature of genre and not medium of expression. Equally, evaluators such as *really* are conventional in narratives. According to Labov, the presence of evaluators, more than any other factor, determines the adequacy or "tellability" of a narrative. *Really*, or more colloquially *real*, is a common evaluator in oral speech. Intensifiers such as *very* play an equivalent role in written narratives. Fundamentally, there is nothing remarkable about narrators attempting to involve their audiences through evaluation in either oral or written narration. Narrators must assert tellability at the outset of and during their story-telling or risk losing the floor to better narrators.

Involvement is a strategy in both oral and written discourse. In the sub-varieties of written instruction and argument especially, reader involvement is a marked feature. A recipe, for example, is a conventionalized set of commands directed to a reader. Directives can be used conventionally in written argument. Throughout his written argument, Chomsky directs his reader to "Consider" the information he is about to present. In written argument the writer requires readers to play the prestigious role of judge in relation to that of disputant. Whether through directives such as *consider* or through use of markers of speaker modality such as *might, may,* or *would,* readers are involved in evaluating the arguments presented to them.

Indeed, interpersonal relations between speaker/listener and writer/reader are most complex in the genre of argument. The listener in oral argument is in fact another co-disputant who does not give up his or her rights to the floor, while in written argument a tripartite relationship of writer, co-disputant(s), reader is set up. The necessary sociality of argument requires that disagreement between parties be constrained if it is to be continued. In oral argument speakers may use collective pronouns to involve their co-disputants in their position. Roles may be superimposed on speakers. In case grammar terms, one speaker may be assigned the role of experiencer of disagreement, while another is assigned the role of agent of disagreement. Further, one speaker may assign him—or herself the role of story-teller or teacher to counteract the perception that he or she is actively disagreeing with his or her co-conversationalist.

In written argument negative evaluation of a co-disputant may be made oblique through the use of impersonal extraposition or cleft constructions which simultaneously reduce the appearance of speaker participation while creating focus on the evaluation supplied. Very complex internal evaluation can also be supplied through a form of characterization of a co-disputant or a co-disputant's position. Impersonal objectivity is often a well-crafted illusion on the part of writers of argument; they have extensive means at their disposal to avoid appearing to evaluate while evaluating. Moreover, co-disputants can be depersonalized by the use of specificatory relative constructions, which simultaneously evaluate and define unnamed opponents: "those who comment on the Cold War." Written speech, like oral speech, has extensive resources for speaker evaluation as well as reader involvement. Detachment in written speech is primarily a strategy, as is reader involvement. Written speech, no more nor less than oral speech, is contextualized speech and so conveys interpersonal meaning, even that characterized by strategic detachment.

This discussion of naturally occurring parallel texts has distinguished different types of variety and analysed the complex interplay of meaning in texts and discourse. Looking at oral and written speech in the context of discourse permits a clearer understanding of how powerful these media are. Oral and written speech correspond to processing varieties and represent the very complex ways in which speakers organize and convey meaning syntagmatically in discourse. They are not neutral in their representation of the world, nor in their impact upon it. Of this fact we may be unconscious, but in such a state we fail to understand our own cognitive and social experience of language itself. I hope that the arguments that I have made will be taken up and further explored. We need to incorporate media analysis into information theory generally as well as into human cognition and memory theory. But above all, we need to see that oral and written media are fundamental and complex aspects of social linguistic expression and not simply adjuncts with neutral valuation.

Appendix: Texts Used

*The Boy in the Mirror/Oral Account of Martin Starret**

Orchard: If you were just waking up what would be the first thing you'd sort of see around?

Starret: The first thing waking up I'd notice the **shadow** from the lamp in the next **room** like in the **dining** room as it would throw **shadow** across if the door was open. If the door was closed it would be **all** dark in there.

Orchard: But what about in the morning though?

Starret: In the morning when you'd wake up you'd see the **sunlight** probably shining on the **window**. There was a vine a virginia creeper vine right there on that side I think or a hop vine something like that and part of the window that is the window from each side was was covered a little bit by the shade from these leaves. But the the full or the two-thirds of the light **part** that is the part that **omitted** the light was **clear**. And I remember the **sun** hitting it there and you'd wake up some mornings you wouldn't be dreaming till you'd just wake wide up and there's the sun. And I'd look around move the neck this side and the other and I'm **home**. **This** this is my **room** I would think.

Orchard: What what was on the walls?

Starret: And I'd look on on the **wall**. And the mirror'd be over there. There was an old fashioned **wash**stand with a **bowl** and a **picture** and so on. But there was a there was a **looking** glass and I remember that that looking glass because it had a a crooked **break** in it. It just **cracked** in the **glass** and then sometimes I'd **smile** a little because I'd remember **breaking** that glass as a very small boy.

After being away visiting my grandparents I returned one time and the **bed** had been **moved** in the room to right alongside of the **glass**, my mother

*Excerpts from the interview with Martin Starret are reprinted courtesy of the CBC. The interview is a record of the British Columbia Archives and Records Service.

not thinking anything a the **glass**'ed be broken. And uh and there were my **grandfather** had **brought** me **up** from Moodyville and he was **talking** to my **parents** in the room and and I looked over to **glass** here 'twas evening then and my I see a little **boy** in there and I said to my brother, "Who who's that what little boy is that there beside you?" "Oh, I don't know. You better **punch** him." So I **punched** the **glass** and that's how it got **cracked**. My mother came in to see what the noise's about an' and she said uh "Wh Why, what happened to the **mirror**?" "Oh Martin **punched** it." "Oh you shouldn't do **thât**. Look how you broke it." She didn't whip me or anything. I said I said I said "Will **told** me to punch it." So I got let out and he was **told** not to **tell** me to do things like that any more.

The Boy in the Mirror/Written Account of Martin Slurret

Upon arriving at Silvervale we were greeted by Father and Mother who were busy at milking time. Being evening we were at once taken into the house where we enjoyed a belated meal, and I was undressed and put into my accustomed bed with my Brother Willie. We were left alone with the bedroom door shut; we could hear our elders conversing in the next room. Our bedroom appeared familiar to me except that our bed had been moved around to a different side of the room so the large old fashioned mirror which hung on the wall and within easy reach was reflecting our likenesses, and the long summer evening gave ample light to show our every movement and detail.

This was the first mirror I have any recollection of looking at, and I became interested in the antics of the little boy reflected on the glass. I asked Willie who that boy was, and he said, "Punch him." This I did and the mirror cracked almost vertically, from top to bottom from the impact of the blow.

Hearing the unusual noise, Mother came in to investigate. When she noticed the cracked mirror, she asked Willie how it had happened and he said, "I told Martin to punch the boy in the glass." Mother told both of us not to touch the glass again and giving my Brother a spank on his barebottom, Mother went out and closed the door again. No doubt I had done something very wrong, but somehow Mother knew Willie was at the bottom of it, and would have chastized both of us plenty, only she had important company, and wanted only quietness.

However the unexpected act on my part, and the warning I received at the time had a tendency to not do always as others advised me to, and also that mirrors were easily broken, a lifelong lesson, as I have not punched any more more mirrors from that day to this.

The Story of Gunninute/Oral Account of Martin Starret

In the fall of nine ss hundred and **seven** I was working in the Whitworth ranch in the Skagit close to the international **border** and a man came to work on that ranch name of Bob **Hume**. He told me about Cataline the packer and he told me about this **Gunninute** the outlaw who who had **killed** these two men at **Hazeltown** and who was out in hiding in the **mountains**. They said the police'll get 'em he can't get **away**. Course he didn't get away but he was **safe** just the same. And ah **he** said that this man had been drinking out at **Two Mile** out a Hazeltown. That's as close as the pack trains camped to town Two Mile little flat and there was a creek running through. And morning after a **drunk** of some kind he'd shot this **packer** and then he'd gone home and shot some of his horses. He only took one or two with him and the dogs I think he left with his wife. His wife **stayed** there. And then he came **back** toward Hazeltown to **get** out to Babine on the Babine trail ˆ to get over to Takla Lake and then **up** Takla Lake and **up** the Driftwood River to a tributary of the **Skeena** up in there ˆ the **Sustut** near Bear Lake. That's where he was heading for Bear Lake or old Fort Connolly north of 56° somewhere. And **it seems** that on his way back into **Hazelton** there was a a **drover** or a **pack train man** running in a bunch of horses just coming out of a **side** road to the one that **Gunninute** was travelling on on his escape toward Babine and he saw this cloud of dust and he saw the man behind it and he **shot** him by mistake. He didn't mean to shoot that man at all he just on alert and he thought that that man was after him and he shot him. That was accident pure accident.

Two years after I went to that country and Bill ˆ **Hamilton** told me **the man** he murdered at Two Mile the name was Alex McIntosh and he was working on a **pack** train. I don't know whose pack train it was Charston or Barrett's or who it was. It wasn't it wasn't **Cataline's** train because Cataline always had a Mongolian crew Chinese crew. And this Bill Hamilton was a a packer along with McIntosh and **he said** that he and this Alex McIntosh was sleeping in the same **tent** and in the morning they got up and built a fire outside to keep the mosquitoes away and to kinda **cook** breakfast while the horses were being brought in and this Indian came along and took a shot at 'em and killed them right there. He had a **grievance**. It seems they'd been mixing up the night before drinking and something to do with this Gunninute's wife. But that's the gist of it that he knew this McIntosh well. He's just slept with him **that night** in those blankets together in **that tent** and the next morning he was **killed** and they they had to bury him before they went out on that ˆ expedition of the **pack** train and that was that and told me how many **years** ago it was and all about it. And my uncle C.V. Smith of Hazeltown was a fur trader at that time then. **He** said that this fellow that was killed deserved killing. He says, "I sympathize with **the Indian**. I don't believe in any these people imposing on **the Indians** at all." He said, "I think he had it **coming**. That's **my** opinion of it." But of course he didn't say it **out loud** because this Alex McIntosh had a whole lot of brothers in Hazeltown and **relations**.

And ah after that I was making a trip from Babine across to Hazelton in **January**. Followed the river road on the ice. And I stopped at what they called the half way place. They called it **MacKenzie's**. He had a white name. An Indian with a white name. He had a little **chunk** of land there and a few **cattle** a couple of **horses** and a **barn** and so on. He stayed there all year round. It was his trapping ground in fact. Stayed there over night ^ and there was a **toboggan** in there from Babine. He was moving freight from the Hudson's Bay. He'd just come in from Hazelton. He had a young kid with him to go ahead o the dogs and help him make **camp** and **cook** and one thing and another. ^ We were in there ^ **talking**. One of the dogs barked outside Bow wow wow wow wow and these Indians looked at one another. And I said, "What the heck's going on out there? I'm the last man in tonight." I was about an hour or two after dark I'd come in then. "Oh," he says, "Maybe **Simon**." I says, "Simon?" I says, "Simon Gunninute?" "Maybe, alltime he come here, somewhere. Nobody know. Maybe just he walk trail. He go now. Maybe he go Hazeltown." "Tonight," he said. Well, that's the way it was ^ in that country. They say, "**Maybe** Simon." They wouldn't afraid to say that. They seemed to know Simon was perfectly **safe**.

Then a few years after that I was talking to Father Coccola the **missionary** in that country and he said ah "I saw Gunninute," he said, "when I was up at Bear Lake." He said, "I told him to give himself up." He said, "The the witnesses are dead." He says, "I don't think you could get anything on him now. I told him to give himself up." He says, "I, I don't doubt a bit that that he will. He said he would this fall or after he got this fall hunting that he'd go down and give himself **up** because he didn't like living this way in the **woods** and somebody else selling his **fur** for him that he'd **catch**. He wasn't getting the **right** money for his **fur** and he wasn't associating in **town** with the **people** like he wanted to." And he said, "I think that's the way it'll **be**." And I heard afterward I was up a Bear Lake a few months after and an Indian in that **village**, Stikine William we called him, he said uh "Simon come back now. He bin **New Westminster** he callim that town. And he stop that scoocum house maybe ah maybe one month. And he lettim go. He home now **Kispiox** he stop somewhere **Kispiox** that's that's he stop **now**." I said, "What did he see down at Westminster?" "Oh," he says, "that white man business not much good. He seeim that **hangum man** that makes **snare** his neck hangum up **rope**. And he said that man stand up somewhere and and fall down that door, man fall down and his **tongue** come out. He said just like **bear** hangum **snare**. He said too much no good. **Eye** too jump out, he said, too bad." "Oh my," he says, "that Simon he don't want that business." "Oh he come back now." "No **hangum**," he said, "that government." "No killum Simon. He allight now." So they must have let him see that **hanging** and scared him good and plenty. Anyway he was a pretty good citizen after. I met him some years afterward in Kispiox. Bought fur from him in fact.

Story of Gunninute/Written Account of Martin Starret

During this season 1907 at Two Mile, the first camp out of Hazelton, a horse wrangler named Alex McIntosh, a half breed, native of Hazelton who was working with one of the most prominant trains, was shot and killed dead early one morning while out herding in the pack animals from night grazing grounds to Two Mile Campground, where the cargo had been placed the previous evening. Another horse haser of another outfit was shot and killed dead that forenoon also by apparently the same Murderer, who by these terrible acts proved or appeared to prove that both deeds had been committed by the same crackshot ability.

A BC Police Constable named James E. Kirby formally from Port Essington Detachment, had reason to believe these two murders had been committed by a Kispiox native named Simon Gunninute, a young capable Indian not only being very capable but also of good repute.

Moccasin Telegraph soon spread the ill news over most of the Carrier Indian domain, Gunninute being a Get-ik-shan (man of the river [Skeena River] Skeena, not a Carrier) by some almost unbelievable source word spread of the tragedy to Ulgatsha to Yukootche, Stuart Lake, to Stella, Cheslatta, Tetachuck Crossing also Kiskagas. Native Telegraph travels fast and far in one day only most of the countryside knew Simon Gunninute had in the forenoon of the eventful day ridden to his home and shot almost all his pack horses and all his train dogs and alone by a round about way had succeeded in dodging the Police Road block and hit the trail to Fort Babine mounted on his best saddle horse and the then capable Police had as much chance of catching him as a mountain Goat which may have been seen on the mountainside the week before last, as so it proved as Gunninute was never found or captured in his vast wilderness domain, from Kispiox North to Telegraph Creek or nearly so thence West to the upper Skeena Waters and East to the Driftood Valley whose waters head near Fort Connelly or Bear Lake. The Police accompanied by an Indian tracker who was acting as a guide also and a competent Whiteman as Deputy once got within a quarter mile of Gunninute's temporary Beaver camp one forenoon they were traversing through a scrub willow swamp with pack dogs at heel, only a Jackpine ridge was now separating the quarry from the Lawmen, when the Indian guide held a hand up as caution to proceed carefully and without noise, the Officer in charge of the little company looked to his weapons to make sure all was in readiness in case Gunninute refused arrest, only a few steps more and somehow by accident or otherwise his rifle discharged in to the ground and the ensuing report echoed from side to side of little Valley.

At this stage of the game everyone stopped and again bent forward and slowly worked his way with more alertness and caution. After gaining the far edge of the Jackpine ridge they had recently crossed the party looked down on a small camp, in which a middle aged Indian woman was busily engaged in making a small meshed gill net for netting fish. Three small native childred were also in this small camp appearently doing nothing. Upon questioning the woman the Guide could only gather that Simon Gunnanute had left early that morning to set Beaver traps in another valley to the North. The Police Officer reasoned that the accidental discharge of his rifle had acted as an alarm and the alerted Indian had snatched up a few neccosities and hot footed out to safer climes. The BC Police unlike the Royal Canadian MP of today of whom are so hampered with restrictions their hands appear to be tied, as the saying goes, and cannot put much law force into action in most intricate cases, entirely different to the Old Canadian NorthWest Mounted Police, who made it a point to inveribly get his man. Today the Law Officer is in danger of the man getting him, and it may not be a full grown man at that. Such is life today!

Astuce (Carrier Creation Myth)/Oral Account of Martin Starret

Orchard: You were talking about the Indian story of the Caribou Hide of that country up in there where the Skeena starts? What about that country there where those rivers start?

Starret: Well, you want the InDîan story the Indian legend how that was how it happened to be there or how she was created?

Orchard: Yes, if you know that, yes, but what is the country in the first place? How would you describe it?

Starret: Well, now I'm telling you what the Indians told me and that was not one Indian but **several** and from two **sections** like from the Babine ^ tribe and from the Stuart **lakers**. They're both **Carriers** but they're kinda cousins you know, different **clans** like. One of them told me I remember the the other one was just ^ **partly** the same thing that ah **years** ago before there wasn't they didn't know anything about any white man. They **always** knew about a supreme a supreme being the Indians in that country and they differ a whole lot from the Indians in the in the southern states like the Navaho tho the Apaches those gentlemen down there. They only believed in **one** supreme being one god. And it seems ^ **they** credit the country like of being created by **that** person. Now, I suppose they had to use their imagination a lot. Although when when it was handed down from generation to generation it it seemed as a **fact** to **them**.

Now there were a **family** of Indians just one family who lived in a remote part **somewhere near** the top near of the summit of the **Skeena Stikine Fraser** watershed way up north of 57° somewhere.

Orchard: Not the Fraser; the Nass, and the Findlay

Starret: The Nass and the Findlay

Orchard: And the Bell-Irving

Starret: Yah that's Peace waters. Yes and the Bell-Irving. It was way up on top there a family lived and they set snares and caught animals and had fish nets. It seems they used to make the fish nets out of **nettle** roots which were very effective. They seemed to be **strong**. I I have read it in the Hudson Bay write-up of that country. The Indians had **nets** before and they tied them with that Weaver's knot just the same as we do nowadays the same knot practically and they used nettle roots in place of ah **hemp** or or ah salmon twine which was made of made of **linen**thread. Didn't have any of that thread then. But anyway they existed way up in there. And the way the story starts (long pause)

Well the ah there was an Indian maiden went for a a drink of water at a **spring**. It wasn't a creek it was a **spring** a a a spring that comes out of the ground. Pure supposed to be **pure** water. There's a fact the springs almost are in that country. Water almost always pure ˆ in that mountain country. And she had a **birch bark** cup or a bowl of some kind. It's birch bark sewed together in such a manner that it'll hold water. And she went to get a drink of water. She dipped in the spring and had this vessel almost full of water but she noticed that there was a a piece of **moss** had come from the bottom or some foreign substance and a small piece of dirt and she put her fingers in and tried to throw it out and it eluded always. You'd try 'an get it you know and you just couldn't get her fingers on it. And the Indian said after hundred times. Instead of dipping for some more water she was thirsty and she drank the whole thing. He said a hundred times well it might have been sixty times or fifty times. Anyway she got tired of trying to get it and she didn't think it was worthwhile so she **drank** it. This this little piece of **foreign** I don't know some kind of dirt or moss or something it wasn't it wasn't any **bug** or anything alive and she swallowed this. Gee whiz afterwards she became became **pregnant** so the story goes. She gave birth to a baby **boy** within a year. And uh this boy showed remarkable intelligence and was built strong physically and everything and she thought an awful lot of this baby boy and she named him **Astace** ASTACE or something like that so the story goes.

And he grew up and when he was in his teens his middle teens I suppose he got to **wander** farther from home and he had a little **bow** and **arrow** and he'd go shootin' grouse and so on maybe catching a few fish. And ah **men** don't ever do very much **work** in the Indian tribes. The **women** do most of the work. The men do most of the **bossing**. Course they go out and do the hunting and hardship or sleeping without **blankets** and **cold** and getting **wet**, all that part of it.

But uh **this** feller went one day and he got a lot of this ah rôots this nettle root. It was in the **spring** of the year and the **swans** had congregated in a little lake. And he'd get this here nettle root into into into a lot. Well you'd call them **pegging** strings now if it was if you were hogtying **calves** in a **roundup** or something like that er for **branding** in a in a **cowboy** country. They were I guess I guess they were pegging strings. His idea was to swim up under the water come up under these swans and tie their **feet** together and then take them into the land and **kill** them. He was smart enough he could come under the water like an otter and just come up. They were **trained** that way those days. A swan wasn't very **wild**; they were rather a tame animal, **foolish** in a way. They'll look at you way more than a goose will or a duck.

Well he he must of got three or four of these tying and tied together and somehow or another when he tried to drag them ashore he wasn't heavy enough. ˆ The swans were **heavier** than **he** was. And so they started to **fly** and he hung on and they lifted him right above the right above the lake and carried him above the tree tops and **landed** him right on the edge of the cloud so the story goes. It was likely on it may have been a little **hill** top or **mountain** top. There must have been **some** land or those people couldn't have lived there. I can't understand that. That isn't **clear** to me.

But anyway when he got on this cloud he sât **down**. He was sitting on the edge of the **cloud** so the Indian told me. And when I questioned him closely about the facts of this he couldn't tell me. Well, that's the way it was told to him. So he sat on this cloud and pretty soon it started to **rain**. And by some reason or other he hada **cup** or a **basket**. The Indian told me a **birchbark basket**. He was carrying it around like like you'd carry a **powder** horn or something. He's carrying this. And he happened to have it when he sat on this cloud and he waited till it **rained** and he held this to get the water. And that got **brim** full of water and when it was full, the rain just about stopped and this Astace straightened up and he walked the cloud and he saw he was on top. And he was inspired in some way or some unknown power and he walked in a kind of a **half** circle around put it carried this in the crook of his left **hand** this this vessel of water and he **sprinkled** the water right out the same as a a **sower** many centuries ago would a like in the Bible times would have sowed seed on the land or **corn** barley or anything like that. And he he threw this water and wherever that drop would hit was a **lake**. And then a little stream started there and she flowed down. And that was supposed to been the head of the **Nass** and the **Skeena** and the ˆ and the ˆ where's that Fort Graham river what do you call that ˆ **Finlay**. That was Peace River waters. The **Turnagain** was the head of the Skeena.The **Bell-Irving** went down into the Nass too. And then the Skeena up in there somewhere the Sustut or some of those she came down the other way.

And he walked this circle round like and then he followed **down** hill away. He didn't want to be up anymore and he followed down till he got **tired** and he was throwing water all the time, for **hours** according to the way the story goes. And when he got down near Spokeshoot which is Port Essington he **tripped** and fell down and the water all spilled. That formed the salt water. That was the Indian story how this world was created according to the **Carrier** legend.

You understand they knew of no ˆ other place or town in the distance other than **Winnipeg** where the Hudson's Bay and the had brought supplies into the country. **They** didn't know anything about Ottawa or Toronto or **England** otherwise than an Englishman was a King George Man. They didn't know that it was across a body of water to get it and they didn't know where the Hudson's Bay was. All they knew was just that little little hell of their own there, that little neck of the woods up there the top of the waters, beginning of the waters. Well that's how they imagined that or how they figured out this world was **created** as it was told me.

Well, when Astace fell down there he slept a long long time before he got up again. He was **tired** and in recovering himself he walked back on this land and up and he settled somewhere up in that Carrier country **way** up in there, Caribou Hide or Medicine **Dan** or some of those places. I guess the Taltan some of the Taltan tribe were his descendants and some of the Carrier, some of the Sickanee and the Sickanee chief river to form the Fort Nelson and so on. His name was **Astace**. Beyond that I'm **just** telling you as it was told me. I don't know anything more about it.

Astace The Indian/Written Account of Martin Starret

Many hundreds of years ago there lived an Indian beyond the place now called Winnipeg. All was space to the north and west of this point. To an Indian lying is a virtue. This man, like other Indians, was very dirty. No doubt he was clever and what was of still more importance, he was able to impress on other Indians that he was smarter than they were. He was also ambitious, more so than others of his tribe. This territory in which he was reared seemed too small for him, and he longed for a new world or country ... something entirely his own ... where he could hold despotic sway. Being very proud like most aborigines, he reasoned that he was much superior in every way, shape, and form to every other man in the tribe or even in the world.

At the time this story commences Astace was a young man of about twenty-five years of age. He was mean, a liar and a thief and an all round rogue generally; but, as has been mentioned, the vicinity in which he lived seemed too small for him. He longed for expansion, and to be great in the eyes of the other young people of his tribe. Astace was fleet of foot; in a race he could give his opponents a mile start, overtake them in a few minutes, and be lost to sight inside the hour without apparent effort. He was slightly over six feet tall, erect of carriage, with long black hair, coarse like a horse's mane which he wore parted almost in the centre of his head. He had a hard, cunning, hatchet face with typical high cheekbones and sharp, cruel, small black eyes; a somewhat prominent nose, straight mouth with jaws resembling a steel trap, and a very determined, strong chin. His brow was high but narrow . . . altogether a mean looking customer to meet on a dark night. His body was strongly constructed with broad shoulders, a small waist and legs and hips built like those of a long distance runner whose every move showed capability of great speed and endurance. The arms were long and, while standing loosely at his sides, the finger tips reached almost to his knees. Astace was inclined to be lacking in sympathy and mean to anyone who happened to be sick, blind or helpless, treating little children cruelly . . . pulling their hair or stepping on their toes if they happened to be standing in his path. He would often go out of his way to kick a dog in the stomach to hear it yelp. In fact, he had no love for anyone but himself. He was kicked out and practically banished from his tribe.

One evening in the early spring, previous to a thunderstorm, Astace climbed to the highest hill west of the village where his people dwelt, and approaching a birch tree, he took from his girdle a flint knife with which he cut a portion of bark from the tree. A little further off there was a spruce tree; digging down into the ground, he took some of the small roots from this tree and with this material he commenced to fashion a rude basket. This completed, Astace's next move was to make it watertight, or as nearly so as possible, and in this endeavour he went to a large balsam tree from which he extracted pitch from the blister in the bark. The pitch thus obtained was smeared over the seams in the basket. Bear in mind that Astace was not at all particular about keeping this balsam pitch from getting on his clothes. The mere fact of smelling like a balsam tree did not worry him. His next move was to fasten a support strap to his basket, which acted as a sort of bail, he put the strap over his right shoulder allowing the basket to be carried firmly under his left arm.

So occupied had Astace been in the construction of his basket, that he had not noticed the immensity of the dark cloud which had been forming close at hand during the past half hour. Astace was now ready so he seated himself comfortably on the boulder and waited for the storm to burst.

Soon thunder began to rumble in the distance accompanied by frequent lightning flashes. A breeze sprung up from the south, which, as the minutes passed, gradually increased to violence. Rain started to fall, and Astace, still sitting leisurely on the rock, drew his knees up before him and placing the basket right side up on his lap, held it in that position so as to catch the raindrops which were now falling thick and fast. The twilight darkened to night very quickly. The storm rose behind him to a gale which increased in volume. His long hair was whipping out from his head in the wind. Before half an hour had elapsed, Astace's basket was filled with rain water and the dark cloud descended lower and lower till the tip of it was even with and almost touched his feet. He realized that the moment had come for the great adventure which he had planned during the long winter months that he had just lived through.

Astace rose to his feet with a grim, triumphant smile on his lips. How he longed at this moment for the smiling glances of the fair maidens of the village he had left behind him down in the valley, for Astace, like all other Indians was proud and wished everyone, especially the fair sex, to realise that he was ASTACE THE GREAT; for was he not smarter, stronger and better than anyone he had ever seen or heard of? Had he not planned beforehand what he would do during the first big storm of the spring? The storm had even now developed to a tempest which seemed to rock the earth, and during a split second in which everything was illuminated in a flash of lightning, Astace could see plainly the dark cloud at his feet, which extended seemingly hundreds of miles to the north and bearing slightly to the west.

Then, as the darkness seemed to press in close around and envelope him, Astace spoke to himself: "I, Astace the Great, will shew that I can create a world of my own, which no one shall enter but those that I wish. I have spoken." So saying, Astace adjusted the basket strap over his right shoulder, and ducking his head through the loop, he swung the water filled basket under his left arm which he used to hug the basket closely to his side, thus making the carrying easy and convenient. Stepping lightly on to the cloud, it immediately and miraculously turned to stone under his feet. Meanwhile the tempest was ever increasing in violence, and Astace, with the aid of the storm, swung to the north west with a long tireless stride which ate up the miles rapidly.

As he settled into his stride, Astace reached over to his left side with his right hand; dipping it into the water in his basket he brought his hand back quickly with a jerk to the right at arms length. Returning it immediately to the basket he again dipped in his hand, but this time he threw the drops of water far out to the left. And so he continued, throwing drops of water far to the right and far to the left alternately. ASTACE THE GREAT ran on and on for hours in the darkness; only during the lightning flashes could he see anything, and then for an instant. The heavy precipitation continued, and Astace seemed to have always ample water in his basket with which to wet his fingers. At times the wind seemed to almost lift Astace off his feet and carry him forward with ever increasing speed. As hour after hour passed, Astace would at times slacken his pace for a change and to recover his breath; but the chill of the storm would soon set his teeth chattering and he would again assume his running stride.

Astace wished to cover all the territory he could for he was making a new world in the far beyond. Where each individual drop of water landed a lake was formed, or a slough, the source of a river. These kept rapidly increasing in size while the storm lasted, and rivers would run off down the hills. The cloud on which Astace ran on this adventurous night is known today as the northern end of the Rocky Mountains.

After running in this direction till about one in the morning, Astace thought his territory extended far enough north and wished the storm to change its course to the west. Everything so far had gone in his favour, so he tried to work over to his left as he ran, still dipping his hand and scattering the drops of water like a husbandman scattering the seed. Astace soon realised that the basket would carry easier if slung from his right side as it would then offer less resistance to the wind while he was working in a more westerly direction, so he paused a moment carefully changing the strap from his right to his left shoulder so that the basket hung under his right arm. On he ran, dipping his left hand now into the basket instead of his right. His left hand seemed to work as well as his right. But was it? The wind seemed to be abating; or was it shifting? Astace knew by instinct that he was travelling more westerly now than an hour ago. Was not that what he had wanted? He kept watching the space far to the west, frequently revealed by the lightning flashes. If he could only get over there a hundred miles or so and then work back toward home, his domain would be large enough for all time.

How could he get there? If he did, would there be another cloud on which he could travel, and would the wind be blowing towards home? So far things had worked his way and Astace thought that if only he wished hard enough everything would work to his advantage. So again self assurance returned to him, and as he ran he threw his head back proudly. Was he not ASTACE THE GREAT? Why should he doubt the power of the great Spirit (the storm in this instance)? So he wished as hard as he could and knew that all things would have to come about as he desired.

Just then the wind started to blow a gale from the east with such force that Astace was lifted off his feet and carried through space at a great speed. As he travelled through the air like a bullet shot from a gun, he realised instinctively that he must take great care of his precious basket and the water it contained. So he strove, and successfully, to keep the water from spilling. Above all things he must preserve his basket, even should he lose the water. It continued to rain hard and he could no doubt collect enough to carry on with. But there were no trees up here in the clouds to collect bark and roots from. At all events then he must keep his basket.

A flash of lightning, to Astace's great joy, revealed a bank of black clouds in his path ahead. Now, if only he could land on these without damaging his basket, he could continue successively on his mission. Just at that instant a cross gale bore down from the north, and in that cross current Astace was shot rapidly through space to the south. This wind was terribly cold. Poor Astace, his hands were blue and his teeth chattered. He was cold right through. If only he could land on a cloud and run as he had done before. But had he not wished for this? Yes, he must now wish again that he might land unharmed on a cloud. With this wind from the north he might almost, if not quite, reach home. The thunder was roaring terribly again, and in a flash of lightning, he saw a nice, fairly level surfaced cloud commencing just ahead of him and a little below. Oh, surely he could land safely on this cloud, so moving his legs as though he were running, Astace clutched his birch bark basket with both hands and gathered himself ready to alight. His moccasined feet touched the cloud and as before it turned to stone under his feet. He caught his balance and carried himself along with the momentum and got into his running stride as before without stumbling or spilling a drop of water.

Dipping his left hand into the basket he again started throwing water to the left and right alternately with a steady, rhythmical action. Astace was now running again at top speed parallel with and in the opposite direction to his earlier travels. This is what is known today as the Coast Range or Cascades on which, many hundreds of years ago on this story night ran Astace, the great Astace, sprinkling water from his basket and forming lakes and rivers which flow to the Pacific Ocean. Although he did not realize it, he was not doing such good work with his left hand as he did with his right, and also the cloud on which he was travelling was not so great as the one on which he had travelled north. Perhaps this is the reason that the Cascades are more broken than the Rockies.

As the storm gradually abated Astace also seemed to be tiring from his long run, although being ambitious he wanted to create all he could this night, as it was the greatest thing he had ever done.

The electric storm gradually abated although the rain still continued to fall in torrents, Astace's moccasins wore through exposing his feet to the bare rock. Without realizing it he was getting fatigued. His strong body needed rest and nourishment. It was now almost dawn of another day. Astace noticed the clouds breaking away in the east. How far was it over there to his home? But what did it matter to him now about home? Was not all this new country behind and to the east his home? Perhaps soon it might stop raining and the sun shine again, then he could lie down and sleep. Now the cloud he was travelling on began to be more and more broken up and he had to leap from one cloud to another. Ah, well, his domain was large enough anyway. The thunder had ceased for some time now and there were no more lightning flashes to see anything by. It was breaking day and growing lighter in the east. Now a breeze seemed to be freshening just ahead of him. The elements which had favoured Astace during the long night seemed now to mock him in his weariness. He slowed down and began to walk, and suddenly became aware that his feet were sore and bleeding. In the half light he glanced down into his precious basket and saw that it was still about half full of water. Just then he stubbed his right foot, and poor Astace, tired after such a long run without rest or food, was unable to recover his balance and fell down hard on his right side crushing his faithful basket beneath him and striking his head. Everything turned black and Astace knew no more. The water thus spilled by Astace in his fall formed that part of the Pacific Ocean west of British Columbia.

Cattle Driving/Oral Description

When the cattle started coming I don't know what **date that** was but it was kind of a an interesting **sight** to to see those **cattle** being loaded. A lot of them were rather **four** sore footed coming across the rocky **trail** and the **wire** edge of the **wild**ness had been **taken** off them en route.

But they you'd see them everybody was ah these storekeepers if there's policemen I never knew any policemen here but there might have been at one time told the people to keep back off because the cattle 'ud be along. So they'd peek through **windows** kids and they'd keep **quiet**. And then the **dogs** would be either **tied** up or or ah put in an **outhouse** or somewhere **warehouse** so they wouldn't bother the **cattle**.

And then one fellow'd be on **point** down the street and the cattle'd be following and they'd be a lot of fellows **wooing** at them and calling and **chasing** them along you know 'n 'casionally you'd hear a **whip** crack from a drover **whip** crack you know but I never see 'im abusin' the cattle any. And they'd get along this street till and and they had a kind of a a receiver **fence** I guess you'd call it along the bank so they wouldn't get over **there** and the gate would open on the other side to make a funnel shape and they'd get them into that corral. And then they'd get the gate shut. And then they'd try uh try to get them **down**. There were **two gates** that closed this now what a **lane** like. A **lane** was also funnel-shaped down to the water's edge from this corral. Ah it was independent of the corral altogether. It was you had to open a gate to get **inta** this lane and then the lane narrowed up till only one at a time could get through the end of it.

And they used to have trouble to get that first **cow** on. The cow would go there and it'd see the gangplank. Well the the uh the effect of the **motion** of the **river** would cause this steamboat just to vary a little to wave a little see to go up and down to flop just a little bit. And the gangplank would move just that little bit and the cow would balk there and wouldn't **go**. So the fellow'd say the fellow that **owned** the cattle would generally be **right** there the man that owned the cattle, **head** of the cowboys and he'd say, "**Hey Tom**, bring that **buckskin** horse here and a **lariat**. Get that **leader** in **there**." So he'd come down with a horse an hit these cattle over the nose and **get** them to other side and **get** them back and then get ah throw a a **rope** over this cattle's **horns** they all had horns those days and then take a a dolly er er **dally** I guess they called swing around two around the horn of the saddle and hold on this way and **put** the spurs to the **horse**. And this horse would go on the gangplank and **drag** that thing right **in** onto the **boat**. When the **first** one went in then the **rest** they **crowded** the other ones right there. They didn't have electric **prods** but they had **sticks** and they'd poke 'em along. When they got the **first** one in well then the rest **followed**. You can imagine it was quite an exciting thing to get that those **cattle** loaded. And then when they got them loaded well they got the **bar** and there they were.

Cattle Driving/Written Description

There was a telegraph service through the Lower Fraser Valley constructed at the time The Old Yale Road was built in the early 1870's this connected with the Cariboo line at Yale, which enabled the Public in general to be informed on the time of Steamboat sailings on River and any changes in stage schudles on the Cariboo Rd. Readiness to ship cattle was governed of course by the time of the Steamboat's sailing, generally the forenoon and as early as it was possible to get the cattle loaded. There being no electric lights in those days to light up the last receiving corral on the Riverbank at the Steamboat Landing which had a capacity of holding twice the livestock one Boat could accomidate at a single trip, some days, three and even four Boat loads would be shipped downriver to New Westminster, where they would be eventually slaughtered.

From the Hudson's Bay pasturefield or from Joe Bowes's feed lot probably the most activity of the season would occur, when the cattle would be moved or driven from these holding enclosures through the edge of town to the waterfront thoroughfare (known now as Water Street) where the Boat Landing corral was located (opposite where Marshall's gift Shop, and Pope's Garage now stand). A substantial gate in the exit of the log fence when being opened allowed the cattle to be driven into a log schute which would allow perhaps three animals to walk abreast down the steep incline to an additional gangplank, built with extra strong braced sides, as the cattle always balked at this point as this was a new experience they were being compelled to pass through. The Steamboat facing down stream was securely tied to the shore by immense hawsers on from the stern whose shore end was fastened to an iron ring attached to a Deadman buried to a secure depth on top of the band, which held the stern of the Boat against the beach, the Bow of the craft was held in place against the shore by another hawser which was secured by tying to a convient tree or stump up on shore. Whenever the Cattle started to walk over the gangplank, their weight would cause the far end to move down a little, and mostly the Boat would rock a little by the action of the river current coming in contact with the moored craft.

This gang-plank motion seemed always to terrify the already, half wild cattle and they would start to mill around in their confined space, the animals crowding in from behind, sensing matters at hand being out of the ordinary refused to advance any further, so a dead lock ensued

At this unusual change of events, the drovers on the rear of the cavalcade would draw together and decide on a more effective manner than having the Cowboys shouting, and whipping the stock in the rear. A Puncher mounted on one of the strongest horses would edge down one side of the shute toward the boat and eventually with much slapping with his stock whip or doubled up rata clear a passage so his horse could get through onto the gangplank at the spear head of the stubbern milling critters. In this position with his mount faced to board the craft, the rider shook his rope out and fashioning a loop swung around over his head and dropped a neat loop over the head of the nearby steer, pulling in the slack on the rope and leaning to oneside in the saddle the puncher threw a dally around the horn of his saddle and still leaning to the side out of the way of the taught rope, he spurred his horse forward the steer fought the rope but the trained roping horse gained inch by inch and gaining momentum soon had the critter very forcibly pulled aboard.

The Cowboys hazing placed at intervals through the oncoming drove, were meantime crowding the living beef animals forward for all they were worth, as with a flock of sheep, cattle when exited into a frenzy will follow the leader, the shrill yells of the Cowboys in the rear pressing forward combined with the cowponies treading on the heels of the steers had the desired effect, and soon the hold would be loaded to capacity, and just before the bars were placed across the enterence into the hold the leading Cowpoke would reappear and would ride through the doorway with his head bowed to avoid it striking on the cross timbers which gave none too much clearance overhead, which in their place supported the upper deck of the vessel. Sometimes this Cowboy would emerge out of the hold minus his hat, having lost it in the melee behind.

No doubt the beef cattle being driven through the side roads and along the waterfront was the most exciting event of the early days in the town of Hope.

The Politics of Love/Oral Exposition*

We all know what needs to be done. Everybody in this audience could conceivably develop a beautiful definition of what it means to be a lover. You **know** what it is. Why aren't you **doing** it that's the question. What's the use of knowing when you don't put it into **action**. You know I had a Buddhist teacher once that said to me "To know and not to do is not really yet to **know**." You'll know that you're a lover when you begin to **act** at being a lover.

And there is **so** much **material** to **cover** if you're going to be a lover. In fact there's so much material it reminds me of ah ah a mosquito in a **nudist** colony. There's so much tempting **stuff** to talk about. But the **first** thing that we're going to have to do if we're going to decide we're going to be **lovers** is you're going to have to develop your sense of **humour**, because my goodness people are going to treat you strangely and you're going to have to learn to **accept** it with a good **laugh**.

Humour is a **wonderful** antidote to cruelty and to rejection and to distrust and to condescension. You know, the wonderful comedian, Victor Borge, says that the closest distance between two people is a good **laugh**. I **love** that. And you know **Mama** taught that to us early. She laughed **all** the time. She used to drive Papa **crazy**. He'd come home with all kinds of **despairing** things and she'd get the **giggles**.

And you know there is nothing so contagious as **laûghter**. **Try** it some time. Just sit there and **laugh** and pretty soon everyone around you will let let you know that they're laughing, they're **roaring** with laughter. We were on the floor wondering what Mama was laughing at. **She** didN't know. It was just the **whole** thing was just funny.

You know sometimes I think people would really become wild when you recognize that **life** is a **great big wondrous** *joke* and you're at the **centre** of it. **You're** the **funniest** thing of all. Have you ever watched, have you ever watched **human behaviour**? It's it's **hystêrical**.

You know I I all during the summer I've been travelling all over the place and I'd like you to know I **love** to sit in airports and watch human behaviour. Here's the family going on the much-needed holiday, you know, here's Mama, here's Papa and here's the six kids and one is on a **leash** and the others are **all over** the **airport** and Papa's saying to Mama "**Get those kids together**, the plane's about to leave." "Where's **Joe**?" "He had to go to the toilet." "**Toilet**! We're gonna miss the flight." And the kids are saying "I don't wanna go," and the other one is saying "When are we going to **get** there?" "I'm **thirsty**." "Well, you can drink on the plane." "I want something to

*Excerpt from *The Politics of Love* by Leo F. Buscaglia used with permission from The Felice Foundation, Los Angeles, CA.

drink **now**." **Oh**, they're having **such** a good time. You see Mama walk on the flight, you know, and she's **had** it. They haven't even taken **off** yet.

Ah I was recently at a concert. It was hilarious. And there was this man. He was **determined** to be the **first one** in the concert hall. I can't explain **why**, but they opened the door and there was this **man** pushing everybody aside with his poor wife on his arm you know he's **pulling** her through and they get inside and then he waits for an hour. You know human behaviour, if it weren't so marvelous, you know, we'd all just freak out.

You know Saint Teresa of Avila had a wonderful philosophy. She said **no nun** will be a part of our order unless she likes to **sleep**, she likes to **eat**, and she like to **laugh**. I'd 'v been a good nun for her. Because, she said, if you like to **eat**, you're usually healthy. If you **sleep** and you like to **sleep** you usually have no big **sins** on your soul, you know, and if you love to **laugh** you will always be **saved**.

You know for **years** and **years** and **years** I was told "Now Buscaglia, you must be serious. You must go you must **plant** you're two feet **firmly** on the ground if you're ever ever going to get anywhere." Well, you know, with my feet firmly pa planted on the ground I couldn't get my **pants** on. Flying in the air I could get them on **anytime** in **any** position.

Abraham Lincoln said, "People are about as happy as they make up their **minds** to be." Isn't that nice? You know, don't expect **others** to make you happy. **You** create the joy and watch what happens. **You'll** be the **one** who is dancing through life and laughing through life. It's such a **nice place** to be. And isn't it interesting that people certainly are happy in all kinds of situations we can't understand. There are poor people that are happy. There are ill people that are happy. There are disabled people that are **seriously** disabled that are happy. Even among the **dying** I have known happy people which tells us something we should all know and that is it isn't the **situation** that makes **you** happy, it's **you** that makes you happy.

I was on a plane recently with a woman who had just lost her husband two weeks before and she was going to visit her **children** and she said some **beautiful** things to me. The two of us **cried** together. You should see me on airplanes. It's unbelievable. I have such an incredible time. It's such a **nice unique** moment where we can **share** intimacy. And then you say good-bye. You may never see each other again. But she told me about her life with her husband and about her **kids** and so on and so forth. **Then** she said, "You know, Leo, the **hardest** time is at **night**. During the day I'm busy. I don't think about it. But at **night** when things are quiet and dark and there's nobody to be **near** you then you realize the **importance** of bringing people **close**." And she said especially after **35 years** having somebody close, just as far as a hand. And she said, you know, when I go back to my kids I know they're going to try to make Mama happy. They're trying to make **her** gonna try to make her smile. My kids are sweet and they're wonderful, but they can't **make** me happy, only **I** can make myself happy again. That got us to **cry** again.

But **how wonderful** when **you** take full respons**ibility** for your joy. Ah just about **two** weeks ago I received a letter that I wanta share with you. And ah **this** was from a woman, very **young** woman, with a small family who who found out at her very young age ah that she was **dying** of cancer and she said the strangest thing happened when she was **told** that she told her family. She said everybody **rallied** around her. All at once her husband who had never shown real affection became **very** affectionate. Her kids **hugged** her and **kissed** her and they **relieved** her of all kinds of mundane duties that she had to **do** all the time. And she said I then found I had a lot of **free** time to **think** about things. And the one thing that occurred to me was that I was living with a **stranger** this is a quote "and the stranger was me." She says, "What was I going to do? I was **absolutely** alone. And I said to this stranger inside of me, "You know we still have time left to get to know each other.' So I started to deal with the things I **think**, and the things I **chose** and the things I **love** and the **books** I **read**. And I decided that these were the things that would get me to know me. And in so doing, Leo, I met a **fantastic** person: **me**. The **best** thing I learned after knowing I had to give up everything was that all that I really had had in the first place was what I **was**." And she ended her letter with this line "Like I told you, I don't have long to live, but I've never been so happy and so alive." So if we are going to be lovers we've got to take full responsibility for our lives.

*Loving Each Other/Written Exposition**

It seems to me that deep relating without joy, laughter, and a sense of humour is an impossibility. That is, perhaps, why all saints are said to be "transcendental clowns." Conrad Hyers, in his book, *Zen and the Comic Spirit*, suggests that "the demons of desire and attachment, ego and ignorance, may be exorcised through laughter, and point us to a kind of cosmic laughter that is to be entered on the other side of this exorcism."

I'm certain that we have all been reminded many times that life is not to be taken causally, that "it's damn serious business!" To a certain degree, this may be true. But, that seems to me to be all the more reason to maintain and develop a keen sense of humor. In fact, I know that I have been saved, again and again, by my ability to see the humorous side of a situation, especially to laugh at myself and my imperfections. I know it takes courage, and a degree of borderline insanity, to smile and laugh in a world where, since the

*Excerpt from *Loving Each Other* by Leo F. Buscaglia used with permission from The Felice Foundation, Los Angeles, CA.

beginning of recorded history, we have continued to kill, rape, desert and hurt each other. We've been, until now, unable to find reason for all of this. Perhaps the giving up of reason and the acceptance of our humanness as the ultimate joke may offer us another alternative.

Mother Theresa of Calcutta, who serves constantly among the despairing, the hungry and the dying, requires that her hospital wards be filled with laughter. She sees the sound of laughter as the strongest force toward health, productivity, strength and spirituality. St. Francis of Assisi wandered the streets like a clown, laughing at despair. St. Theresa of Avila always looked for novices who knew how to laugh, eat and sleep. She was sure that if they ate heartily, they were healthy, if they slept well, they were more than likely free of serious sin, and if they laughed, they had the necessary disposition to survive a difficult life.

The symbol of the laughing Buddha, fat and healthy, represents the essential joy of Buddhism. In fact, among the Zen Buddhists, laughter and happiness are the core of their teachings. There is a level of humor to be found sprinkled lightly over every religious sect.

Philosophers throughout our history have stressed the necessity of joy for survival. In 451 BC Sophocles, for instance, reminded his students that, "The man from whom the joys of life have departed is living no more, but should be counted as dead." The philosopher George Santayana has said, "Happiness is the only sanction of life. Where happiness fails, existence remains a mad and lamentable experiment." "There is no duty we so much underrate," Robert Louis Stevenson reminded us, "as the duty of being happy." Even the constitution of the United States guarantees us "the pursuit of happiness" as part of our constitutional rights.

Still, in our time, there is pitifully little joy demonstrated. There seems to be something not quite right about those who are happy. It is common belief that there must be something wrong with contented people. We look at them as either fools, frivolous, or totally lacking in ordinary common sense. They are suspect.

Most of us actually feel guilty when we're happy! We're convinced that we will either be punished for it or that gloom will not be too far behind. D. Raymond Moody, in his fine book, *Laugh after Laugh*, states that,

It is well to recognize that some persons are actually fearful of joy, elation, pleasure or other usually positive emotional states. In many of these people being joyful causes them to have feelings of guilt, shame or unworthiness.

This is certainly strange.

Scientists almost totally avoid the study of joy, laughter, humor and happiness and its relationship to human well-being. Lin Yutang writes, "I have always been impressed by the fact that the most studiously avoided subject in Western philosophy is that of Happiness."

It is rare that we hear spontaneous, uproarious laughter. If we do, we are certain that the revelers must be ne'er-do-wells or drunk. We pay large amounts of money to get professional comics to make us laugh. We tumble over with laughter when they mimic our "sane" behaviors and in this way reveal our follies. We love clowns. In strange attire, they participate in outrageous antics and engage in divine madness to help us see the simple truth about humanity. For a time, their behaviors set us free from the straightjacket of convention, the predictability of a routine life and expectations of behavior. They teach the deep desire within all of us to let go of inhibition and get in touch with our natural spontaneity, our natural madness. In a very real sense, we are all of us clowns—some more fearful and inhibited than others—but, nonetheless, potential clowns.

Comics view life through a microscope and are, therefore, able to show us clearly what we already know unconsciously, that life is a wonderful joke, and that we human beings, in our studied seriousness, are often at the center of it!

I was recently asked to help plan, with some friends, a "real Italian wedding." As with most ethnic groups, weddings are for Italians only slightly less important than births. In this case, the planning had taken on monumental proportions, all leading to loud, lusty arguments and empty solutions. It all reached a peak when it was announced that the mother of the bride was a vegetarian! It took Grandma to set everything straight. Laughing all the time, she pointed out how silly everyone was being. "So, don't worry about the vegetarian. I'll stuff her a zucchini!" Everyone roared. The wedding was planned, and Giacomo Leopardi, the Italian philosopher, was proved right again when he said, "He who has the courage to laugh is almost as much a master of the world as he who is ready to die." We are funny! All we need to do to affirm this is to look about us. A wedding which should be the height of togetherness, love, and joy had almost come apart because someone didn't eat meat!

Observe people in airports, in crowds, at parties, on busy freeways. How can we keep from laughing? A man is just informed that his flight has been cancelled due to serious mechanical difficulties. He insists that the plane *must* fly or he will miss his Chicago connection! A lovely girl sits at a party, unwilling to make the slightest effort to mix, and leaves exclaiming what a dull party it was and how unfriendly the people were. A person pushes or shoves his way to the box office only to have to wait an hour for the movie to start. The driver goes at breakneck speeds to pass you up, only to have to wait at the next stop signal as you drive up smiling next to him. These are certainly laughable behaviors which we observe daily in our lives. Human beings are very comical creatures and life provides us with so many opportunities for laughter. Now, all we need is to learn to laugh again.

Victor Borge said that, "Laughter is the closest distance between two people." There is no more sure way of coming together with other human beings than through laughter. George Bernard Shaw, the great cynic/philosopher, agreed that only "by laughter can you destroy evil without malice, and affirm good fellowship without mawkishness." We have all known experiences when a shared laugh has changed what was just moments before a strained, anxious relationship into a warm, joyous, productive one.

Happiness is connected etymologically, and in reality, with the word "happen." It is always part of a "happening" in life which comes and goes. Only a fool expects to find happiness continually, or to hold onto it once found. Happiness is always a by-product of some feeling or action. Even knowing this, there are many of us who spend our lives frantically *looking for happiness* constantly in mad pursuit of *joy*. We complain that our relationships are dull. We act as if these things are to be found *out there somewhere*. We seldom come to terms with the idea that happiness is in *us*. Soren Kierkegaard recognizing that when "a man, who is a physical being is always turned toward the outside, thinking that his happiness lies outside him, finally turns inward and discovers that the source is within him," is one of life's great insights.

We cannot look for joy as we do a lost article of clothing. We make our own happiness. We define it for ourselves and experience it in our unique way. No one can be happy for us nor tell us what should make us happy, though people will always try. The sad fact is that we fall into Madison Avenue traps which convince us that happiness is the right drink, the flashy automobile, the scented deodorant, bursting-with-health cereal or the special snack food. Even the wisest among us are seduced by the exuberant TV ad or the seductive graphic into believing that we, too, can change our lives if we switch to a new mouthwash. We never stop to think that there is nothing in the world which can be given or denied us that will bring us happiness unless we decide it. In fact, the happiest people in the world would probably still be happy if stripped of everything except life.

I recall when I was travelling through Asia that I was constantly encountering people who existed, according to our standards, at barely above a starvation level, yet they lived in genuine joy. Their lives were filled with smiles, song, dance and celebration of whatever they had. Of course, I am not advocating the naive illusion of the "happy peasant." All who so desire should be able to rise above whatever social condition in which they were born and attain whatever prize they want for what they believe to be their betterment or happiness. What I'm saying is that nothing but *life itself* is necessary for humans to know joy and happiness.

I constantly had this affirmed in my work with handicapped individuals. I saw quadriplegics who smiled and laughed their way through life, while those working with them, with every physical advantage, were often miserable, unsatisfied and depressed. It is strange that some of the happiest people I have ever known were those who seemed to have no particular cause to rejoice. They were simply happy. They seemed to have in common a singular courage, a willingness to risk, to fail and to let go, a belief in themselves, a wonderful resourcefulness, a trust in their creative uniqueness and an ability to hold on to their dream.

Perhaps much happiness is lost in the pursuit of it. Hawthorne in his *American Notebooks* said that happiness always comes incidentally. "Make it the object of pursuit," he stated, "and it leads us on a wild goose chase and is never attained." He suggests that we should lose our way and follow something totally unrelated. In that way we often happen on happiness without ever dreaming it would be there.

We are far too rational in our relationships, far too ordered, organized and predictable. We need to find a place, just this side of madness and irrationality, where we can, from time to time, leave the mundane and move into spontaneity and serendipity, a level that includes a greater sense of freedom and risk—an active environment full of surprises, which encourages a sense of wonder. Here, ideas and feelings which would otherwise be difficult to state can be expressed freely. A bond of love is easy to find in an environment of joy. When we laugh together we bypass reason and logic, as the clown does. We speak a universal language. We feel closer to one another.

Joy, humor, laughter—all are wonderful, easily accessible tools for bringing comfort into a relationship. They can be used to overcome inhibitions and tension. Dr. William Fry of Stanford University has just recently reported that laughter aids digestion (give up your antacids), stimulates the heart and strengthens muscles (give up jogging), activates the brain's creative function and keeps you alert (give up artificial stimulants). All this with a good guffaw.

Joy and happiness are simply states of mind. As such they can help us to find creative solutions. When we feel joyful, euphoric, happy, we are more open to life, more capable of seeing things clearly and handling daily tensions. When one laughs, the body secretes a special hormone that is a natural painkiller. Norman Cousins claims to have cured himself of a terminal illness with, among other things, the power of laughter. Good uproarious laughter of the roll-in-the-aisle type, causes all the vital organs to vibrate and jostle, much like what happens to us when we jog. So, if we are too lazy to jog, we can laugh our way to health! Throw out the aspirins and giggle away despair.

For years, I had been told that I was taking life too casually, that my attitude would surely lead me to wrack and ruin. A man of my professional background should be an example—firm, serious, with his "feet planted firmly on the ground." With my two feet "firmly planted on the ground," I found I couldn't get my pants on! With my feet in the air, it's easier now!

"Joy comes in our lives," Joseph Addison says, "When we have something to do, something to love, and something to hope for."

Live fully and with abandon. Love totally and without fear. Hope splendidly and never relinquish the dream. These will help us but joy will only be ours when we choose it. As Abraham Lincoln reminded us, "Most folks are about as happy as they make up their minds to be."

Many a relationship has been saved by a good belly laugh.

Yogurt and Yogurt Cheese/Oral Instruction*

Hi and welcome to my **cheese** factory. Today I'm gonna make **cheese** for you outa **yogurt**. That's the oldest cheese we have in the world. **Now**, the question is **who** invented yogurt and the answer is **nobody**. Yogurt is a member of the **family** of foods that have come to us ah as a gift of god, that is to say that we **discovered** things, but they were **already** planned out. I **really** believe that. **Wine** and **bread** and **cheese** are our three most **ancient** food products. All discoveries of **yeast** on the desert. All **blessings** of yeast on the desert. Old old food products. And yogurt is one of **those**.

In the old days when they began ah taking **care** of **herds** of **goat** and **cattle** and they would milk these creatures you see. When they'd leave the milk set about **natural** yeasts in the air, bacteria in the air in the desert, would land in the milk and cause it to to ah **ferment** as ah **yogurt**. Ah the term *yogurt yogurti*, I think it is in **Turkish**, probably where it began, the Turks and the (unclear) of the desert people, marvelous times. In any case it would preserve the cheese. So they began to **save** the starters you see, save the yogurt and pass it on among generations.

The **other** method of thickening a milk or causing it to curdle was discovered when they began **saving** the **milk** itself in ah the **stomach** linings of a **cow** or of a **goat**. If you put it into a **goat's** stomach or a **cow's** stomach you see the natural rennet inside the **skin** causes the **cheese** to form and of course that preserves the **cheese**. Wine and bread and cheese were **all** discovered when we were trying to **save** stuff for the wintertime. Isn't that fascinating?

Well today I'm going I'm ready to fly with you here. Lots of **marvelous** things that we can make with **yogurt**. When you make your own yogurt, the equipment is very simple. You need a **stainless steel** pan. You can't do it in aluminum or enamel see. Put it into a stainless steel kettle. And you need a **thermometer**, a **good** cheese thermometer. These are not hard to find. One that will go from what does mine go from? from ah from about 20 degrees

*Excerpts on yogurt from *The Frugal Gourmet* by Jeff Smith. Copyright © 1984 by Jeff Smith. Reprinted by permission of William Morrow & Co.

centigrade to about 250 degrees you see. You want to be able to control this **very very** carefully. Then I want you to buy a **heat diffuser**. These are very simple to find. It's ah a **cheap** gadget, but a **marvelous** thing that ah will on ^ the burner, you see, it functions as a **double boiler**. It makes the heat **very very** even. And you want to put that under your pot because stainless steel is **generally too thin** to use ah for normal cooking. For me, everything burns, but use a heat diffuser and it won't.

So here we go. I've thrown I'm making a gallon at a time. **Easy** to do. Put a **gallon** in my stainless steel pot, brought it to a 180 degrees and I cooled, let it cool to 115 degrees. Got that. That's **very** important, the 115 degrees. Bring it to a 180 because you are going to **pasteurize** it. That was the number that ah Louis Pasteur decided on, remember. And then you bring it down to a 115, because then it's **just** warm enough to excite the starter, that is to say the yogurt bug that we're going to add to this, and it is a **bug**, it is a bacteria. **Marvelous** creature. So I have some yogurt left over from my last batch and at this point I'm going to add oh a **good cup** to my gallon here, previously made yogurt. You can buy yogurt starters in the market, in sometimes a supermarket but always in a health food store. And uh a **good** middle eastern deli will have a very **tart** one for you. **I** was **raised** on a yogurt that was brought from **Lebanon**, a yogurt starter that was brought by Mrs. **Selma Abdo**. She's a **marvelous** lady. Ah she died when I was oh I don't know seven years old. I still remember her recipes. I've **talked** with her about you before. I talked about **her** with **you** before. And she had she had a yogurt starter that was **so tart** and it's still in the family. **Years** and **years** and **years** ago. Oh **Lord** it's **tart**. It's **marvelous** stuff.

All right, the yogurt is mixed now. My starter is mixed into the gallon of milk that had been heated to a 180 cooled to a 115 and we're ready **now** to put it into **jars**. And I'm going to simply use **some** more gallon jars. You might also use a ladle, but I think I can just pour this in here. We'll see how far I get; don't want to make a mess. And we're going to ^ I'm just using corn jars. Be sure they're **clean**, for **heaven sake's** be sure they are good and clean or you'll have terrible trouble. And you'll get the idea.

All right here we gooo. (pouring) There's one. Be sure and stir your starter in carefully. You don't want to ah you don't want to have one jar alive and the other jar dead. You know what the term for yogurt is in Lebanese? The word is *leben* L E B E N which is connected with the **German** term for some reason, we don't know, for life, *leben* 'life,' *leben* in German. **Why** would they use such a word? Well, **because** this milk is now **alive**. It has a **bug** in it. And the bug will keep the milk alive and uh literally preserve it. A **marvelous marvelous** concept.

Now we'll seal these up and I'm going to put them in a **bucket** of water, a **kettle** of water that is **exactly** at the **same** temperature that I have my **milk** which means a 115 degrees. Now this is very simple to do but you need a

second thermometer. And you see my kettle is **all** set here. And you know how I'm keeping it **warm**? We want to keep this warm for oh about **8–10 hours**. And my water's in the bottom at exactly 115 degrees. See my my thermometer is right here. And you **know how** I'm keeping it warm? There it is. I have **Betsy's mother's heating pad** right underneath the bottom **and I have it on medium**. And I'm just gonna let it **sit** overnight. And after you make a **gallon** of yogurt in nothing flat. I would by the way I would by the way suggest that you ah once the thing's going you see keep the lid on it to ah **preserve** conserve the heat. And in the morning you wake up and you've got an entire gallon of yogurt. No sweat. You don't need those little yogurt starters. **Besides** they **don't make enough**. If you are going to **cook** with yogurt as **I** do **you've** got to have a **gallon** at a time.

Did you get the recipe? 180 in in the kettle. Cool it down to 115. Add your starter. Put it in jars. Put it in a kettle of water that is at exactly 115 degrees on a heating pad overnight. You've got it. Allright.

So today I've made yogurt for you ˆ **by the gallon**. We prepared yogurt with **eggs** which is a a Middle Eastern dish, little garlic and a little onion. We prepared a yogurt **sauce** that we put over a **chicken**. We prepared an herbed ah an herbed cheese that we placed a little crock for you here, a little garlic and lively herbs. We prepared the yogurt **balls** packed in olive oil and garlic and finally we make a **dessert** for you out of yogurt with **chocolate** in it. That can also be used as a cake icing. There it is. Talk about versatile! I think the stuff is terrific. **So** make some and enjoy yourself. Keep the **tartness** down by not keeping your starter too long and you'll be in good shape. I'm glad we could cook today. Until I see you again this is the Frugal Gourmet. I bid you peace. Bye bye.

Yogurt and Yogurt Cheese/Written Instruction

Yogurt and Cheese—Make Your Own

Cheeses and yogurt, the original cheese, are easy to make and much cheaper than those you buy from the market. Besides, you can control the salt and fat content.

Yogurt is probably the oldest cheese that we know. Originally it was discovered by nomads in the desert when natural yeasts that were present in the air landed in their milk products and preserved them. The yeasts or yogurts were saved and used to thicken and preserve more batches of milk. Milk was also stored in bags made of the stomach of an animal, thus providing a natural rennet that would turn the milk to a curd.

We can find terrific yogurt starters in most delicatessens and all health food stores. You may have to try more than one until you find one that is to your liking, perhaps not as sweet as the commercial yogurt. The starter will live for years if you care for it and continue to make fresh batches.

Yogurt

The rules here are simple. Just remember that you can kill the yogurt by getting it too hot. On the other hand, the yogurt will not grow if you do not keep it warm enough. So use the old heating pad method.

EQUIPMENT 6- to 8-quart stainless steel or enamel kettle
Cheese or yeast thermometer (needs to go from about 100 degrees to 220 degrees Fahrenheit)
Heat diffuser or flame tamer
4 quarts fresh milk
4 1-quart widemouthed canning jars with lids, sterilized
Heating pad

Heat the milk to 180 degrees Fahrenheit in a stainless steel or enamel kettle. You may use skim, low-fat, or whole milk. Remember that flavor is not terribly affected by butterfat. I prefer using low-fat milk for yogurt so that the final product can be used in low-fat/low-salt dishes.

Cool the milk to 115 degrees. Add starter to yogurt from your last batch. You generally need about 1/2 cup of a previous yogurt to 1 quart of new milk. Blend it in carefully so that the yogurt will be smooth. Place the mixture in a sterile jar, and cap with lid.

In another kettle (any kind will do), place water that is 115 degrees, right on the button! Put the jars of new yogurt into the water, which should come up about three-fourths of the way to the lid of the jar. Cover the kettle, and place it on a heating pad set for medium heat. Eight hours later you will have fine yogurt. Refrigerate before using.

The above method works for any amount. I usually make a gallon at a time, so that I have enough yogurt around for the following recipes.

*Noam Chomsky and Fred Halliday in Conversation**

Halliday: Noam, both you and I have written books on what we call the New Cold War and we seem to **agree** on the fact there is a new Cold War, a **worsening** of East/West relations and particularly U.S./Soviet relations since the late Seventies. This characterized by an increased arms race, by break-

*Excerpt from *Voices*, Channel 4, Great Britain, June 1985, reprinted courtesy of the BBC

down in substantial negotiations between East and West but also by a
change in climate **within** the two **camps**, by an emphasis on ideological
purity whether it's on orthodox Marxism-Leninism in the Soviet Union or
on conservative values in Britain and the United States and by **greater**
concern to **marshall** control in the **Third** World to control the allies be it in
Afghanistan on the one hand or in the case of the United States in Central
America. So we **agree** that just as there was a Cold War in the late Forties
and early Fifties so there seems to be a **new** Cold War **now**.

But I also get a sense that there's some **disagreement** between us, that you
lay greater more stress on control **within** the domains of each power. You
say the United States and Soviet Union are **losing** influence have been
losing influence over their respective allies since the Sixties or since the the
great days of the Fifties for both of them and that in a way they're **using** the
Cold War rhetoric they're **using** the idea of conflict between them I think **not**
to prosecute a conflict against each other which I think in **your** view is
largely mythical or not so substantial but to **control** the people who are
subordinate to them. And I think you've even said that the **real** enemies of
the United States is not the Soviet Union so much as Japan, Western Europe
that they are seeking seeking

Chomsky: potential enemies

Halliday: they're seeking to control those things, whereas in **my** view there is
of course there is this **element** of controlling the situation at home of Britain
controlling its own population, United States controlling its population,
controlling the weaker allies in the Third World, but I give I think a much
more **weight** to the **reality** of the East West conflict. I **do** think the United
States and the Soviet Union have a **lot** to conflict about and that you can't
understand this new Cold War if you **don't** see that the conflict has in fact
got a lot of substance to it.

Chomsky:I think what the Soviet Union has wanted is essentially to be able
to run their own dungeon without internal interference ah and to compete
for influence in the Third World at targets of opportunity. The **American**
version of the world order has been much more expansive uh and I I think
that essentially reflects the relative **power** of the two states. In particular
immediately after the Second World War ah the United States was in a
position of **global** dominance which probably has no historical parallel and
they were literally producing 50 percent of world output and using roughly
50 percent of the world's resources. There's and they they **knew** it you know
they were conscious of it. The United States is an **extremely** open society on
nothing like it in the world. We have **tons** and **tons** of documentary evidence
and it's very very **explicit** the there was very careful and very explicit planning for the post-war world and it **didn't** in it it was supposed to be a world
which was **going** to be open to penetration and exploitation uh by uh
American-based uh ultimately international uh uh uh uh corporations.

Halliday: Hm, hm.

Chomsky: Now the Soviet Union was plainly an **impediment** to that, first by its **existence**, that is it was simply not incorporated into what American planners called the Grand Area, the area subordinated to American influence and **secondarily** because it **did** support ah to some extent at least never to the extent **claimed** but to some extent it provided some protection for ah movements towards independence elsewhere in the Third World. And that's an impediment. And in fact in the early Fifties the ah late Forties and the early Fifties the United States **was** pursuing a roll-back strategy. It was still hoping to **break up** the Soviet Union and incorporate it in the system.

Uh uh, but what I think **has happened** over the years is that the Cold War has increasingly come to serve have a certain functional utility for the super powers. They can **use** it. It's useful for them and I think that's a **major** reason for its persistence. It's not a zero-sum game. It's not a competition in which one gains where the other loses. And I think you can see that by looking at the **incidents** of the Cold War. So for example if you take the Soviet Union uh which **has** to mobilize its own population as a uh even a totalitarian state must do when it carries out aggressive or brutal actions uh so from the beginning in fact from the intervention of East Berlin to the invasion of Afghanistan it has always appealed to the threat of the foreign enemy and the uh the you know the Americans stand there waving their missiles and uh carrying out savage acts therefore we have to defend ourselves. And the United States has been doing the **same** thing. The in fact from the beginning I mean Acheson actually takes **pride** in his memoirs uh for his success in ah ah **convincing** Congress by a series of sh sheer **deceptions** uh that they had to move in in Greece and Turkey to defend themselves against the Russians. And that goes on up to the invasion of Granada. You know, you invade Granada: "Well we have to defend ourselves from Russian attack." Uh now that's the **that's** been a **very** successful device for mobilizing the American population for what are in fact acts of aggression and intervention. And there's a **second** factor, too, which has to be emphasized and that is that in the United States **maybe** in the Soviet Union but certainly in the United States the uh the ah ah military system has become essentially the technique of ah industrial policy management. Uh if **when** the government has to intervene to subsidize high technology **industry** as it repeatedly does it does it does it through the military system and in order to do **that** ah you need a foreign enemy that you are defending yourselves against. Hence you consist you **continually** see in America in recent American history the conjunction of **major** military expenses interv ex ex extended intervention overseas and confrontationist tactics with uh and appeal to the Russian threat. Now **that's** become an extremely useful system and we're locking into it and I think it's a major reason for the persistence of the Cold War.

Halliday: Yah. I follow some of what you say, but I still don't agree. What you

understate is two things. First of all you understate the degree to which they still **do** dispute. In other words this is **not a stable** competition. It is not, I think you once used a phrase "a dance of death" in which each knows its place, its role and how far they can **go**. They do know how far they can go in terms of nuclear weapons and there haven't been many incidents recently or since the Cuban missile crisis when **rules** of the dance of death have been unknown. But when it comes to the **Third World** there **really** are not any rules and there's not any agreement on where they should step and **not** step and **I** see the onset of the second Cold War from the late Seventies onwards as a response by the United States **not just** to disorder within their own realm not just to you know **lengthening** queues of unemployed in Cleveland, Ohio or to rebelling peasants in Nicaragua but to the intersecting of revolt in the Third World on the one hand with Soviet power on the other. And that that seems to be the history of the post-war world. **Towards** the end of the Seventies there was a a **wave** of Third World revolutions by my count **14** countries which went through Third-World revolutions. There was Vietnam, there was Ethiopia, there was Iran with very spectacular consequences, there was Central America and there were others. Now these revolutions in themselves would support **your** view. There were revolts within the U.S.domain.

Chomsky: Hm, hm.

Halliday: But at the same time they intersected with the conflict between East and West. Who was giving the Vietnamese the weapons to fight and kill Americans? Who was **it** who assisted the guerrillas in Africa to weaken the Portuguese? Who was it who was encouraging Nicaragua if not Cuba and in some way the Soviet Union too?

Chomsky: In **case** after **case** it has **not** been a major concern to American policy if a **newly** independent area becomes allied to the Soviet Union. In fact we **drive** them to do that and in fact we even **want** the United States even **wants** them to do that. You can see why. I mean when if we can drive Nicaragua into becoming uh a Cuban or Soviet client that will give a justification for the further attacks that we **intend** to carry out to prevent them from **extri**cating themselves from the world system that the United States controls. And you see it's a **very** striking fact notice that this is totally systematic. It happens in **every** case. In every case if we cannot **crush** and **destroy** one of these revolutionary movements we will act in such a way to drive them into the hands of the Russians.

Halliday: But this is why I think you understate the reasons why in most cases the Prussians win or as we put it in most cases the **militarists** win or the **hawks** win, which is that Nicaragua, Algeria many of these other cases represent **not** just national control of the economy not just independence as you construe it but something more than that they represent an alternative

model of organizing society, an alternative **politics** and **therefore** the **resistance** while it **can** be overcome in a few cases goes to the heart of the
American system, the American system of how a domestic polity should be
run, the American view of how the world strategic and political structure of
relations between states should be run **requires** it to oppose, to crush, to try
and role back revolutions. If one looks at the conflicts between major world
powers in the nineteenth century between **Britain** and France, **Britain** and
Russia, one can say that these were societies and polities which were organized in **roughly** similar ways, but which were competing for territory,
economic influence, strategic weight and so forth. Now all of these elements
are present in the rivalry between the United States and the Soviet Union
but there's something further which is that there are societies and political
systems which are organized in very different ways, and which **do** present a
threat to each other even though they **exaggerate** the degree of the threat,
there is a **real** threat and both of them would like to **gain** ground at the
expense of the other and ultimately **eliminate** the other from the face of the
earth. The Russians would like to see a world organized in the way they are
organized and the Americans would like to see American-style capitalism.
Their view of the free world would prevail everywhere. Now, of course they
live together because neither is powerful enough to overthrow the other and
there is the small matter of nuclear weapons which threatens the destruction of everything so there are **controls** on this rivalry, but, nevertheless, the
rivalry **has** a **deep** reality to it. Their values are very different. People often
say there is no Cold War because nobody believes in communism nobody
believes in capitalism; Mrs. **Thatcher** believes in capitalism; Ronald **Reagan**
believes in capitalism and would have thought that Konstatin **Ostainivitch**
Chernenko believes in communism as well. And they certainly believe in
nationalism and in their nationalism being reflected in different social systems as well. So there is a conflict of values. Secondly I think that there's no
doubt that the societies **are** organized in a **profoundly** different way. As
people in Russia ah often say if you think this is capitalism you should come
and **look** at it. It isn't capitalism
Chomsky: Hm, hm.
Halliday: There is no McDonald's. There is no Bank of America. There is no
no no Coca Cola advertisements on Kurtasovsky prospect or Red Square in
Moscow. And in the United States people are not given the kind of housing
social services securities that people in the East have and so forth. **Power,**
wealth are organized and distributed in quite different ways in these countries. And **both** of these systems have a hegemonic intent, a hegemonic
element. **Thirdly,** in the disputed area which is the Third World at the
moment, but in the past was Europe and could become Europe again the
Spanish Civil War and after the Second World War it **was** Europe. There is a
competition for influence. Now we **agree** that the revolutionary upheavals in

the Third World are not created by the Soviet Union. They're not dredged out of the blue by communist subversion or communist proxies or whatever the Cold War language might be, but that this this rivalry between the two major powers and the two systems intersects with these insurrections in the Third World in a way that has a reality beyond the myths of right-wing propaganda. It may well be true that in 1954 Guatemala was not about to go into the Soviet camp. But the overall **pattern** of upheaval in the Third World since 1945 have been that many of these revolutions have turned to the Soviet Union, driven to them in some ways, but turned to out of affinity in others and affinity was very important in the Vietnamese case. And **therefore** the the the **American** refusal to **accept** these revolutions is **not** merely a policy mistake in White House.

Chomsky. Nobody's

Halliday: It's **not** merely a refusal to accept independence or autarchy in general. It's reflects ultimately the refusal to accept this alternative **social** system which is based on **different** values and **different** systems of organization. And **that's** what lies at the **core** of the Cold War.

Chomsky: Well you see I think your pa part of what you say is true but part of it in my view is simply **mystical**. The talk about about alternative social systems and **values** and so on I think is really mysticism. If if

Halliday: You say it's mystical to say that the Soviet Union and United States

Chomsky: They're **different** but that's **not** the problem. I mean if the Soviet the Soviet if the Soviet you **got** to the point when you said that there's no McDonald's and there's no Pepsi-Cola and so on and so forth. The United the the the the United the the the **existence** of the Soviet Union is incompatible with the American view of world order **because** it is **not** freely open to penetration by American capital. It's resources are not **freely** available.

Halliday: But **Japan** is not freely open to American capital.

Chomsky: Eh eh eh Japan is **very** open, **highly** open and where it is **not** open there is continual conflict. Uh after the during and after the Second World War the United States **planned** uh a structure of world order what it the planners called the Grand Area. Uh and that was to be in their terms the area strategically uh necessary for world control, the area that would be essentially subordinated to the needs of the American economy. But the point was that ah there had to be **free** possibility for export capital for exploitation of resources ah for uh ah ah **investment** overseas and so on. **This** region had to be open to American penetration and economic control. That's the crucial part. Ah now the United States is not omnipotent, but it has **acted** in such a way as to maximize these objectives and uh uh it is uh uh if we look through the **incidents** of the Cold War, whether it's the intervention in whether it's the rebuilding European capitalism in terms which would be ah integrated with and in and in large part subordinated to the United States, if we look at **Middle East** policy if we look at **Asia** policy we look at Central America policy, we discover this unifying thread. Always the attempt to **ensure** that some region will **not** be will **not** ah develop in such a way that it will refuse to complement the industrial societies of the West primarily the United States. The the United States **has** acted and will continue to act to try to create ah a system in which what they used to call in the nineteenth century free-trade imperialism will work.

Halliday: Much of what you've said so far suggests that the analysis of the Vietnam War both **how** it developed but also what its outcome is is perhaps a central **focus** of the different ways in which we look at post-war **history**. I mean in my view first of all the whole **development** of Vietnam War from the Fifties but particularly since the serious American involvement from the late Fifties onwards **demonstrated** that the **view** of the world of the strategic planners was erroneous, that whatever they **thought** they were doing about controlling the Grand Area they did not understand the forces involved **and** that there **was** in their perception of Vietnam and in its strategic importance a very clear awareness that there was conflict between the capitalist American way of running the world and the Soviet communist way of the world with the Chinese addition as well, that the **war** was not just any old war in the Third World it was a **war** between armies representing very different social systems and indeed armies organized in very different ways and that the outcome of the war was a **very** signal defeat for the United States, not only the **only** major defeat the United States has ever suffered in a war, it greatly **weakened** the United States economy internally and vis-à-vis its competitors and it **sent** a signal around the world to other revolutionary movements that the United States could be defeated by as the Vietnamese would say a combination of military, political and diplomatic activity. That it greatly encouraged the defeat of the Portuguese colonies in Africa. It made possible the Cuban intervention in Angola. It encouraged the revolutions in Central America and so forth. And that so it was a loss of American prestige as well as of American life and of American **treasure**. **Of course** the Vietnamese paid a terrible price over two million dead. Of course their society their ecology had been terribly damaged for decades maybe hundreds of years but nevertheless a country of 60 million people did defeat the United States. That regime has consolidated itself. They have **now** of course also extended their influence through the war with Cambodia to Cambodia itself and in overall terms it was a major defeat for the United States and nothing could illustrate this more clearly than the fact that even ten or more years after the last American troops left Vietnam there is still an enormous and **healthy** reluctance in the United States to sending troops abroad. For all that Reagan said in his first term about intervening in the Third World and overcoming the Vietnamese syndrome eh all they could drum up was this pathetic sort of promenade militaire in Granada which was of no military significance. Eh, the reason they had to pull their troops out of Lebanon was

American public opinion wouldn't wash it. One of the major problems they
have in sen sending troops to Central America is American public opinion
however bellicose it is won't buy it.

Chomsky: That's true.

Halliday: So the Vietnamese not only **defeated** the United States inside **Vietnam** but they defeated the United States globally and the impact of it is still
with us. So in and I would see that as a very major a very very major
development and a very major defeat for the United States.

Chomsky: Um well, I agree with everything you've said and I think it's
exactly half the story. Ah now let's turn to the other half. Here we have to
ask what the American **goals** were. And those we know very well from the
documentary record. I mentioned before let me repeat this the ah American
policy with regard to Indochina was set pretty well in the late 1940s and
early 50s within the general framework of Grand Area planning motivated
by the goals that Cannon and others describe. Uh an international order
which will be open to the penetration of uh uh uh American-based enterprise and its exploitation of resources and so on, **that's** the Grand Area;
that's what we try to reconstruct.

Why was Vietnam important? It wou Vietnam was was important **not** for
itself. There were virtually no American interests in Indochina despite some
talk by Eisenhower about zinc, tin and tungsten and so on. That was very
minor. Ah it was important on the within ah the framework of the Domino
Theory, now I mean the **rational** Domino Theory. The theory **was** that an
independent South Vietnam under so-called communist control ah would
be able to carry out mass mobilization ah ah ah and some degree of modern-
ization and industrialization ah leading to the form a **social** form which
would be meaningful in terms of the Asian poor and could have a demonstration effect elsewhere, in Thailand, in in Malaysia, in Indonesia ah ultimately leading to a system in which South East Asia and South Asia would
be **extricated** from the Grand Area under communist control. It could be a
communism opposed to the Russians or opposed to the Chinese ^ that
didn't matter ^ it would be **out of** American control and not free not open to
not **part** of the international capital system of exploitation and investment
and so on. **Then** the next step and that's the **crucial** step ah would be that
what John Dower calls the super domino would fall, namely Japan, and
Japan which they always recognized would be the industrial centre of ah ah
of Asia would be had had its natural markets and sources of resources in this
region and would be forced to accommodate to it and in effect what we
would have is a system **like** the one that Japan was attempting to construct
oh in the 1930s, a new order. Ah ah a system in large parts of Asia ah with an
industrial Japan at its heartland from which the United States would be
excluded and the United States was **not** prepared in the late 1940s to lose
the Second World War. **That** was the picture that they had in mind. Well,

now let's look at the outcome. We talked about the **negative** effects for American policy but there's another side. Ah Vietnam is **not** going to have a demonstration effect which will lead to development of independent and successful peasant-based movements in Thailand, Malaysia, Indonesia. **In** Vietnam itself they didn't achieve their their ends. Vietnam is not part of the American system **clearly** but in the **region** they achieved their ends. And the concern over Vietnam was a **regional** concern. It was not a Vietnamese concern. So therefore I think the **conventional** view, namely that the United States suffered a victor a a **defeat** is partially true but only but **crucially** only partially true ah there there was a regional victory.

Halliday: Looking at the issue of intervention and what lies behind it that the new buildup of American power in the Second Cold War and the question arises which is this: **Is** the buildup in American power, is the increase in military rhetoric, is the increased emphasis on **strength** and on American power, is the **vastly** increased military expenditure of the United States and its allies, can this be primarily explained by the Third World or not? Can it primarily be explained by the need to intervene in the Third World to **discipline** the Grand Area which I take to be your argument

Chomsky: Hm, hm.

Halliday: or has it not got a lot to do with the Soviet Union?

Chomsky: Well all you have to do is this

Halliday : My own view is this, that clearly the Arms Race serves multiple functions. It serves a domestic function as we said earlier, the the function of military Keynesianism, of boosting domestic expenditure. I **still** think that it's different from military Keynesianism in the Forties and Fifties in that the effects are much more contradictory. It can have inflationary effects; it can draw people away from scarce employment and so forth. But nevertheless there is a military Keynesian effect for some sectors of the American economy and **that's** what the arms lobbies are all about in Washington. So there is a **military** industrial complex which simply derives a domestic benefit. Fine. There is an ideological benefit for if you get people to believe in the army, if you raise the status of the army, if somebody walking down the street in uniform is saluted and all the school children run after him then after her as is currently the case in the United States clearly **that** serves to strengthen conservative values. When it comes to to foreign issues and to foreign purposes and I would stress that in my view I think they are still the most important ones, I think we can't get away from the fact that the Arms Race particularly the Arms Race as pursued by the United States **has** as commonsense suggests it has a **primary** target which is the Soviet Union. In other words it can't just be explained, the the **expenditure** the **values** the **propaganda** about the Arms Race and the Soviet threat, are **not** just about the Third World and I would argue are not **primarily** about the Third

World. They **point** to the reality, the enduring reality, of this East/West conflict.

Chomsky: Well, I feel each of the factors you've mentioned is **real**, but I think that you have failed to see the connection between them. I suspect that's where we primarily differ. So let's take a look at you see for example let's take I I think you **very** much underestimate the military Keynesian effect. It's not a matter of an arms lobby, so for example

Halliday: With the country the the United States has the largest deficit in its history?

Chomsky: It's not look look yes because this is a very **costly** means of industrial policy management but nevertheless for quite good reasons it's the only one we have. Come back to the reasons, but it's a fact and it goes way beyond the arms lobby. So let's take for example the development of computers. That's not the arms lobby. Now in the 1950s uh the government was **virtually** the **sole** purchaser of computers. In the 1960s it was still purchasing if I recall up to about 50 percent and paying for the development. Uh there's now a race so-called for developing what they call fifth generation computers su super-computers mainly with Japan. Europe is right out of it. Ah now in Japan that's controlled that's organized by **their** industrial management system.

Halliday: Nothing to do with military.

Chomsky: It has **nothing** to do with the military. But **how** does it work in the United States. Well, the funding for super-computer development is coming from the Pentagon, ARPA, Advanced Research Project Agency, the Pentagon, from the Department of Energy which is primarily a military department producing nuclear weapons and from NASA which is again largely a military ah organization. The way in which the United States for **good** historical reasons that we could go into but the fact is the **way** it organizes industrial production, the way it develops high technology that's the cutting edge of the economy. The way it encourages sunrise industry is by creating a government **guaranteed market** for high technology production and paying the research and **development** costs for it. Now let's turn to the second case, the question of the the second two factors, the Third World and the the conflict with the Soviet Union. They **both** exist, but I think you're wrong to disso-ciate them. They're **very** closely related. And in fact again ah since the United States is an open society we can turn to the documentary sources which explain the relationship. So for example ah let's not talk about about Reagan. Take Harold Brown. As as both you and I have both pointed out it was in the **late** Carter Administration that the new phase of the Arms Race developed, prior to the Iran hostages and prior to Afghanistan. It was in '78 in fact that Carter offered his you know proposal for a major increase in the military budget. In the last um um ah statement to Congress of the Penta-gon in the Carter Administration Harold Brown who was then secretary of defense ah gave an explanation as to why we have to have a big strategic **weapons** build-up and the way he put it which I think is essentially correct is this: he said that ah he said our strategic weapons system is the **foundation** of our security as he put it.

Halliday: Hm.

Chomsky: And he said within the framework of the strategic weapons system our **conventional** forces become **meaningful** instruments of political and military control. Now **that's** correct.

Halliday: Why is Reagan launching this arms race?

Chomsky: Carter

Halliday: It and Carter why did Carter? Yah and why did the majority of the American people support it? **Well** one reason is a lot of nonsense about the Russians having military superiority which on **any** possible criterion except conventional forces in Europe **cannot** be justified. One is that the Russians are more powerful in the Third World which is nonsense too. But nevertheless the Arms Race **has** this symbolic importance as being this central symbol. Nuclear weapons are the central symbol of power. They are the **potency** symbol of international power for the United States and unfortunately for much of the U.S. population as well **not** unrelated to the fact that the United States has never had any real **experience** of war. So there is this militaristic **culture** and this militaristic association of power in which nuclear weapons are very important, but there is also this control of the Third World on which we agree and how **what** percentage of the U.S. budget goes for intervention or how many of arms we can debate but **that** is important. It is a **central** factor.

Chomsky: That doesn't and it could be any

Halliday: And and the third but there is this **third** and irreducible element of **direct** rivalry with the Soviet Union

Chomsky: And **what** is the rivalry over?

Halliday: And and and

Chomsky: And **what** is the rivalry over?

Halliday: Not . . . the rivalry is over Soviet power and the increase of Soviet power.

Chomsky: Well the the

Halliday: **Both both** in terms of its geographical extension in the Third World and **also** in terms of this symbolic element

Chomsky: Hold it

Halliday: of how strong is the Soviet Union.

Chomsky: But notice that this notice what we're **agreeing** on.

Halliday: **Yes.** Can can I go on to say that **what** we **do** agree on and this is where you and I would disagree with many of those in the peace movement is that the arms race while it does have an irrational element and while it is extremely dangerous is also in part motivated by rational political concerns.

Chomsky: Absolutely.

Halliday: It is **not** out of control. It is not a a a **behemoth** or a monster which is simply spreading and which human beings cannot control. It is **not** merely the product of a group of conspiratorial scientists or of secretive people in bunkers here there and everywhere. It is a product of government decisions of political decisions taken and repeated and at least in my view and in your view I think a different way it is a product of a political and social conflict and **this** cannot explain it completely. It cannot comprehend the moral horrors involved in this arms race, but we would put ourselves into a small minority of people who think that the arms race is controllable, is rationally explicable and therefore can be rationally and politically controlled.

from *The Making of the Second Cold War*/Halliday

2 CONSTITUENT ELEMENTS OF WORLD POLITICS*

It might, at first sight, appear fruitless to search for underlying factors which shape the course of international relations: a system involving over one hundred and sixty states, many non-governmental forces, and several levels of interaction, allows of no simple explanation. But if it is intellectually implausible to reduce world politics to being the expression of some single cause, a Hegelian essence or a *primum mobile*, it may be less outrageous to suggest that there are certain theoretical approaches which can, without undue simplification, provide coherent explanations of recent world history by highlighting deep trends within it. Rather than proffering one single cause of the current Cold War, analysis of such theories suggests that it can be explained by reference to a set of constituent elements which, in their interaction, profoundly shape world affairs.

Theories of Cold War

It is remarkable how many of those who practice or comment upon international politics do, in fact, make assumptions about what its constituent elements are. These assumptions may be presented explicitly, and justified by reference to recent events, history or what is said to be common sense. They may be implicit, but known to both exponent and audience. At the risk of some condensation of the argument, it is possible to identify at least eight major schools of thought, each of which purports to offer an explanation of

*Chapter 2 from *The Making of the Second World War* by Fred Halliday (1984) reprinted by permission of Verso Editions, London, England

contemporary world politics and hence of why Cold War II began.

1. *Soviet threat theorists* place the blame for the current world crisis on the policies of the USSR. It is, they argue, Soviet expansionism and aggressiveness which underlies the major problems of the contemporary world, and which have ruined Detente. Whether such a Soviet orientation is due to the workings of Marxist-Leninist theory or to more embedded features of Russian society that predate 1917 is of secondary importance: the fact of Soviet actions being primarily responsible for the crisis of world politics is said to be evident whichever explanation is accepted.

2. *US Imperialism theorists* produce what is, in some respects, a mirror image of the Soviet threat account. Again, responsibility is ascribed to the actions of one major state, and the actions of the other innocent one are not seen as having contributed to the deadlock. US imperialism theorists locate the aggressiveness and belligerence of the west in the workings of a social system, capitalism, which they argue requires confrontation and military production for its survival.

3. The *super-power theorists* place the blame on the two major powers together, arguing that the USA and the USSR have conjointly subordinated the world to their common interests and to their remaining differences. Popularised by China in the 1960s, the 'superpower' theory identifies the two major powers as, in Peking's phrase 'colluding and contending' to dominate the world. This explanation has won particular support amongst those who see themselves as building a third alternative in world politics, be they European conservatives, anti-Soviet Marxists, or third world nationalists. It has the attraction of avoiding identification with one or other of the major blocs and of suggesting that, were the world to be rid of these two disputant and dominant states, then other problems and tensions could the more easily be resolved.

4. *Arms race theorists* single out the stockpiling of weapons, and particularly of nuclear weapons, as the central factor in recent world politics. The danger of potential destruction of much of the social, economic and cultural fabric of the world by nuclear weapons, and the apparent lack of control over the arms race, are seen as of such overriding importance that they are invested with the power of explaining the course of world events. The stopping and reversing of this arms race is therefore seen as the key to reducing international tensions. Such theories tend to a considerable extent to equate the political and social impact of this arms race in east and west. They abstract the problem of arms from other, it is argued, secondary and distinguishing, features of these societies, be they political intentions or social interests.

5. *North-south theorists* present the dynamic of world politics as lying primarily in the conflict between rich and poor nations, between imperial and colonial, dominant and dominated states. The great importance which this issue has attained since 1945 and the continuing immiseration and subordi-

nation of hundreds of millions in the third world are factors that, it is argued, override morally and strategically the east-west and other conflicts and provide the motor for these. The production of weapons and the disputes of richer states are, in the first instance, seen as motivated by the intention of consolidating their influence over weaker and poorer countries. In a north-south perspective it is the difficulty of maintaining this control over third world peoples and a competitive advantage over rival dominating states that underlies the deterioration of international politics in the late 1970s.

6. The *west-west theorists* argue that world politics is determined by the conflict between richer capitalist states, just as it was in the period before 1914. For them, the conflict with the USSR is but a pretext used by the USA for waging conflict with its major capitalist rivals—the EEC and Japan. It is the sharpened rivalry between these OECD countries which has produced the Second Cold War. Military buildups are a means of reimposing US control over its competitors; the Soviet Threat is the only ideological tool available for reuniting the major capitalist states; the turmoil in the third world is fuelled and aggravated by these intercapitalist rivalries.

7. The *intra-state theorists* locate the primary causes in the inner workings of the major world powers. Thus international relations are seen as fundamentally the expression of domestic factors. Changes in foreign policy are related to shifts in internal power structures, new economic weaknesses or strengths, and changes in the social composition of the country concerned. The politicians in charge of foreign policy may pretend to their respective constituencies that they are responding to the actions of forces and states outside their own countries; but they are above all using these international events to resolve internal tensions and to gain ground over domestic competitors.

8. *Class conflict theorists* see international politics as determined by the ebb and flow of social revolution, and of the conflict between capitalism and communism, on a world scale. In such a perspective, it is the simultaneous unity and variety of the world as transformed by capitalism which accounts for the turmoils of the postwar epoch. This conflict may at times be expressed primarily in rivalry between the major states of each bloc. But this is not necessarily so. At other times class conflict is reflected in the spread of revolutionary activity in the third world, at others still, at least potentially, in the level of class conflict within the major capitalist states.

All of these eight theories claim to provide some plausible explanation of world events. They all identify factors which must be taken into account in explaining the onset of the Second Cold War. Yet each also raises certain difficulties. The *Soviet Threat* and *US Imperialism* theories can only be sustained by denying an active role, any responsibility, to the other, exempted, state and by suppressing discussion of the rivalry between the two. Both powers helped to bring on the Second Cold War, as they did the First, albeit in different ways. The *super-power* approach overstates the degree to which the USA and USSR actually share common interests and exaggerates their ability to influence the course of world events: the USA and USSR 'contend' far more than they 'collude', and there are many factors in world affairs which are beyond the control of Moscow and Washington. This is indeed why the two major powers have been persistently unable to reach a negotiated settlement of their main differences. The *arms race* clearly constitutes a major factor in world politics, but it is itself fuelled by other tensions and purposes which must themselves be addressed: rather than being irrational or beyond human control, the arms race reflects conscious aims pursued by political actors, and it is these that have to be identified. Important as the *north-south* issue has become it cannot on its own explain the course of world politics, since so much of the power—industrial, political, military—which influences the conflicts of the south and those tensions between north and south is located outside the third world. The north-south conflict has not been waged in isolation from the east-west and west-west conflicts, but it has rather articulated with them and has been greatly accentuated, and rendered more lethal, precisely by this articulation.

The misleading attraction of the *west-west* theory is that it dispenses with the need to account for Soviet behaviour at all: yet in so doing it implies that the USSR, and the third world revolutionary movements associated with it, play no active instigatory role in the course of world politics. Not only does this go against the rather substantial evidence of a deep concern in western states about the policies and actions of the USSR, but it also downplays the importance of recent Soviet involvement in third world revolutionary advance. The *intra-state* theory has similar intellectual seductions in that it avoids the problem of analysing east-west conflict itself; but it reproduces the limitation of the *west-west* approach. World events do impinge on individual states—however strong the latter are— through military and economic challenges, through political threats, through ideological influence. Whilst the internal plays a more significant part than foreign policy experts usually admit, the course of international relations cannot be reduced to the domestic alone. The *class conflict* theory has the special merit of seeking to relate state and class politics within one approach. But it can suffer from two limitations. First, it downplays the importance of the conflict between rival *states*; in particular it underestimates the manner in which the US-Soviet conflict takes effect in other countries. Secondly, in its unrevised reassertion of a classic Marxist perspective on international affairs, it runs the risk of neglecting the degree to which the introduction of nuclear weapons has altered the nature of world politics in the postwar epoch.

EAST-WEST RIVALRY AND THE ARMS RACE

There is no need to deny the importance of any of these theories and the elements to which they draw attention. It is, rather, possible to explore more carefully how such elements interrelate and how, in any particular period, one or other of the main factors in world politics comes to play a leading role. It is in this connection that an attempt will be made here to suggest what the constituent elements of recent world politics have been, so that the course of events leading up to the Second Cold War and the articulation of these different constituents can become somewhat more intelligible. It is these elements which, in their individual evolution and their mutual inter-action, have generated the crisis and the changes of direction that have marked the postwar epoch, and it is they which can explain the causes and course of Cold War II.

The starting-point for such an investigation is 1945, the end of the Second World War, for it was then that the international political system as we know it today was born. Since that time two elements have above all else dominated international relations, to such an extent that they have often been elided with each other. These are the conflict between two rival social systems, capitalist and communist, what Isaac Deutscher termed 'the Great Contest' and the nuclear arms race. The one has come to form the structure within which international relations are worked through, the other has introduced an element of potential annihilation that has transformed not only the nature of any future war but also the risks and methods of diplomacy in time of peace. The theory being suggested here is, put simply, an extension of the class conflict theory to encompass both of the single-state theories—the Soviet Threat and US Imperialism variants—and the arms race itself.

Both the Great Contest and the arms race have to be accorded their due importance. To focus only on the conflict of east and west, of Soviet Union and United States, is to diminish the attention which must be paid to these new weapons of mass destruction and to the deep changes in the nature of international relations and political conflict which they have introduced. Yet to see this span of history in terms of the arms race alone is to obscure the very real political and social issues around which international affairs have revolved and which have themselves to a great extent determined the course of that arms race. Tempting as any single-factor analysis may be, it is not one or other of these constituent elements but rather their unpredictable and unprecedented combination which has made the postwar period so unique, and so perilous.

Although these two major constituent elements are all too familiar in the 1980s, it has to be remembered just how novel they are. The competition of the two social systems differs from previous great power rivalries in three respects. First, it is a rivalry that is *globalised*, i.e. it involves the whole world in its political and military dynamics. Whilst unable to control or programme much of world events, the major powers nonetheless tend to impose their own competitive logic upon them. Secondly, the rivalry rests upon a *bipolar* conflict between the USA and the USSR, the two states which emerged as dominant forces in their respective domains at the end of World War II. In the nineteenth century Britain was supreme in its international influence. In the period between the First and Second World Wars a variety of states competed for dominion. The bipolar conflict dates from the period since 1945 and from the emergence of these two and only two great powers of the nuclear age. They are endowed with economic, geographic and political weight at a time when the possession of large nuclear arsenals has given each of them additional superiority over other states within their own camp. Thirdly, this conflict is *systemic*. It is not just one between rival states, a realisation of the prediction made by de Tocqueville in the 1830s that Russia and America would one day be rivals for world domination. It is a conflict in which aspects of this great power rivalry are grafted onto a rivalry between two social systems that remain, with all necessary qualification, in continuing conflict. However much the leading states do act or appear to act simply like great powers in the traditional mould, there is something more at stake in their competition. There are underlying reasons, inherent in their respective social orders, which dictate that they cannot permanently resolve their disagreements.

The globalised and bipolar nature of the conflict is perhaps evident enough; but there are many who doubt the inter-systemic element, whether out of a belief in the underlying similarity or convergence of capitalist and communist states, or because of skepticism about the rival ideological claims of the two states involved. The right has less difficulty in recognising this reality than the left. With all due caution about believing the claims each camp makes about itself, it is worthwhile summarising the reasons why such a conflict does still have this systemic character. The eminently justified rejection of the way in which the 'Soviet threat' is presented in much western analysis should not lead to the mistake of denying that an east-west conflict exists.

The fundamental nature of the conflict between the two social systems can be seen in three aspects of their interrelationship. First, these societies are organised on the basis of contrasting social principles: private ownership of the means of production in one, collective or state ownership in the other. This antagonism is, however, rooted not just in the contrast of social organisation but ultimately in the different social interests which they represent. For the capitalist world has, since 1917, faced an opponent where capitalist rule has been overthrown and replaced by a society of a fundamentally different kind. The original hope of those who made the Russian revolution, that a society in which workers' democracy could be established, was belied; instead a system based on the dictatorship of the party leadership, and of a social group tied to it by bonds of power and privilege, emerged. But for all the betrayal of the intentions of those who made the Bolshevik revolution, a contrasted social system, representing different social interests and classes, was produced and it is this difference which above all else underlies the Great Contest as it continues to this day.

This difference is reflected in a second distinction, that both systems stake an ideological claim to be world systems, ideal societies which others should aspire to follow. However hypocritical such proclamations may at times be, and however much each side seeks to find accommodation with the other, there are conflicting appeals embodied in both systems which direct state policy and state responses to events elsewhere. Thirdly, the search for even limited bilateral accommodation between the USSR and the USA cannot proceed smoothly because of the outbreak of the conflicts in other countries which draw the two major powers into antagonistic involvements. Systemic conflicts override attempts at state-to-state accommodation. For the very social interests embodied in the leading capitalist and communist states are present, in a fluid and conflicting manner, in third countries; the result is that the clash of the two blocs is constantly reanimated and sustained by developments in these other states that may be supporters or allies of one or other bloc. While state advantage and competitive opportunity play a part in this, the pull towards involvement in other societies and conflicts has its roots in the systemic imperatives of both camps. It is in these three dimensions that the inter-systemic conflict of capitalism and communism resides; and it is above all this inter-systemic nature of the conflict which marks the era of postwar international politics off from that of inter-state competition in the pre-1945 period.

CONFLICT IN THE THIRD WORLD

The very category of the 'third world' reflects a certain dubious distinction. For it implies a greater difference between these poorer states of the world and the major components of the eastern and western blocs, and, by the same token, implies a greater unity between the 'third world' countries than in fact exists. One thing these states do share is a certain poverty, although even here there is much to link an Argentina, a Kuwait or a Singapore more to the richer capitalist, or 'second', post-capitalist worlds, and political movements of the south are similarly ones that seek to establish societies that would themselves follow one or other model. For this reason, the internal diversity of 'third world' states, there is no common character to the movements and states that emerge there and hence to the kind of challenges they pose to the advanced capitalist countries; the conflicts of the USA and

Britain with Vietnam or Cuba differ profoundly from those with Saudi Arabia or Argentina. The former seek to challenge the capitalist system as such, the other to negotiate a new position within it. Yet precisely because of the systemic linkage of both the capitalist and post-capitalist components of the third world to the first and second worlds, the rise of new forces and states since 1945 has directly affected relations between the major powers of east and west.

In their own bilateral negotiations, the Soviet Union and the USA have, in different ways, sought to minimise the impact of third world upheavals upon their own relations while taking advantage of each other's difficulties. But the American and more general western attempt to subdue the south and to secure Soviet acceptance of this has failed time and again on the rocks of third world revolution and nationalism themselves. These have defied the terror of metropolitan armies and the diplomatic injunctions of Soviet caution. Thus Stalin's obstinate compromise in Europe after 1945 was dramatically upstaged by the independent initiatives of the Chinese and Korean communists in the Far East. Later Khrushchev's search for agreement with America was stopped by US retaliation against the Cuban revolution of 1959, by Chinese stubbornness over 'peaceful coexistence' and by the renewed determination of the Vietnamese communists to unite their country. Brezhnev's pursuit of Detente in the early 1970s was undermined by the revolutions that swept the third world from 1974 onwards.

Yet while both the Soviet Union and the USA have been affected by the insurgencies of the third world, the two have reacted asymmetrically, since the USSR has to a certain extent made itself the ally of third world emancipation and has provided support—military, economic, diplomatic— for those resisting control by the major western states. In certain countries, the leadership of the nationalist movements has itself been assumed by communist parties or other forces sympathetic on ideological grounds to the USSR. There are many cases where the USSR has not provided significant aid, or indeed any; but, on balance, the USSR has acted and has been perceived as acting in support of third world movement, however reluctant and partial that support has been. This Soviet role has served to link the struggles between metropolitan and dominated third world countries to that between social systems and has, in so doing, provided a political advantage to the USSR, comparable to that provided to the capitalist world in the realm of political and economic achievement. The reason for the USSR's involvement in the struggles of the third world are [sic] often said to be great power interest and tactical advantage alone. Such factors and calculations must play a role; yet, on closer examination, these cease to be sufficient explanation. It is certainly true that some of the states aided by the USSR—Egypt and India, for example—have remained part of the capitalist bloc, and that here state interest seems to be primary in Soviet motivation. But other examples of economic and military support, from China in the 1950s to Afghanistan, Cuba, Vietnam and Nicaragua in the 1980s, represent the drive to consolidate these as extensions of the post-capitalist world.

The major capitalist states are also and have, to some extent, given expression to these conflicts by rivalry with each other in the third world. There has since 1945 been competition between different western European states, the USA and Japan for influence in the Middle East. But this inter-capitalist conflict has had clear limits and is quite distinct from that between the USA and the USSR. No capitalist rival of the USA's has offered to guarantee the security of Cuba against US attack, has armed Vietnam to fight the American intervention forces, or has airlifted weapons to Angola and Ethiopia. There is, in other words, a more fundamental dimension to this Soviet involvement in the third world, one that goes beyond mere inter-state rivalry. It is here that the systemic character of the Great Contest arises again: the Soviet Union is committed by its own ideology and social interests it represents to competing with the USA in the third world and to supporting those states that have themselves sought to break from the capitalist world order.

DIVISION WITHIN BLOCS

The third, final, contributory factor is one which many writers have seen as the core of contemporary international conflict, namely the desire of the leading powers, the USA and the USSR, to maintain control within their own camps. Its appeal lies behind the 'west-west' and 'intra-state' theories already mentioned. In this perspective, the conflict between camps is a convenient issue around which the maintenance of internal order can be justified. It is a diversion, a ritual, an excuse, which masks the primacy of conflicts within the societies and between the states of both camps. The easiest way to discredit opponents is to accuse them of being agents of the enemy camp. In the early 1980s this was the fate of Solidarity in Poland and the guerrillas of El Salvador, the one accused of working for the CIA, the other of being tools of Soviet expansionism. The easiest way for a stronger state to impose policy on a weaker ally is to remind the latter of the dangers from which the stronger is protecting it. The easiest way to mobilise domestic support for a course of action is to justify it as a response to the threat from outside. As Edward Thompson has argued, such ideological 'bonding' serves important functions in both east and west.

This 'internal' analysis is an approach especially attractive to those who are in opposition within either camp. Those in capitalist societies who seek to focus criticism upon the actions of their own governments can do so the more easily if they ignore the conflict with the communist world, and put all the blame for the world's problems upon their own politicians. Yet this can only be done by suppressing the degree to which the USSR is itself an actor in world politics, with aims and policies at variance with those of the west. No account of the Second Cold War, any more than that of the First, can portray one of the two major constituents as simply a passive element. Those in communist countries, struggling for democratic freedoms, finds [sic] it convenient to blame all on their ruling parties and Politburos. Yet, in so doing, they ignore some elementary but significant facts: that the USA has sought since 1945 to maintain a military superiority over the USSR and its allies, that the west has used a wide variety of economic pressures to harass the communist states, and that the metropolitan capitalist states have waged a series of barbaric wars in the third world under the justification of fighting communism. On both sides such dissident analysts, in the attempt to criticise their own governments try to portray the official enemy as either politically innocent or analytically irrelevant. It is for this reason that both the opposition in the Soviet bloc and the peace movement in the west have tended to understate the degree of inter-systemic conflict *and* to downgrade the role of third world revolt in international tensions.

There is much to recommend this 'internal' perspective, but its insight can be preserved only so long as it does not exclude the other constituent elements. The intra-bloc conflicts between major capitalist or communist powers, between the USA on one side and the EEC and Japan on the other, have figured prominently in recent years, as has for a longer period the dispute between the USSR and China. Threats to metropolitan control posed by third world resistance of various kinds have often been met by casting all of these as the product of a Soviet grand design. Just as the First Cold War was accompanied by the mobilisation of anti-communist sentiment in a Red Scare, so the Second Cold War has involved a concerted rollback of social and political changes in the advanced capitalist countries and renewed emphasis upon the need to control the third world. Domestic interests and tension and conflicts between states within one system do play a major role in influencing international relations. They are linked to the conflict between systems by the rhetoric of those who seek to discredit forces for support from outside their own system.

Yet despite the ferocity of these intra-blocs conflicts, and their contribution to international relations, they cannot on their own account for the course which the latter take. Beyond the disputes of the Russian and American governments with their respective allies and populations, there lies the Great Contest, the ongoing dispute between the two systems itself, to which the maintenance of order within each camp is linked. The inter-systemic conflict is not fought out as its main protagonists claim, and there is much that is ritualistic, diversionary and misleading in it. But this is a long way from saying that the conflict between capitalism and communism is a mirage; it remains the focal point of world politics, the globalised conflict around which other constitutive elements, for all their independence and unpredictability, must develop. If these constituent elements provide the framework within which international politics work themselves out, they do not, on their own, provide explanation of the specific events of any one period. And to explain the onset of the Second Cold War, it is necessary to look in more detail at those developments which combined to alter the east-west climate from one of Detente to one of Cold War. It is this closer examination which the following chapters attempt, concentrating on five major causes of the Second Cold War, from the arms race through to the conflicts between the major capitalist states.

The central role of the Great Contest needs, however, to be underlined once again, because it is easy to lose sight of it in the rush of individual incidents and because there are many who, as indicated earlier in this chapter, deny its importance. For opponents of the arms race, it seems to be a complicating factor, one that can make the abolition of nuclear weapons appear more difficult, and introduce divisive issues into the campaign against them. For the left, critical of the revolutionary pretensions of the USSR and the 'Soviet Threat' rhetoric of the right, it is equally unwelcome. Yet it is also important to stress the unequal character of this Contest, and the continuing superiority, in resources and initiative, of the USA and its allies. It is they who bear the primary responsibility for launching the Second Cold War because of what was seen in Washington and its allied capitals as an erosion of the superiority, military and political, which the west had previously had. The responsibility for Cold War II is shared between east and west, as was that for Cold War I; but it is the west which, precisely because it has the upper hand, took the initiative in introducing a new level of competition which it believes will restore the primacy in world politics which recent developments have taken from it. It is this theme, of the shared but unequal responsibility of east and west for the Second Cold War, which the subsequent chapters discuss.

from "Towards a New Cold War"/Chomsky*

These essays have so far focused on relations between intellectuals and the state at one particular historical moment, in the aftermath of the Vietnam war. The consequences of the war for the international system were not negligible, but it led to no structural or institutional changes in Western societies. It is therefore to be expected that the programs of counterrevolutionary intervention rooted in these institutional structures will persist as they have through the "post-colonial era," taking new forms in the context of conflicts over scarce resources and the conditions of exploitation. But such programs require a docile and obedient population. It has therefore been imperative to overcome what is now called the "Vietnam syndrome," that is, the reluctance on the part of large sectors of the population of the West to tolerate the programs of aggression, subversion, massacre, and brutal exploitation that constitute the actual historical experience of much of the Third World, faced with "Western humanism." In part as a consequence of the Indochina wars, dangerous feelings of sympathy for oppressed and suffering people developed in Western society. These had to be reversed and the image of Western benevolence restored, a difficult task, but one that was forthrightly addressed and carried out with great skill by the Western propaganda system.

It is unrealistic to suppose that the propaganda campaign was planned or centrally orchestrated. Rather, it was conducted on the basis of perceived self-interest, with the willing cooperation of the secular priesthood in conformity with traditional and quite intelligible tendencies towards service to the state. Opportunities were seized and exploited as they arose. Nixon's petty criminality provided an occasion to personify the evil that could not be denied and to expunge it from the body politic, its institutional structures protected from scrutiny; his serious crimes—the merciless bombing of Laos and Cambodia and the murderous "pacification" campaigns in South Vietnam, the domestic terrorism of the national political police that was exposed during exactly the Watergate period, vastly exceeding in scale and significance anything charged against Nixon—were no part of the Watergate farce. Now cleansed and purified, the U.S. government embarked on a noble campaign to defend human rights everywhere—at least, everywhere east of the Elbe—to the applause of its allies, eager to reap what benefit they might from the exercise. Meanwhile, the docile intellectuals of the Western world assumed the task of presenting in the most lurid light the suffering, brutality, and terror to be found throughout the shattered societies of Indochina, often effacing the Western role and responsibility. As for the bitter consequences of Western actions elsewhere, these are noted at most on an episodic basis, rarely subjected to systematic analysis or traced to their causes. Whenever the flimsiest opportunity arises, the West is portrayed as a victim, not an active agent in world affairs, suffering the blows of its legitimate interests and the values it proclaims.

These and other noteworthy propaganda successes have helped set the stage for a renewed commitment to militarization as a mechanism for imposing order on a domestic and international society that is regarded as dangerously "out of control." By the latter stages of the Carter Administration, the predictable and predicted moves were already evident. In late 1978—long before the Russian invasion of Afghanistan or the taking of the hostages in Iran—President Carter stated that "our goal . . . is to increase the real level of defense expenditures." Later, he proudly announced that whereas "defense spending dropped by one third in those eight years before I became President," since he assumed office "outlays for defense spending [have] been increased every year." In November 1978, the *New York Times* reported that "Administration sources said that the Defense Department was especially gratified because Carter has decided to cut about $15 billion out of the normal growth of a range of social and domestic programs" while raising military spending by some $12 billion. "Officials indicated that the 'guns and butter' argument waged within the Administration has now, in fact, been settled by Carter in favor of the Defense Department." Meanwhile, in direct violation of campaign promises, the Carter Administration stepped up arms sales, while also accelerating the development of new strategic weapons and pressuring its allies to install nuclear missiles (with, it is reported, a flight time of five minutes to Moscow) in Western Europe.

It goes without saying that Western initiatives are only one element in this race towards disaster, which have led many commentators to speak ominously of the mood of 1914 and 1939. But they nevertheless constitute one significant component. What deserves specific mention in this context is the contribution to this dangerous state of affairs that has been made by the remarkably effective campaign to reconstruct the ideological system that was battered by the Indochina wars.

The taking of the American hostages in Iran was also exploited, not without cynicism, as a target of opportunity in the process of overcoming the "Vietnam syndrome." Shortly after the crisis erupted, the *New York Times* ran a front-page story by Hedrick Smith headlined "Iran is Helping the U.S. to Shed Fear of Intervening Abroad." Smith reported "an important shift of attitudes" in Washington "that, many believe, will have a significant long-term impact on the willingness of the United States to project its power in the third world and to develop greater military capacities for protecting its interests there." "We are moving away from our post-Vietnam reticence," one policymaker said. Democratic National Chairman John White stated that "we may have reached a turning point in our attitude toward ourselves, and that is a feeling that we have a right to protect legitimate American interests anywhere in the world." Senator Frank Church indicated support for military intervention in the Middle East "if our interests were threatened." The "lesson of Vietnam," Smith reports, is that we must be "more selective" in the use of military power with a more careful calculation of the costs to us, as we consider intervention "in such troubled regions of potential American influence as the Middle East and the Caribbean." Consider what must be intended if our influence in these regions is regarded as only "potential."

Such reactions are a very natural culmination of the process of reconstruction of imperial ideology that has been progressing step by step for the past years. It is hardly surprising that in Kuwait and other Middle Eastern states bitter resentment is expressed over the concept of "legitimate American interests" that may be "protected" by U.S. armed force, a fact little noted or appreciated here since it is assumed that the resources of the world are ours by right. On similar assumptions, the respected political commentator Walter Laqueur suggested that Middle East oil "could be internationalized, not on behalf of a few oil companies but for the benefit of the rest of mankind," though his concern for the benefit of the rest of mankind did not extend to the natural conclusion that the industrial and agricultural resources of the West should also be internationalized and made generally available.

In January 1978, Secretary of Defense Harold Brown ordered the pentagon to plan for a rapid deployment force of 100,00 men backed by air and naval units for possible intervention in the Persian Gulf region or elsewhere, renewing plans that had been blocked by a Congress hobbled by "post-Vietnam reticence"—for example, by the conservative Senator Richard Russell, who warned that "if it is easy for us to go anywhere and do anything, we will always be going somewhere and doing something," with consequences that were dramatically evident at the time. The lesson of the hostage crisis in Iran is supposed to be that we should overcome our "reticence," develop more destructive strategic weapons, deploy forces prepared for rapid intervention throughout the world, "unleash" the CIA, and otherwise demonstrate our pugnacity.

That such lessons should be drawn from the taking of the hostages in Iran is quite revealing. It is obvious on a moment's thought that a rapid deployment force, now estimated at 200,000 men, would be no more effective than the MX missile system in rescuing the hostages or preventing the takeover of the embassy (or deterring the USSR in Afghanistan); and that it was precisely the policies of military intervention and subversion that led to the Iranian debacle, while subjecting Iranians to a quarter century of torture, murder, and suffering—"progressive methods of development," as U.S. ideologists describe what was taking place when the U.S.-trained secret police were gouging out eyes of children and much of the rural population was being driven to miserable urban slums while the agricultural system collapsed and Iran practically sank into the sea under the weight of American armaments. The hostage crisis served as a useful opportunity to advance policies that derive from other interests and concerns.

As the decade of the 1970s came to an inauspicious end, NATO, under U.S. pressure, agreed to deploy in Western Europe new advanced missiles targeted against the Soviet Union, the USSR invaded Afghanistan, and the Carter Doctrine was proclaimed, calling for still further increases in the military budget, including not only intervention forces but also preparations for a peacetime draft and the MX missile system, vast in scale and cost and a major contribution to an escalating arms race. War clouds are gathering. We are entering the period of what some are calling "the New Cold War."

If there is indeed a renewal of superpower confrontation, it is likely to resemble the Old Cold War in certain respects but to be crucially different in others. Consider first some likely similarities. The Cold War is generally described as a "zero-sum game" in which the gains of one antagonist equal the losses of the other. But this is a highly questionable interpretation. It would be more realistic to regard the Cold War system as a macabre dance of death in which the rulers of the superpowers mobilize their own populations to support harsh and brutal measures directed against victims within what they take to be their respective domains, where they are "protecting their legitimate interests." Appeal to the alleged threat of the powerful global enemy has proven to be a useful device for this purpose. In this respect, the Cold War has proven highly functional for the superpowers, which is one reason why it persists despite the prospect of mutual incineration if the system misbehaves, as sooner or later it very likely will. When the United States moves to overthrow the government of Iran or Guatemala or Chile, or to invade Cuba or Indochina or the Dominican Republic, or to bolster murderous dictatorships in Latin America or Asia, it does so in a noble effort to defend free peoples from the imminent Russian (or earlier, Chinese) threat. Similarly, when the USSR sends its tanks to East Berlin, Hungary, Czechoslovakia, or Afghanistan, it is acting from the purest of motives, defending socialism and freedom against the machinations of U.S. imperialism and its cohorts. The rhetoric employed on both sides is similar, and is generally parroted by the intelligentsia in each camp. It has proven effective in organizing popular support, as even a totalitarian state must do. In this respect, the New Cold War promises to be no different, and can be understood in part as a natural outcome of the effort to overcome the "Vietnam syndrome."

Another typical gambit is the pretense that only a show of force will deter the superpower antagonist from its relentless marauding and subversion. The actual dynamics of the Cold War system suggest a rather different conclusion. Typically, acts of subversion, violence, and aggression, or development and deployment of new weapons systems, have had the predictable effect of reinforcing those elements of the antagonist state that are committed, for their own reasons, to similar practices, a recurrent pattern throughout the Cold War period. Examples that are cited in support of the standard thesis regularly collapse on examination, e.g., Angola, where the U.S.-backed South African intervention is generally disregarded in Western propaganda on the Cuban menace, and a more accurate assessment would take note of "the manner in which Kissinger tried to foment and sustain a civil war in Angola simply to convince the Russians that the American tiger could still bite." It does not, of course, follow that a willingness to seek accommodation would mechanically lead to a relaxation of tensions and a reduction of international violence, but its role as a possible factor should not be discounted.

One persistent element of the Cold War system is the portrayal of the superpower antagonist in the most menacing terms. In Soviet propaganda, the United States is led by warmongers deterred from their limitless drive for expansion only by Russian power. In the West, it is now an article of faith that the Soviet Union is outspending its rivals in a race towards military domination of the planet. There is some basis of truth in these competing claims, as is usually the case even in the most vulgar propaganda exercises, but it is revealing to disentangle the element of truth from the web of distortion. The claim that the USSR is unrivaled in its commitment of resources to military production is based largely on CIA analyses which estimates the dollar equivalent of the USSR military effort; thus the question asked is what it would cost the United States, in dollars, to duplicate the military force deployed by the USSR. As a number of commentators have observed, these calculations have a built-in bias. The Soviet military force is labor-intensive, in contrast to the military system of the West with its superior technological level and higher cost of labor relative to capital. It would be highly inefficient, and extremely costly, for the United States to duplicate a technologically less advanced Soviet military machine that relies heavily on manpower. Hence calculations of dollar equivalents considerably exaggerate Russian power. For the United States to duplicate the Russian agricultural system, with its intensive use of human labor power and low level of technology, would also be extremely expensive. But we do not therefore conclude that the Russians are outmatching us in the field of agricultural production. For similar reasons, calculations of dollar equivalents give a highly misleading picture of relative military strength. . . . I have been discussing some features of the Old Cold War that one may expect, I believe, to persist if it is successfully resurrected. But there will also be differences. The world is not what it was a generation ago. It is doubtful that the United States, no longer in a position of overwhelming dominance, can devote its resources to the production of waste while maintaining its position in international trade—of course, apart from sales of military equipment, which continue to increase, not solely from the United States. Efforts to pressure U.S. allies to "bear their share of the burden" of military expenditures are not likely to prove too successful. Europe and Japan have shown little enthusiasm for the new crusade. East-West trade in Europe is now quite substantial, as traditional relationships are being reestablished, and it is unlikely that the Europeans powers will be willing to sacrifice it. American allies may choose to take their own independent initiatives, not only towards the USSR but also towards the Middle East and other resource-rich areas, realizing long-term fears of American planners. It is worth recalling Henry Kissinger's warning, in explaining the thinking behind the "Year of Europe" in 1973, about "the prospect of a closed trading system embracing the European Community and a growing number of other nations in Europe, the Mediterranean and Africa" from which the United States might be excluded. The proper organization of the world system, he explained, should be based on the recognition that "the United States has global interests and responsibilities," while our allies have "regional interests"; the United States must be "concerned more with the overall framework of order than with the management of every regional enterprise," these being accorded to our allies, as he elaborated elsewhere. But this version of "trilateralism" is unlikely to survive for long.

The Trilateral Commission, which was formed in 1973 to come to terms with the problems of fragmentation within the First World of industrial capitalism, was quite correct in describing the international system that arose from World War II in these terms: "For a quarter century the United States was the hegemonic power in a system of world order"—correct, at least, if we interpret the phrase "world order" with the appropriate irony. It is true that in the system that arose from the ashes of World War II, the United States was in a position of quite considerable power, sufficient to materially influence historical developments though not to control them completely in its interests. It is hardly surprising, then, that it attempted to organize a global system, or at least a Grand Area, in the interests of those who held domestic power. The USSR created its own power bloc in Eastern Europe and to some degree China. This was the basic structure of the Old Cold War, but the world is now radically different. China is an American ally and a bitter enemy of the USSR, a major shift in the balance of world power in favor of the United States. And the capitalist world is drifting towards a kind of trilateralism which may eventuate in three partially closed trading blocs—a dollar bloc, a yen bloc, a European Currency Union bloc—as a recent OECD study suggests, with international consequences that are uncertain, and in many ways ominous. Those who recall the mood of 1914 and 1939 do so with some reason.

There is no doubt that U.S. power has waned as the bipolar system of the postwar years has gradually evolved to something more complex. The same is true of Soviet power. A recent study of the Center for Defense Information in Washington, tracing Russian influence on a country-by-country basis since World War II, concludes quite reasonably that it reached a peak in the late 1950s and has since declined to the point where by 1979, "the Soviets were influencing only 6% of the world's population and 5% of the world's GNP, exclusive of the Soviet Union." For reasons already discussed Cold War ideologists in both camps like to pretend that their adversary is marching from strength to strength, but the facts hardly support these conclusions.

Though their capacity to destroy grows steadily, neither the United States nor the Soviet Union now has the power it once was able to wield in world affairs, and this process is not likely to be reversed.

Europe and Japan pose a greater potential threat to u.s. world power than the Soviet Union, if they move towards a more independent role. And a u.s.-sponsored New Cold War may press them in that direction, raising the possibility of new and unanticipated crises and alignments. In the shorter term, one may expect the superpowers to create new and more awesome forces of destruction and to try to subjugate those who stand in the way of their global ambitions, marching toward nuclear catastrophe.

The recent steps towards Armageddon have evoked little articulate pro-test in the United States, though there is a substantial ground swell of popular concern. This testifies again to the great success of the campaign to overcome the "Vietnam syndrome." A few recent examples will illustrate the astonishing achievements of the efforts to restore what Hans Morgen-thau once called "our conformist subservience to those in power"—though as noted in these essays, the distance that had to be traveled was far less than is often supposed. First, some additional words of background.

The war against the world's poor and oppressed reached its peak under the liberal democratic administrations of the 1960s, with the considerable amplification of the doctrine and practice of counterinsurgency and coun-terrevolutionary subversion and violence. A plague of new-fascist states spread through Latin America and elsewhere as well. Brazil, because of its size and power, was a particularly significant example. The u.s.-backed mil-itary coup of 1964 placed in power a repressive and murderous regime that carried out an "economic miracle" while keeping the great mass of the population in conditions of grinding poverty and actually lowering the already miserable standard of living for many of them. It also had a noticea-ble "domino effect," contributing to the spread of u.s. backed military dicta-torships committed to repression and violence. As always, u.s. support for the Brazilian coup was justified on the grounds that "the nation needed it in order to free itself of a corrupt government which was about to sell us out to international communism (General Andrew O'Meara, Commander of the u.s. Southern Command, testifying before Congress in 1965). President Kennedy's ambassador to Brazil, Lincoln Gordon, described the Brazilian "revolution" as the "the single most decisive victory for freedom in the mid-twentieth century." Similarly the Indonesian coup a year later was wel-comed in liberal circles as a vindication of the u.s. policy of standing firm in Indochina, while the resulting massacre of hundreds of thousands of land-less peasants, if noted at all, was dismissed as an unfortunate reaction to Communist plotting. The revolution in Cuba, in contrast, was understood to pose such threats to human rights and civilized values that the leader of the Free World subjected Cuba to invasion, subversion, embargo. Terrorism, poisoning of crops and livestock—and now, after this record, stands in judgment over Cuba for its violation of human rights.

The situation in Latin America has not gone unnoticed in establishment media. Richard Fagen writes in *Foreign Affairs* (Winter 1979) that the Linowitz Commission was accurate in describing the "plague of repression" that had settled over Latin America by 1976: "At no time in the recent history of the hemisphere had the incidence of military rule been so high, the gross violations of political and human rights so widespread, and the use of officially sponsored assassination, torture and brutality so systematic." But in journalistic or scholarly discussion these facts are rarely related to u.s. initiatives; rather, these developments show that it is not within the power of the United States to eliminate inequality and poverty, as it has been striving so desperately to do for so many years in Brazil, Paraguay, Nicaragua, Guatemala, and elsewhere within the domains of its influence and control.

Actually, it is interesting to inquire into the relation between human rights violations and u.s. aid and support. There does, in fact, appear to be a correlation, which has been noted in several studies, one of them by Edward S. Herman and myself (see our *Political Economy of Human Rights*, vol. I). We found, as did Michael Klare in an independent study, that the deterioration of the human rights climate in some Free World dependencies tends to correlate rather closely with an increase in u.s. aid and support. Of course, one must be cautious with statistical correlations; the correlation in question should not be interpreted as implying that the u.s. government is rewarding some ruling group for the increase in torture, death squads, destructions of unions, elimination of democratic institutions, decline of living standards for much of the population, etc. These are not a positive priority for u.s. policy; rather, they are irrelevant to it. The correlation between abuse of human rights and u.s. support derives from deeper factors. The deterioration in human rights and the increase in u.s. aid and support each correlate, independently, with a third and crucial factor; namely, improvement in the investment climate, as measured by privileges granted foreign capital. The climate for business operations improves as unions and other popular organizations are destroyed, dissidents are tortured or eliminated, real wages are depressed, and the society as a whole is placed in the hands of a collection of thugs who are willing to sell out to the foreigner for a share of the loot— often too large a share, as business regularly complains. And as the climate for business operations improves, the society is welcomed into the Free World and offered the specific kind of "aid" that will further these favorable developments. If the consequences are, for example, that crops are produced for export by wealthy landowners or transnational agribusiness while the population starves, that is simply the price that must be paid for the survival of free institutions.

The humanitarian missions to which the u.s. government is devoting its energies out of its deep compassion for the suffering people of Southeast Asia deserve more attention than I can devote to them here. The zealous efforts of the industrial democracies to help implement Indonesian atrocities in East Timor are merely a by-product of their relations to Indonesia, which has thrown itself open to their plunder since the military coup of 1965. The United States, Japan, France, and their allies have no positive interest in the massacre of the population of East Timor, contrary to what is suggested by consideration of their action. It is merely that the fate of the Timorese is of null import given the higher importance of exploiting the wealth of Indonesia. The case of Indochina is more complex. The United States did win a significant victory in Indochina, a fact that is crucial to the understanding of postwar events. True, it did not achieve the goal of retaining Indochina within the American system, so that its people could enjoy the happy life of the peasants, urban slum-dwellers, torture victims, and child slave laborers of Thailand, Indonesia, the Philippines, and Latin America. But that was always a secondary goal. The primary goal was to ensure that "the rot would not spread," in the terminology favored by the planners. In South Vietnam itself, the United States did win the war. The battering of the peasant society, particularly the murderous post-Tet accelerated pacification campaigns, virtually destroyed the indigenous resistance by eliminating its social base, setting the stage for the northern domination now deplored by Western hypocrites—exactly as had been predicted many years before. In Cambodia, the horrendous bombing campaign of 1973, which was directed primarily against the peasant society, was a significant factor in brutalizing the Khmer Rouge victors, a conclusion supported by u.s. government studies and other sources. In Laos, the prospects for peaceful development in one of the world's poorest countries were destroyed by American subversion and military attack. North Vietnam, while not conquered, was left in ruins.

The terrible prospect of successful economic development has been overcome for a long time, perhaps permanently. No one knows when, or if, the land and people poisoned by chemical warfare and bombed to ruin will be restored to a viable social order. The postwar policy of refusing reparations, aid, or normal relations with Vietnam and blocking assistance from other sources where possible is perfectly rational, as a further contribution to ensuring maximal suffering. It also succeeded in driving Vietnam into alliance with the Soviet Union as the only alternative remaining, again a consequence eagerly exploited by the Western propaganda system. By systematically creating conditions under which existence is reduced to virtually the zero grade, Western power has attained its primary ends throughout Indochina. The West has once again taught the lesson that European civilization has offered to the world for centuries: those who try to resist the technologically advanced but morally primitive Western societies will pay a bitter price.

Notes

1 Cited by Angus McIntosh 1957:40.
2 I use these particular terms because I wish to view processing varieties as subtypes of language rather than as languages. I am employing the term "speech" abstractly to designate a category of language of which two variants (oral or written) are available to the speaker. These terms are also employed by Lev Vygotsky in *Thought and Language* with the addition of a further form of speech, inner speech.
3 Halliday distinguishes embedding from subordination; embedding primarily involves use of relative clauses and nonfinite verbal phrases, while subordination involves use of adverb and noun clauses.
4 Gregory (1967) distinguishes between two major oral speech groupings: spontaneous oral speech and non-spontaneous oral speech. Within the second grouping, Gregory further distinguishes recitation, oral performance, and lectures. Gregory, in fact, categorizes written speech in terms of its degree of relatedness to oral speech, for, as he points out, much that is written is done so with a listener and not a reader in mind. Thus, most talk on television is scripted and performed.
5 Thus Jean Ure and Jeffrey Ellis specifically refer to register in generic terms: "Register is a certain kind of language patterning regularly used in a certain kind of situation. It is a social convention" (1977:7).
6 The related genres of argument and persuasion are difficult to distinguish, although both have a world to word direction of fit. In argument, where speakers are co-conversationalists, debate occurs on the basis of difference of view or opinion, whereas in persuasion, where only one speaker has the floor, speech is used to change the behaviour of another and is not genuinely persuasive unless a change of state has occurred. Persuasion is best exemplified by advertisements which are

constructed so that consumers will purchase specific goods. Conversely, debate can occur between speakers without change in the mental state of either speaker. Although the purpose of argument is to cause such change in the mental state of another, it does not require such a change. Argument is a non-telic activity.

CHAPTER TWO: ORAL AND WRITTEN NARRATIVE

1 In this narrative told by Della about Fernandez, Della gets Fernandez, who thinks of himself as a good dresser, to mimic the dress of another young male who has dressed to reveal his chest and figure to the fullest extent. Della appears to be a black American engaging in the verbal combat and challenge typical of members of the black subculture in the U.S.A.

2 As Ong points out, "In his *Arts Poetica*, Horace writes that the epic poet 'hastens into the action and precipitates the hearer into the middle of things' (lines 148–9)" (1981:14). Therefore, literate poets such as John Milton "interpreted Horace's *in medias res* as making *hysteron proeteron* obligatory in the epic" (14).

3 De Saussure articulates a similar conception of such evocation in his analysis of "associative relations" which "unite terms *in absentia* in a potential mnemonic series" (1966:123).

4 Pawley and Syder isolate several features which they correlate with oral speech: vernacular relative clauses (deeply embedded NP's) dependent clauses functioning as relatives, delayed relative clauses, pseudo-clefting with complete basic clauses as complement, conditional clauses as nominals governed by a preposition, left-dislocation, right-dislocation, parallelism, right-dislocated reduced modifying clauses, and the use of *like* in conversation. Their research calls attention to the extent that sequencing of larger syntactic structures such as clauses differs in oral speech from that in written speech. They focus not so much on the absence or presence of certain word groups in these two media, but rather on differences in processing strategy which in turn result in syntactic differences.

5 Interestingly, Alan S.C. Ross designates these very same lexemes as sociolinguistic variants. The oral *looking glass* represents U or "upper class" speech, while the written *mirror* represents non-U or "non-upper class" speech (1962:102). Lewis Carroll identified himself as a U-speaker by entitling his second most famous narrative *Through the Looking-Glass*. In Canadian English, however, the Latinate *mirror* would mark prestige in speech, while the composite Anglo-Saxon *looking glass* would be neutral as a social marker (or be thought of as an archaic usage).

6 *Mirror* would also have +breakable as a semantic feature, but by virtue

of its glass composition. Breakability is therefore a primary feature of *glass* and a feature of *mirror* only in its association with glass.

7 Beaman assumes, as does Chafe, that "nonfinite clauses pack more information into fewer words" (1984:66).

8 Wald states that "there is no known record of its use before the 1930s," but since this feature shows up in the speech of an adult male born in 1888, "the recentness of new-this" is not "beyond dispute" as Wald maintains. Wald suggests that it is children and not adults who initiated this usage and that this feature shows up more in their speech than in that of adults. Martin would have had no opportunity to acquire this usage from children since he spent most of his life in the bush. It seems reasonable, then, that this feature existed in his oral speech well before the 1930s and that he continued to use it into his 80s during the 1960s. The new-*this*/a dichotomy must have existed in Modern Oral English for at least a hundred years and possibly longer.

9 Halliday would note here the use of "grammatical metaphor" whereby the acts themselves prove or corroborate their own relationship. Such a usage depresses the reader's awareness that an interpretation has in fact been made and so more strongly suggests the self-evident factualness of the proof.

10 Interestingly, Harold Innis notes that "Oral tradition permits painters on vases to attempt to show several scenes at once but written tradition compels a concern with time and painters use scenes with fixed space and time" (1972:69).

11 Martin Starret's first wife, however, was a member of the Carrier Indian tribe, as was his son.

12 It is also common in oral epics for agents to boast about their deeds as a way of portraying themselves, but again a story within a story ensues, such as that of Beowulf's famous swimming adventure.

13 Auerbach interprets the function of these "digressions" as "retarding" plot, but he argues nonetheless that digressions in oral narrative never provide background to the main events in a particular narrative since the narrator goes seamlessly from one narrative event to another. However, Starret's episodic digressions do provide background, as do those in oral epics, because they explain through narrative the history or background of a particular character, feature or object.

14 As Halliday notes, "As far as action clauses are concerned, an intransitive clause is one in which the roles of 'affected' and 'agent' are combined in the one participant; a transitive clause is one in which they are separated, the process being treated as one having an external cause" (1971:353).

15 In Halliday's analysis, the agent in action clauses functions as cause.

CHAPTER THREE: ORAL AND WRITTEN DESCRIPTION

1 Schank and Abelson (1977) pioneered the concept of the script whereby
an archetypal experience such as going to the dentist or to a restaurant
is made up of an equally archetypal chain of events. In the description
of a "visit" to the dentist, by virtue of a shared script between speaker/
writer and listener/reader, certain activities may not have to be
explained, such as being seated in a chair or having a final rinse once
the "checkup" is complete. Shared knowledge of the dentist checkup
script obviates the need for certain details. However, any invocation of
a script will require certain events in the chain to be described or the
script will lack generality as a type of experience. Fillmore (1975a) uses
the terms "frames" and "scenes" to denote archetypal activities such as
writing, differently conceived in the West than in the East, and associative contexts of situation. The concept of "schemas" goes back to the
work of Bartlett (1932) on memory, wherein he demonstrated the means
by which new experience was necessarily accommodated to already
existing schemas in the mind for storage and recall.

CHAPTER FOUR: ORAL AND WRITTEN EXPOSITION

1 Quoted in Howell 1971:498.
2 The term "state present" is used by Quirk et al. (1985) to designate the
use of the simple present to convey "general timeless statements" or
"eternal truths."
3 Havelock demonstrates that epic poetry in oral Greek culture functi-
oned "not on the grounds that we would offer, namely poetry's inspirational and imaginative effects, but on the ground that it provided a
massive repository of useful knowledge, a sort of encyclopedia of
ethics, politics, history and technology which the effective citizen was
required to learn as the core of his educational equipment" (27).
4 To arrive at these percentages, I have divided the number of clauses by
the number of sentences to determine an approximate percentage. Of
course, some sentences may have one, two, or more clauses, but to gain
an average percentile I have used gross numbers.
5 Buscaglia did research before presenting his findings to his listening
and reading audiences. Of the 1000 questionnaires he sent out, each
with seven basic questions, 600 were returned completed. The definition of a lover Buscaglia presents in both texts is based on the
responses found in the returned questionnaires.

CHAPTER FIVE: ORAL AND WRITTEN INSTRUCTION

1 In *Preface to Plato* (1963) Havelock explicates Plato's antagonism to oral poetics as a hypnotic influence on the rational mind.

2 I have included an excerpt of the full half-hour program in my appendix. There should be no confusion between the length of this excerpt and the length of the entire text.

3 In miniature these two contrastive texts parallel Martin Starret's respective oral and written process descriptions. Both oral texts are pseudo-narratives, while both written texts delete information which is not thematically useful and place emphasis upon key aspects of a process.

4 Schmandt-Besserat (1978) demonstrates that hollow clay bullae and enclosed clay tokens used in the Neolithic period in Western Asia for purposes of record keeping were the earliest precursors of actual writing.

5 John Chadwick, who aided Michael Ventris in deciphering Linear B, reputedly employed this term.

CHAPTER SIX: ORAL AND WRITTEN ARGUMENT

1 To arrive at a syntactic profile of each speaker (Tables 8 and 9), Noam Chomsky and Fred Halliday, I have isolated four smaller sub-texts within the three larger main texts.

2 Unable to examine Halliday's entire book, I have focused attention on his thesis chapter, which primarily delineates the arguments he opposes as well as his own position.

3 Jonathan Steele, *The Guardian*. Quoted on the back cover of *The Making of the Second Cold War*.

4 Bernardo (1979) distinguishes between two major types of relative clause, "informative relative clauses" and "non-informative relative clauses." Informative relative clauses are used to convey new information: "A--nd they come across his ha ̆t, . . . that he neglected [.55] to pick up" (542). Non-informative relative clauses convey "identificatory" information: "The man who's picking pears" (544). Such relative clauses convey known information which is used as a means to identify a particular individual or thing. Bernardo further distinguishes non-informative clauses which are "specificatory." Such clauses are used to "specify the nature of a new referent by mentioning a defining property of the referent": "Something that I noticed about the /movie/ particularly unique was that the colors . . . were [.35] just [.5] veˆry straˆnge" (540). In my view such specificatory relative clauses are a sub-variety of

informative relative clauses. These relative clauses are restrictive, and it
is the information in these relative clauses which conveys significant
new information to the listener about a newly defined but independently vague topic, usually an indefinite pronoun such as *something* or a
demonstrative pronoun such as *those*.

CHAPTER SEVEN: CONCLUSION

1 Beaman's data were taken from the Pear Stories, a set of narratives told
by speakers after having seen a film in which a young boy steals a pear
from a man picking pears in his orchard. The stories were not naturally
occurring in that they concerned subject matter selected and determined in all ways by the linguistic researchers.
2 As Mathesius points out, "In regular two-element sentences that contain the theme (T) and the rheme (R) it is of importance in which order
these two elements are arranged. Two arrangements are possible, T–R
and R–T, and both are found. When we realize the relations between
the speaker and the hearer we find that the order T–R takes into
account the hearer. The speaker starts from what is known and proceeds to what is new. This is the so-called objective order since the
speaker takes into account the particular situation and conforms to the
usual mental procedure" (83).
3 In *Basic Word Order: Functional Principles*, Russel S. Tomlin has recently
(1986) shown that word order in languages has a strong relation to
what he calls the Theme First Principle. Here the Theme First Principle
is actively employed in the structure of sentences as they appear in
sequence.
4 Use of *etc.* in written speech and *and so on* in oral speech is comparable
to the employment of the *ejusdem generis* rule in legal discourse. This
rule equally permits the discontinuation of listing of like or other examples in a series.

Bibliography

SOURCES

Buscaglia, Leo. *Loving Each Other*. Toronto: Holt, Rinehart and Winston 1984
—. *The Politics of Love*. PBS. November 1985
Chomsky, Noam. "Towards a New Cold War." In *Towards a New Cold War*. New York: Pantheon 1982
Halliday, Fred. *The Making of the Second Cold War*. London: Verso 1984
"Noam Chomsky and Fred Halliday in Conversation." *Voices*. Channel 4. Great Britain. June 1985
Smith, Jeff. *The Frugal Gourmet*. New York: Ballantine Books 1984
—. "Show 116. Yogurt and Cheese: Make Your Own." *The Frugal Gourmet*. PBS. March 1986
Starret, Martin. *Journal (Add. Mss. 364)*. Victoria: British Columbia Archives and Records Service
—. *Mss. Relating to Northern B.C. (Add. Mss. 364)*. Victoria: British Columbia Archives and Records Service
—. *Astace the Indian (Add. Mss. 364)*. Victoria: British Columbia Archives and Records Service
—. *Interview with Martin Starret (1963-9)*. With Imbert Orchard. CBC Radio (No. 399:1-21). Victoria: British Columbia Archives and Records Service

GENERAL

Akinnaso, F. Niyi. "On the Differences between Spoken and Written Language." *Language and Speech* 25 (1982):97-125
Aristotle. *The Rhetoric of Aristotle*. Trans. Lane Cooper. Englewood Cliffs, NJ: Prentice-Hall 1960
Auerbach, Erich. "Odysseus' Scar." *Mimesis: The Representation of Reality in Western Literature*. Princeton: Princeton University Press 1953, pp. 3-23

Bakhtin, M.M. *The Dialogic Imagination*. Ed. Michael Holquist. Austin: University of Texas Press 1981

Bar-Lev, Zev, and Arthur Palacas. "Semantic Command over Pragmatic Priority." *Lingua* 51 (1980):137-46

Baron, Naomi S. *Speech, Writing, & Sign*. Bloomington: Indiana University Press 1981

Bartlett, F. *Remembering*. Cambridge: Cambridge University Press 1932

Beaman, Karen. "Coordination and Subordination Revisited: Syntactic Complexity in Spoken and Written Narrative Discourse." In *Coherence in Spoken and Written Discourse*. Ed. Deborah Tannen. Norwood, NJ: Ablex 1984, pp. 45-50

Becker, Alton. "A Tagmemic Approach to Paragraph Analysis." In *The Sentence and the Paragraph*. Urbana, IL: National Council of Teachers of English 1966, pp. 33-8

Bernardo, Robert. "The Function and Content of Relative Clauses in Spontaneous Oral Narratives." *Proceedings of the Fifth Annual Meeting of the Berkeley Linguistics Society*. Berkeley: Berkeley Linguistics Society 1979, pp. 539-51

Biber, Douglas. "Spoken and Written Textual Dimensions in English: Resolving the Contradictory Findings." *Language* 62 (1986):384-412

Black, John B., Deanna Wilkes-Gibbs, and Raymond W. Gibbs Jr. "What Writers Need to Know that They Don't Know They Need to Know." In *What Writers Know: The Language, Process, and Structure of Written Discourse*. Ed. Martin Nystrand. London: Academic Press 1982, pp. 325-43

Blankenship, Jane. "A Linguistic Analysis of Oral and Written Style." *Quarterly Journal of Speech*, 48 (1962):419-22

Bloch, Maurice. "Introduction." In *Political Language and Oratory in Traditional Society*. Ed. Maurice Bloch. London: Academic Press 1975

Bloomfield, Leornard. *Language*. New York: Holt 1933

Bolinger, Dwight L. "Visual Morphemes." *Language* 22 (1946):333-40

Bradley, Henry. "Spoken and Written English." In *The Collected Papers of Henry Bradley*. Oxford: Clarendon Press 1928, pp. 168-88

Brazil, David. "Intonation and Discourse: Some Principles and Procedures." *Text* 3 (1983):39-70

—. "Phonology: Intonation in Discourse." In *Handbook of Discourse Analysis*, Vol. 2. Ed. Teun A. van Dijk. London: Academic Press 1985, pp. 57-75

Brown, Gillian. "Understanding Spoken Language." *TESOL Quarterly* 12 (1978):271-83

— and George Yule. *Discourse Analysis*. Cambridge: Cambridge University Press 1983

Brown, P. and Levinson, S.C. "Universals in Language Usage: Politeness Phenomena." In *Questions and Politeness*. Ed. E.N. Goody. Cambridge: Cambridge University Press 1978

Carrell, Patricia. "Cohesion Is Not Coherence." *TESOL Quarterly* 16 (1982):479–88

Chafe, Wallace. "Givenness, Contrariness, Definiteness, Subjects, Topics, and Points of View." In *Subject and Topic*. Ed. C.N. Li. New York: Academic Press 1976, pp. 26–55

—. "The Recall and Verbalization of Past Experience." In *Current Issues in Linguistic Theory*. Ed. R.W. Cole. Bloomington: Indiana University Press 1979, pp. 215–46

—. *The Pear Stories: Cognitive, Cultural and Linguistic Aspects of Narrative Production*. Norwood, NJ: Ablex 1980

—. "Integration and Involvement in Speaking, Writing and Oral Literature." In *Spoken and Written Language: Exploring Orality and Literacy*. Ed. Deborah Tannen. Norwood, NJ: Ablex 1982, pp. 35–53

— and Jane Danielewicz. "Properties of Spoken and Written Language." In *Comprehending Oral and Written Language*. Eds. Rosalind Horowitz and S. Jay Samuels. San Diego: Academic Press 1987, pp. 83–113

Champagne, Roland. "The Resurrection of THOTH, the God of Writing: Jacques Derrida's Arguments for the *machine à écrire*." *Centrum* 2:1 (1974):5–13

Clanchy, M.T. *From Memory to Written Record: England 1066–1307*. London: Arnold 1979

Clancy, Patricia. "Analysis of a Conversation." *Anthropological Linguistics* 14 (1972):78 86

Comrie, Bernard. "Aspect and Voice: Some Reflections on Perfect and Passive." In *Syntax and Semantics, Vol. 14: Tense and Aspect*. Ed. Philip Tedeschi and Annie Zaenen. New York: Academic Press 1981, pp. 65–78

Cook-Gumperz, Jenny, and John J. Gumperz, "From Oral to Written Culture: The Transition to Literacy." In *Variation in Writing*. Ed. Marcia Farr Whiteman. Hillsdale, NJ: Erlbaum 1981, pp. 89–109

Cooper, Marilyn. "Context as Vehicle: Implicatures in Writing." In *What Writers Know: The Language, Process, and Structure of Written Discourse*. Ed. Martin Nystrand. London: Academic Press, 1982, pp. 105–128

Coulthard, M., and M. Montgomery, eds. *Studies in Discourse Analysis*. London: Routledge and Kegan Paul 1981

Danes, Frantisek. "A Three-Level Approach to Syntax." *Travaux linguistiques de Prague* 1 (1964):225–40

Danielewicz, Jane M. "The Interaction between Text and Context: A Study of How Adults and Children Use Spoken and Written Language in Four Contexts." In *The Development of Oral and Written Language in Social Contexts*. Eds. Anthony D. Pellegrini and Thomas D. Yawkey. Hillsdale, NJ: Erlbaum 1984, pp. 243–60

Derrida, Jacques. *L'Ecriture et la différence*. Paris: Editions de Seuil 1967

DeVito, J.A. "A Quantitative Analysis of Comprehension Factors in Samples of Oral and Written Technical Discourse of Skilled Communicators." Diss., University of Illinois 1964

—. "Comprehension Factors in Oral and Written Discourse of Skilled Communicators." *Speech Monographs* 32 (1965): 124-8

—. "Psychogrammatical Factors in Oral and Written Discourse by Skilled Communicators." *Speech Monographs* 33 (1966a):73-6

—. "The Encoding of Speech and Writing." *The Speech Teacher* 15 (1966b):55-60

—. "Levels of Abstraction in Spoken and Written Language." *Journal of Communication* 17 (1967):354-61

Drieman, G.A.J. "Differences between Written and Spoken Language." *Acta Psychologica* 20 (1962):36-58, 79-100

Durmosoglu, Gul. "The Notion of 'Parallel Texts' and Its Place in Contrastive and Applied Linguistics." Diss., University of Exeter 1983

Edmondson, W. *Spoken Discourse*. London: Longman 1981

Ehrich, Kate. "Eye Movements in Pronoun Assignment: A Study of Sentence Integration." In *Eye Movements in Reading: Perceptual and Language Processes*. Ed. Keith Rayner. Academic Press 1983, pp. 253-65

Fillmore, Charles J. "The Case for Case." In *Universals in Linguistic Theory*. Ed. E. Bach and R. Harms. New York: Holt, Rinehart and Winston 1968, pp. 1-88

—. "An Alternative to Checklist Theories of Meaning." *Proceedings of the First Annual Meeting, Berkeley Linguistics Society*. Berkeley: Berkeley Linguistics Society 1975a

—. *Santa Cruz Lectures on Deixis*, 1971. Bloomington: Indiana University Linguistics Club 1975b

Firbas, Jan. "On Defining the Theme in Functional Sentence Analysis." *Travaux linguistiques de Prague* 1 (1964):267-88

Firbas, Jan. "Non-thematic Subjects in Contemporary English." *Travaux linguistiques de Prague* 2 (1966):239-56

Fisher, John H. "Chancery and the Emergence of Standard Written English in the Fifteenth Century." *Speculum* 52 (1977):870-99

Frazier, Lyn. "Processing Sentence Structure." In *Eye Movements in Reading: Perceptual and Language Processes*. Ed. Keith Rayner. New York: Academic Press 1983, pp. 215-36

Gibson, J.W., C.R. Gruner, R.J. Kibler, and F.J. Kelly. "A Quantitative Examination of Differences and Similarities in Written and Spoken Messages." *Speech Monographs* 33 (1966):444-51

Givón, Talmy. *On Understanding Grammar*. New York: Academic Press 1979a

—. "From Discourse to Syntax: Grammar as a Processing Strategy." In *Syntax and Semantics, Volume 12: Discourse and Syntax*. Ed. Talmy Givón. New York: Academic Press 1979b, pp. 81-115

Glatt, Barbara S. "Defining Thematic Progressions and Their Relationship to

Reader Comprehension." In *What Writers Know: The Language, Process, and Structure of Written Discourse*. Ed. Martin Nystrand. London: Academic Press 1982, pp. 87-103

Goffman, Erving. *Forms of Talk*. Philadelphia: University of Pennsylvania Press 1981

Golub, L.S. "Linguistic Structures in Students' Oral and Written Discourse." *Research in the Teaching of English* 3 (1969):70-85

Goody, J. and Ian Watt. "The Consequences of Literacy." In *Comparative Studies in Society and History* 5 (1963):304-45

Graesser, Arthur C. and Sharon M. Goodman. "Implicit Knowledge, Question Answering, and the Representation of Expository Text." In *Understanding Expository Text*. Eds. Bruce K. Britton and John B. Black. Hillsdale, NJ: Erlbaum 1985, pp. 109-72

Green, J. "A Comparison of Oral and Written Language: A Quantitative Analysis of the Structure and Vocabulary of the Oral and Written Language of a Group of College Students." Diss., New York University 1958

Gregory, Michael. "Aspects of Varieties Differentiation." *Journal of Linguistics* 3 (1967):177-98

Grice, H. Paul. "Logic and Conversation." In *Syntax and Semantics, Vol. 3: Speech Acts*. Eds. Peter Cole and Jerry L. Morgan. New York: Academic Press 1975, pp. 41-58

Grimes, Joseph E. "Topics within Topics." In *Analyzing Discourse: Text and Talk*. Ed. Deborah Tannen. Georgetown University Round Table on Language and Linguistics, 1981. Washington, DC: Georgetown University Press 1982, pp. 164-76

Gruner, C.R., R.J. Kibler, and J.W. Gibson. "A Quantitative Analysis of Selected Characteristics of Oral and Written Vocabularies." *Journal of Communication* 17 (1967):152-8

Gulich, Elisabeth, and Uta M. Quasthoff. "Narrative Analysis." In *Handbook of Discourse Analysis*, Vol. 2. Ed. Teun A. van Dijk. London: Academic Press 1985, pp. 169-97

Haber, R.M. and Lyn R. Haber. "Visual Components of the Reading Process." *Visible Language* 15:2 (1981):147-82

Halliday, M.A.K. "Linguistic Function and Literary Style: An Enquiry into the Language of William Golding's *The Inheritors*." In *Literary Style: A Symposium*. Ed. Seymour Chatman. New York: Oxford University Press 1971, pp. 330-63

—. *Halliday: System and Function in Language*. Ed. Gunther Kress. London: Oxford University Press 1976

—. "Differences between Spoken and Written Language: Some Implications for Literacy Teaching." In *Communication through Reading*. Eds. Glenda Page, John Elkins, and Barrie O'Connor. Proceedings of the Fourth Australian Reading Conference, Adelaide: Australian Reading Association,

Vol. 2, 1978, pp. 37-52

—. *Spoken and Written Language*. Victoria: Deakin University Press 1985a

—. *An Introduction to Functional Grammar*. London: Arnold 1985b

—. "Spoken and Written Modes of Meaning." In *Comprehending Oral and Written Language*. Eds. Rosalind Horowitz and S. Jay Samuels. San Diego: Academic Press 1987, pp. 55-82

— and Ruqaiya Hasan. *Cohesion in English*. London: Longman 1976

Harrell, Lester E., Jr. "A Comparison of Oral and Written Language in School-age Children." *Monographs of the Society for Research in Child Development* 22, Serial No. 66 (1957), Lafayette, IN: Child Development Publications

Haslett, Betty J. "Children's Strategies for Maintaining Cohesion in their Written and Oral Stories." *Communication Education* 32 (1983):91-105

Havelock, Eric A. *Preface to Plato*. Cambridge, MA: Harvard University Press 1963

—. "The Preliteracy of the Greeks." *New Literary History* 8 (1976-7):369-91

Havránek, Bohuslav. "The Functional Differentiation of the Standard Language." In *A Prague School Reader on Esthetics, Literary Structure, and Style*. Ed. Paul L. Garvin. Washington, DC: Washington Linguistics Club 1955, pp. 3-16

Heath, Shirley Brice. "Standard English: Biography of a Symbol." In *Standards and Dialects in English*. Eds. Timothy Shopen and Joseph Williams. Cambridge, MA: Winthrop 1980, pp. 3-31

—. "Protean Shapes in Literacy Events: Ever-Shifting Oral and Literate Traditions." In *Spoken and Written Language: Exploring Orality and Literacy*. Eds. Deborah Tannen. Norwood, NJ: Ablex 1982, pp. 91-117

—. *Ways with Words*. Cambridge: Cambridge University Press 1983

Hinds, John. "Organizational Patterns in Discourse." In *Syntax and Semantics, Volume 12: Discourse and Syntax*. London: Academic Press 1979, pp. 135-57

Horn, E.H. "A Basic Writing Vocabulary: 10,000 Words Most Commonly Used in Writing." Iowa City: University of Iowa Monographs in Education, 4, 1st series, 1926

Horowitz, M.W. and A. Berkowitz. "The Structural Advantage of the Mechanism of Spoken Expression as a Factor in Differences in Spoken and Written Expression." *Perceptual and Motor Skills* 19 (1964):619-25

—. and J.B. Newman. "Spoken and Written Expression: An Experimental Analysis." *Journal of Abnormal and Social Psychology* 8 (1964):640-7

Howell, Wilbur Samuel. *Eighteenth-Century British Logic and Rhetoric*. Princeton: Princeton University Press 1971

Hunt, Kellogg W. *Grammatical Structures Written at Three Grade Levels*. Monographs of the Society for Research in Child Development 22, no. 3, serial no. 66. Lafayette, IN: Child Development Pubs. 1965

Hymes, D. "Toward Ethnographies of Communicative Events." In *Language and Social Context*. Ed. Pier Paolo Giglioli. New York: Penguin 1964, pp. 21–43

Innis, Harold. *Empire and Communications*. Toronto: University of Toronto Press 1972

Jarret, Dennis. "Pragmatic Coherence in an Oral Formulaic Tradition: I Can Read Your Letters/ Sure Can't Read Your Mind." In *Coherence in Spoken and Written Discourse*. Ed. Deborah Tannen. Norwood, NJ: Ablex 1984, pp. 155–71

Jarvella, Robert J. "Syntactic Processing of Connected Speech." *Journal of Verbal Learning and Verbal Behavior* 10 (1971):409–16

Kaump, E.A. "An Analysis of the Structural Differences between Oral and Written Language of One Hundred Secondary School Students." Diss., University of Wisconsin 1940

Kay, P. "Language Evolution and Speech Style." In *Sociocultural Dimensions of Language Change*. Ed. B.G. Blount and M. Sanchez. New York: Academic Press 1977, pp. 21–33

Kinneavy, James L. *A Theory of Discourse*. New York: Norton 1971

Kopperschmidt, Josef. "An Analysis of Argumentation." In *Handbook of Discourse Analysis*. Ed. Teun A. van Dijk. London: Academic Press 1985, pp. 159–67

Kress, Gunther. "The Social Values of Speech and Writing." In *Language and Control*. Eds. Roger Fowler et al. London: Routledge and Kegan Paul, 1979, pp. 46–62

—, ed. *Learning to Write*. London: Routledge and Kegan Paul 1982

— and Michael Rowan. "The Expression of Causality in Children's Language." In *Learning to Write*. Ed. Gunther Kress. London: Routledge and Kegan Paul 1982, pp. 157–77

Kroll, B. "Combining Ideas in Written and Spoken English: A Look at Subordination and Coordination." In *Discourse across Time and Space*. Ed. Elinor Keenan and Tina Bennett. Southern California Occasional Papers in Linguistics, 5. Los Angeles: University of Southern California 1977, pp. 69–108

Labov, W. and David Fanshell. *Therapeutic Discourse*. New York: Academic Press 1977

Labov, W. "Some Principles of Linguistic Methodology." *Language in Society* 1:1 (1972a):97–120

—. "The Transformation of Experience in Narrative Syntax." In *Language in the Inner City: Studies in the Black English Vernacular*. Philadelphia: University of Pennsylvania Press 1972b, pp. 354–96

—. "The Logic of Nonstandard English." In *Language and Social Context*. Ed. Pier Paolo Giglioli. New York: Penguin 1980, pp. 179–216

Lakoff, Robin Tolmach. "Persuasive Discourse and Ordinary Conversation, with Examples from Advertising." In *Analyzing Discourse: Text and Talk*. Ed.

Deborah Tannen. Georgetown University Round Table on Language and Linguistics, 1981. Washington, DC: Georgetown University Press 1982a, pp. 25-42

—. "Some of My Favorite Writers are Literate: The Mingling of Oral and Literate Strategies in Written Communication." In *Spoken and Written Language: Exploring Orality and Literacy*. Ed. Deborah Tannen. Norwood, NJ: Ablex 1982b, pp. 239-60

—. "Expository Writing and the Oral Dyad as Points on a Communicative Continuum: Writing Anxiety as the Result of Mistranslation." Unpublished manuscript. Cited in Beaman

Levin, Harry, Susan Long, and Carol A. Schaffer. "The Formality of the Latinate Lexicon in English." *Language and Speech* 24 (1981):161-71

Linde, Charlotte and William Labov. "Spatial Networks as a Site for the Study of Language and Thought." *Language* 51 (1975):924-39

Longacre, R.E., ed. *Discourse, Paragraph, and Sentence Structure in Selected Philippine Languages*. Santa Anna, CA: Summer Institute of Linguistics 1968

Longacre, R.E. *An Anatomy of Speech Notions*. Lisse: Peter de Ridder 1976

—. "The Paragraph as a Grammatical Unit." In *Syntax and Semantics, Volume 12: Discourse and Syntax*. Ed. T. Givón. London: Academic Press 1979, pp. 115-34

—. *The Grammar of Discourse*. New York: Plenum Press 1983

Lord, Albert. *The Singer of Tales*. Harvard Studies in Comparative Literature 24. Cambridge, MA: Harvard University Press 1960

Magoun, Francis P., Jr. "The Oral-Formulaic Character of Anglo-Saxon Poetry." In *An Anthology of Beowulf Criticism*. Ed. Lewis E. Nicholson. London: University of Notre Dame Press 1980, pp. 189-222

Mair, Walter N. "Français parlé et français écrit." *Lingua e Stile* 16 (1981):151-62

Mann, William C. and Sandra A. Thompson. "Relational Propositions in Discourse." *Discourse Processes* 9 (1986):57-90

Mathesius, Vilem. *A Functional Analysis of Present Day English on a General Linguistic Basis*. Ed. Joseph Vachek. The Hague: Mouton 1975

Matthei, Edward, and Thomas Roeper. *Understanding and Producing Speech*. Bungay, Suffolk: Fontana 1983

McIntosh, Angus. "'Graphology' and Meaning." *Archivum Linguisticum* 13 (1961):107-20

—. "The Analysis of Written Middle English." *Transactions of the Philological Society*. London: Oxford University Press 1957, pp. 26-55

McLuhan, Marshall. *The Gutenberg Galaxy: The Making of Typographic Man*. Toronto: University of Toronto Press 1962

—. *Understanding Media: The Extensions of Man*. New York: McGraw-Hill 1964

Mehler, J., T.G. Bever, and P. Carey. "What Do We Look at When We Read." *Perception and Psychophysics* 2 (1967):213-19

Morrison, Robert E. and Albrecht-Werner Inhoff. "Visual Factors and Eye Movements in Reading." *Visible Language* 15:2 (1981):129-46

Mulkay, Michael. "Agreement and Disagreement in Conversations and Letters." *Text* 5 (1985a):201-27

—. *The Word and The World: Explorations in the Form of Sociological Analysis.* London: Allen and Unwin 1985b

Newman, Jean E. "Processing Spoken Discourse: Effects of Position and Emphasis on Judgments of Textual Coherence." *Discourse Processes* 8 (1985):205-27

Nosek, Jiri. "Notes on Syntactic Condensation in Modern English." *Travaux linguistiques de Prague* 1 (1964):281-8

Nystrand, Martin, ed. *What Writers Know: The Language, Process, and Structure of Written Discourse.* London: Academic Press 1982

O'Donnell, R.C., W.J. Griffin, and R.C. Norris. "A Transformational Analysis of Oral and Written Grammatical Structures in the Language of Children in Grades Three, Five and Seven." *Journal of Educational Research* 61 (1967):36-9

O'Donnell, R.C. "Syntactic Differences between Speech and Writing." *American Speech* 49 (1974):102-10

Ochs, Elinor. "Planned and Unplanned Discourse." In *Syntax and Semantics Volume 12: Discourse and Syntax.* Ed. T. Givón. London: Academic Press 1979, 51-80

Olson, David R. "From Utterance to Text: The Bias of Language in Speech and Writing." *Harvard Educational Review* 47 (1977):257-81

—. "On Language and Literacy." *International Journal of Psycholinguistics* 7 (1980):69-83

Ong, Walter J. "The Writer's Audience Is Always a Fiction." In *Interfaces of the Word.* Ithaca and London: Cornell University Press 1977, pp. 53-81

—. "Literacy and Orality in Our Times." *Journal of Communication* 30 (1980):197-204

—. "Oral Remembering and Narrative Structure." In *Analyzing Discourse: Text and Talk.* Ed. Deborah Tannen. Georgetown University Round Table on Languages and Linguistics 1981. Washington, DC: Georgetown University Pres 1981, pp. 12-24

—. *Orality and Literacy.* New York: Methuen 1982

Pawley, A., and F.H. Syder. "Natural Selection in Syntax: Notes on Adaptive Variation and Change in Vernacular and Literary Grammar." *Journal of Pragmatics* 7 (1983):551-79

Polanyi, Livia. "Telling the Same Story Twice." *Text* 1 (1981):315-36

Perlman, A. "*This* as a Third Article in American English." *American Speech* 44 (1969):76-80

Pomerantz, Anita. "Agreeing and Disagreeing with Assessments: Some Features of Preferred/Dispreferred Turn Shapes." In *Structures of Social Action.*

Eds. J.M. Atkinson and J. Heritage. Cambridge and New York: Cambridge University Press 1984, pp. 57–101

Poole, M.E. and T.W. Field. "A Comparison of Oral and Written Code Elaboration." *Language and Speech* 19 (1976):305–11

Pratt, Mary Louise. *Toward a Speech Act Theory of Literary Discourse*. Bloomington and London: Indiana University Press 1977

Price, Connie C. and J.T. Price. "The *Phaedrus* and the *Sundiata* Epic on Speech and Writing." *Second Order* 2 (1976):37–44

Quirk, Randolph, Sidney Greenbaum, Geoffrey Leech, and Jan Svartvik. *A Comprehensive Grammar of the English Language*. London: Longman 1985

Radar, Margaret. "Context in Written Language: The Case of Imaginative Fiction." In *Spoken and Written Language: Exploring Orality and Literacy*. Ed. Deborah Tannen. Norwood, NJ: Ablex 1982, pp. 185–95

Rayner, Keith. "Eye Movements in Reading and Information Processing." *Psychological Bulletin* 85: 3(1978):618–60

—. "The Perceptual Span and Eye Movement Control during Reading." In *Eye Movements in Reading: Perceptual and Language Processes*. Ed. Keith Rayner. New York: Academic Press 1983, pp. 618–60

Redeker, Gisela. "On Differences between Spoken and Written Language." *Discourse Processes* 7 (1984):185–98

Rensky, Miroslav. "English Verbo-Nominal Phrases." *Travaux linguistiques de Prague* 1 (1964):289–99

Ross, Alan S.C. "U and Non-U: An Essay in Sociological Linguistics." In *The Importance of Language*. Ed. Max Black. Englewood Cliffs, NJ: Prentice-Hall 1962, pp. 91–106

Sacks, Harvey, Emanuel A. Schegloff, and Gail Jefferson. "A Simplest Systematics for the Organization of Turn-Taking For Conversation." *Language* 50 (1974):696–735

Sanders, Gerald and Jessica R. Wirth. "Discourse, Pragmatics, and Linguistic Form." In *Beyond the Sentence: Discourse and Sentential Form*. Ed. Jessica R. Wirth. Ann Arbor: MI: Karoma 1985, pp. 1–20

Saussure, F. *Cours de linguistique générale*. Paris 1916, 1967

—. *Course in General Linguistics*. Toronto: McGraw-Hill 1966

Schafer, John C. "The Linguistic Analysis of Spoken and Written Texts." In *Exploring Speaking-Writing Relationships: Connections and Contracts*. Eds. Barry M. Kroll and Roberta J. Vann. Urbana: University of Indiana Press 1981, pp. 1–31

Schegloff, E.A. "Notes on a Conversational Practice: Formulating Place." In *Language and Social Context*. Ed. Pier Paolo Giglioli. New York: Penguin 1980, pp. 95–135

Schmidt, Siegfried J. "Some Problems of Communicative Text Theories." In *Current Trends in Textlinguistics*. Ed. Wolfgang Dressler. Berlin and New York: De Gruyter 1977, pp. 47–60

Scholes, Robert, and Robert Kellogg. *The Nature of Narrative*. London: Oxford University Press 1966

Scinto, Leonard F., Jr. "Relation of Eye Fixations to Old-New Information." In *Eye Movements and the Higher Psychological Functions*. Eds. John W. Senders, Dennis F. Fisher, Richard A. Monty. Hillsdale, NJ: Erlbaum 1978, pp. 175-94

Scribner, Sylvia, and Michael Cole. *The Psychology of Literacy*. Cambridge, MA: Harvard University Press 1981

Searle, John. *Speech Acts: An Essay in the Philosophy of Language*. Cambridge: Cambridge University Press 1969

—. "Indirect Speech Acts." In *Syntax and Semantics, Vol. 3: Speech Acts*. Eds. Peter Cole and Jerry L. Morgan. New York: Academic Press 1975, pp. 59-82

Sewell, P.M. *Enquête sur la presse: Parallel Texts for Comparison and Analysis*. Cambridge: Cambridge University Press 1981

Shaklee, Margaret. "The Rise of Standard English." In *Standards and Dialects in English*. Eds. Timothy Shopen and Joseph Williams. Cambridge, MA: Winthrop 1980, pp. 33-61

Shank, R.C. and R.P. Abelson. *Scripts, Plans, Goals and Understanding*. Hillsdale, NJ: Erlbaum 1977

Shanon, Benny. "Room Descriptions." *Discourse Processes* 7 (1984):225-55

Siegel, Jeff. "Developments in Written Tok Pisin." *Anthropological Linguistics* 23 (1981):20-35

Schmandt-Besserat, Denise. "The Earliest Precursor of Writing." *Scientific American* 238 (1978):50-9

Smith, Adam. *Lectures on Rhetoric and Belles Lettres*. Ed. John M. Lothian. Edinburgh: Heath 1970

Smith, Edward L. "Text Type and Discourse Framework." *Text* 5 (1985):229-47

Smith, Frank. "Psycholinguistics and Reading." In *Psycholinguistics and Reading*. Ed. Frank Smith. New York: Holt, Rinehart and Winston 1973

Stubbs, Michael. "Can I Have That in Writing, Please? Some Neglected Topics in Speech Act Theory." *Journal of Pragmatics* 7 (1983a):479-94

—. *Discourse Analysis*. Chicago: University of Chicago Press 1983b

Tannen, Deborah. "Spoken/Written Language and the Oral/Literate Continuum." *Proceedings of the Sixth Annual Meeting of the Berkeley Linguistics Society*. Berkeley: Berkeley Linguistics Society, 1980, pp. 207-18

—. "Oral and Literate Strategies in Spoken and Written Narratives." *Language* 58 (1982):1-21

Thompson, Sandra A. "Grammar and Discourse: The English Detached Participial Clause." In *Discourse Perspectives on Syntax*. Ed. Flora Klein-Andrew. London: Academic Press 1983, pp. 43-65

Todorov, Tzvetan. "The Origin of Genres." *New Literary History* 8 (1976-7):159-70

Tomlin, Russell S. "Interaction of Subject, Theme and Agent." In *Beyond the Sentence: Discourse and Sentential Form*. Ed. Jessica R. Wirth. Ann Arbor, MI: Karoma 1985, pp. 61-83

—. *Basic Word Order: Functional Principles*. Croom Helm Linguistic Series. London: Croom Helm 1986

Traugott, Elizabeth Closs. "On the Origins of 'And' and 'But' Connectives in English." *Studies in Language* 10-1:137-50

Turner, Victor. "Social Dramas and Stories about Them." In *On Narrative*. Ed. W.J.T. Mitchell. Chicago: University of Chicago Press 1979, pp. 137-64

Ure, J.N. "Lexical Density and Register Differentiation." In *Applications of Linguistics: Selected Papers of the Second International Congress of Applied Linguistics*. Eds. G.E. Perren and J.L.M. Trim. Cambridge: Cambridge University Press 1971, pp. 443-52

Vachek, Joseph. "Written Language and Printed Language." *Recueil Linguistique de Bratislava* 1 (1948):65-75

—. *The Linguistic School of Prague*. Bloomington: Indiana University Press 1966

—. *Selected Writings in English and General Linguistics*. The Hague: Mouton 1976

—. "Some Remarks on the Stylistics of Written Language." In *Function and Context in Linguistic Analysis: A Festschrift for William Haas*. Eds. D.J. Allerton, Edward Carney, and David Holdcraft. Cambridge: Cambridge University Press 1979, pp. 206-15

van Dijk, Teun A. "Episodes as Units of Discourse Analysis." In *Analyzing Discourse: Text and Talk*. Ed. Deborah Tannen. Georgetown University Round Table on Language and Linguistics 1981. Washington, DC: Georgetown University Press 1982, pp. 177-95

Voelker, C.M. "The One-thousand Most Frequently Spoken Words." *Quarterly Journal of Speech* 28 (1942):189-97

Vygotsky, Lev. *Thought and Language*. Cambridge, MA: MIT Press 1962

Wald, Benji. "Variation in the System of Tense Markers of Mombasa Swahili." Diss., Columbia University 1973

—. "Referent and Topic within and across Discourse Units: Observation from Current Vernacular English." In *Discourse Perspectives on Syntax*. Ed. Flora Klein-Andreu. New York: Academic Press 1983, pp. 91-115

Weltner, K. *The Measurement of Verbal Information in Psychology and Education*. Berlin: Springer-Verlag 1973

Werlich, Egon. *A Text Grammar of English*. Heidelberg: Quelle and Meyer 1976

Wilson, Deirdre and Dan Sperber. "On Grice's Theory of Conversation." In *Conversation and Discourse*. Ed. Paul Werth. London: Croom Helm 1981, pp. 155-78

Index